Society's
Impact
on
Television

SOCIETY'S IMPACT ON TELEVISION

How the Viewing Public Shapes
Television Programming

GARY W. SELNOW
and
RICHARD R. GILBERT

PRAEGER

Westport, Connecticut
London

Library of Congress Cataloging-in-Publication Data

Selnow, Gary W.
  Society's impact on television : how the viewing public
shapes television programming / Gary W. Selnow and Richard R.
Gilbert.
      p.   cm.
  Includes bibliographical references and index.
  ISBN 0-275-94390-9 (alk. paper)
  1. Television programs—United States—Planning. 2. Television
viewers—United States—Attitudes. I. Gilbert, Richard R.
II. Title.
PN1992.55.S4 1993
791.45′0236′0973—dc20   92-23455

British Library Cataloguing in Publication Data is available.

Library of Congress Catalog Card Number: 92-23455
ISBN: 0-275-94390-9

First published in 1993

Praeger Publishers, 88 Post Road West, Westport, CT 06881
An imprint of Greenwood Publishing Group, Inc.

Printed in the United States of America

The paper used in this book complies with the Permanent
Paper Standard issued by the National Information Standards
Organization (Z39.48—1984).

10 9 8 7 6 5 4 3 2 1

This book is dedicated to Ralph Daniels—
"Class of the networks, conscience of the industry."

Contents

Acknowledgments

This book could not have been written without the gracious help of these people who generously gave their time, ideas and comments.

Susan Baerwald
Robert Bellah
David Bollier
Charles Brackbill
Holmes Brown
Beverly Campbell
Marcy Carsey
Anderson Clark
Steve Colson
William D'Angelo
Ralph Daniels
Richard Daw
Frank Dowling
Corydon Dunham
William Emerson
Betsy Evans
Duane Evans
Thomas Galvin
Theodore Gill
Richard Gitter
Gary David Goldberg
Julian Goodman
Maurie Goodman
Morton Hill

Bettye Hoffmann
James Holland
Benjamin Hooks
Betty Hudson
Reed Irvine
Lane Kirkland
James Kuhn
Hal Lacy
Jo Laverde
Norman Lear
Arthur Link
Doug Marlette
Martin Marty
Ronald Milavsky
David Milch
Arthur Miller
Ellis Moore
Michael Ogiens
James Poteat
Arthur Price
Nelson Price
Fred Rotandaro
William Ruebens
Irwin Sieglestein

Alan Sloan   Grant Tinker
Frank Stanton   Perrin Wright
Tom Stites   Alan Wurtzel
Rabbi Marc Tanenbaum

Society's **Impact** on Television

1

Introduction

Writers and producers . . . breathe in a huge variety of experiences . . . and
then breathe them out in scripts.
                                    —Gary David Goldberg, writer-producer of
                                       "Family Ties," "Brooklyn Bridge"

Three years ago, Gary David Goldberg was the first in a vivid band of writers, producers and network programmers to be asked the question, "To what extent are your characters, your plots, your tastes and your values affected by such forces as network censorship, advertising sensitivities, pressure group tactics and public opinion itself?"

The writer-producer looked out the window of his trailer and into the studio park named for "Lucy." He glanced over at a portrait of his black Lab, Ubu. Worried by his silence, we quickly added, "We know all about *your* influence on the public. What we want to know is, what is the influence of the public, if any, on *you*?"

Like Norman Lear, Grant Tinker and many other television-makers we interviewed, Goldberg was accustomed to being told by scholars, critics and the press that his programs profoundly affect the tastes and values of millions of viewers. He had never, he said, been approached serendipitously from the other direction and asked to consider the various forces, outside of his own skills and imagination, which pilot and regulate the kinds of things he can say on primetime television.

It was at this point that Goldberg came up with the metaphor of "breathing in" a variety of experiences and "breathing them out" into characters and stories.

This book is about the breathing-in phase, all the things that influence the work or shape the tastes and values of TV-makers. Our research took several forms.

We started by haunting the halls of network leaders, censors, advertisers, heads of pressure groups, technocrats and government regulators—all those who have a part in creating the atmosphere and culture that triangulates from Hollywood to New York to Washington, D.C., and ultimately sets the coordinates for what writers can write and programmers can air. Call these the working influences in the creative environment of America's pop art.

Physically speaking, breathing in is no easy task in Los Angeles where the creative community lives and moves. For example, a bulletin board in Burbank displays each day the condition of the air. Cruising into the NBC parking lot in their Mercedes and BMWs, young programmers and senior executives dock at their designated parking slots. Passing security, the network people pay little attention to the environmental bulletin boards. Why bother?

But one advisory will catch their attention. When the air gets even yellower than usual, a smog alert is issued. That grabs them. Protected by air conditioning until lunch, they wonder if one day they will have to emerge wearing one of those gauze nose cones used so widely in Tokyo.

Similarly, TV-makers seldom consider their cultural atmosphere. Unconscious of the value system they live in, enjoying it more or less reflexively, they have no reason to think about it until someone issues a smog alert. That could be an advertiser who jerks a program because it offended a minority. Or a pressure group protesting sleaze. Or someone on the abortion watch accusing networks of taking sides. Or the PTA raising hell about a particularly violent show. Or the government in the person of some politician threatening to reregulate the whole industry. It could even be a bean counter from New York City asking for smaller staffs, tighter budgets and better quality in sexually suggestive violent shows that are off the wall, offensive to no one and pulling a 40 share.

When such smog alerts appear, the storytellers (writer-producers) and the story developers (network programmers) sniff the air to see just how yellow it is. If the offending pollution is minor, they ignore it. If major, they attach temporary nose cones to upcoming programs until the alert is over and normal pollution can return.

This book tries to breathe that same air, report its qualities and make some suggestions for purifications.

Readers familiar with the format for the television game show "Jeopardy" know that Alex Trebek supplies the answer to which the contestants must give the question. In our book, writers and programmers give their answers in the first two chapters. Each, however, presupposes a basic question: Outside your own talent, skills, imagination and value system, what forces set the parameters for your shows on primetime entertainment?

We tried to aim this question at TV-makers from a good many angles. Do you merely reflect what you see "out there"? Do you back off or resist the muscle of the network, of advertisers, of pressure groups? And since everybody from scholars to viewers talks about your staggering influence on the tastes and values of the public, do you think your shows are really that powerful, that inculcating, that indoctrinating? Is it just possible that your influence on society is not as great as society's influence on you?

With this approach, we reverse the direction usually taken by serious books about America's most popular art. While most examine the impact of television on the viewers and society, we look at how viewers, their representatives and other forces in society impact the medium. We ask, "What ingredients in that social, governmental, special interest broth shape the content of television programming?"

A surprising number of people, including scholars and everyday viewers, assume that the impact of television on society flows in one direction only. The traffic of influence moves from the content of a given program to the behavior of those who view it. If a show is too exploitative or violent or stereotypical, it supposedly transforms the minds of those who watch it in some proportionate manner. Both common sense and research attest to this assumption: After all, anything that captures the attention of the average American for four hours a day must influence that viewer inescapably. Over the years there is bound to be a conditioning effect from a medium that constitutes one-sixth of the environment lived in by most Americans during their time on planet Earth.

When research psychologists test children who are heavy viewers of violent programs and find them more aggressive in their behavior than children who are lighter viewers, they make the case for the one-way influence that travels from producers of programs to consumers of programs. When parents complain that the sexual content of television contributes to promiscuity, they make much the same point. When civil rights leaders protest a racial slur or feminists decry a sexist image on the air, they are attesting to television's power to foster harmful behavior. And when journalists proclaim that television "sets the agenda" for society, they reinforce the conviction that the social influence of the tube is like bumper-to-bumper traffic flowing from the set to the public.

It is this tidal wave of influence that drives observers to use such metaphors as "the national nervous system" when they try to evaluate the one thing most Americans have in common. In light of such widespread belief bordering on the mythic, can anyone doubt that the national "Thing" influences society more powerfully than any social force since the established church and that the direction of that influence is one way only?

As Sportin' Life sang in *Porgy and Bess*, "It ain't necessarily so." This book maintains that the one-way social influence theory is only half true. The full truth, in our judgment, is that even as television makes its impact on society, society makes its impact on TV, and often with more noticeable effect.

One of the first to notice the boomerang effect on writers was Gary David Goldberg, father of "Family Ties," a sitcom that launched the career of Michael J. Fox, and did nothing to harm the popularity of two other actors, Meredith Baxter-Birney and Michael Gross. "Family Ties" was a top-five show every year it ran during the eighties, second only to the "Cosby Show," and now enjoys a robust syndication.

Evaluations of its influence, however, were mixed. Goldberg's characters and plots drew praise from liberals who approved the way he and his team explored social topics – racial prejudice, teenage sexuality, right-wing politics, corporate ethics, divorce and death. This was television helping society.

On the other hand, conservatives threw brickbats at "Family" complaining about the "permissive" attitudes on sex, the alleged left-of-center politics and tendencies of writers to bootleg their social ideology into situation comedy. This was TV harming society.

Despite a 180-degree difference in these evaluations, both parties were in total agreement on one-way social influence. Protesters and supporters, liberals and conservatives, social psychologists and viewers at large agreed that the show made a powerful impact on its regular viewers who could not help but be affected by the tastes and values in "Family Ties."

When we interviewed Goldberg about the alleged infectiousness of his program, he did not deny its inducements, but he did interject a thought that fits the direction of this study.

> Writers and producers, and for that matter, programmers and standards people, don't live in isolation. People tend to believe that we are unaffected by the world around us. If that were so, we couldn't successfully produce. Our best material comes from the fact that we are fathers, brothers, sisters, voters, consumers. We read. We talk with lots of people. We watch the news. We serve in community organizations. In some ways, writers are more influenced by the world than the world is influenced by us.

Another writer-producer, Bill D'Angelo ("Webster," "Alice," "Flo," "A Family for Joe," "Top Cops") described for us the same reverse influence.

> Let me give you an example of radical change in programming content and you tell me if the catalyst was Hollywood or society. I'm talking about cigarettes and liquor. When you see old movies on TV, half the time they are puffing and drinking, right? Hell, they were virtually props. Astaire's cigarette was as much a part of his routine as his top hat. Gable was as likely to order a cocktail as kiss the girl. Even ten years ago, TV cop shows and westerns relied heavily on rolling a butt and downing a shot. But look at it now. The whole damn tube is sanitized. Today if I allowed the casual use of smokes or drinks on my shows unrelated to the plot, the network would scream and half a dozen pressure groups would jump my bones.

Did writers dream this up? Clearly it came from the outside.

What caused the change? In all probability, writer-producers were deeply influenced by simultaneous forces – the Surgeon General's reports (i.e., government pressure), pressure groups, network censorship and by their own reading of the public mind. One can argue about how much impact the sanitizing of television smoking and drinking has had on society. Chances are, it has conditioned viewers a bit, but since television is only one of the many influences on social behavior, its distinctive impact is hard to measure—a difficulty largely ignored by those who confidently patrol the one-way street of social influences.

What no one can doubt in this instance is the effect of social pressure on TV programmers, beginning with the writer-producer who makes the product for the networks. The pressure to take cigarettes and alcohol out of drama came from public forces exterior to the industry.

We suggest that the one-way theory—the prevailing wisdom—is only one side of the coin, and that the flip side—usually overlooked—is the other-way theory. Taken together, they form a continuous process. The action is something like a billiard ball when hit below the center of gravity. Called "english," the blow puts a reverse spin on the cue ball so that when it hits the object ball, it not only moves the object but rebounds itself at the same time. Both balls are affected. In a sense, a ball with reverse spin on it is coming and going at the same time.

Such is the rhythm of television influence. The producer moves the public with his program but a reverse spin caused by the collision of program and public moves the producer as well. For example, a series that treats women in a certain way may occasion a feedback (negative or positive), which then affects the way producers shape future episodes in the series. As a total process, the influences are coming and going at the same time.

Is there any empirical evidence to back up reverse spin? Curiously, the busiest researchers to address this phenomenon are those from a Marxist orientation on the one hand and a neoconservative orientation on the other. One viewpoint maintains that the ingredients that go into primetime television are predetermined by the capitalistic establishment of sponsors and networks whose aim is to keep the people too busy buying products to fight the powers that be. The point: He who pays the piper calls the tune. And since the writer and the network are paid by the advertiser, guess who calls the tune?

Another well-known view draws from research that approached a small sample of Hollywood names with a "values" questionnaire and concluded that the creative community, being mostly secular and left of center, inevitably bootlegs these values into programs under the very noses of right-wing sponsors who pay the bill. Having made these pronouncements, however, supporters from neither group have backed up these claims with convincing data on the relationship between ideology and program content. Such generalizations about either the conspiratorial liberalism of the creative community or the economic conservatism of advertisers miss the mark. They are not adequate evaluations of network entertainment.

It is easy to understand why most researchers and writers have avoided the "other-way" influence of the public upon the producer. For one thing, writers are notoriously and deliciously anecdotal. A question about network boundaries might elicit a funny story about the latest scatological gaffe by the male star whose physical beauty far outshines his ability to memorize a script. A question about FCC rules on decent language might be met with the "how's that again?" of one who has never really thought about it. A question about the revolutionary practice of viewers "grazing" about the dial with their clickers might generate a stream of consciousness on the latest storylines that had been coursing through the writer's imagination, followed by the responsive question, "How does this beat (incident in a story) strike you? Think I can slip it by standards?"

The best one can do is to try to distinguish between the external influences (e.g., censorship, government regulations, pressure groups) that interest us in this study and the built-in factors of imagination, experience and craft, which make that person a writer or programmer. We did, however, retain some of the idiosyncratic dialogue if for no other reason than to show the serendipity of the nondiscursive mind. Like butterflies, writer-producers refuse to fly in formations.

Norman Lear, who talked to us over a period of several months, was delightfully unpredictable. For those who were not around when "All in the Family" first appeared (can any teacher believe that Archie was born before any member of the freshmen class of 1992?), the reception accorded this sitcom was decidedly mixed. After years of sweetness and light on family shows, Archie Bunker became the "equal opportunity offender" for every minority, religion and good cause. But it was tricky. On the one hand Archie used taboo words never heard on television but on the other he was definitely the "heavy" who absorbed the liberal putdowns of sociologist son-in-law Mike and limousine-liberal Maude.

Musing on the reception, Lear said, "One of my best friends called me a bigot and it hurt. The first complaints did not come from conservatives at all. They got me later. The rocks were thrown by liberals who said that I gave all the good lines to Archie. Which supposedly played into the hands of bigots. Funny, I remember Martin Marty [popular Lutheran theologian] telling me that Luther was harshly criticized for setting sacred hymn lines to popular drinking songs. Luther answered, 'Why should the devil have the good tunes?' "

Lear paused as if savoring the line for inclusion in a later script. Then he added, "That's all very true. But in situation comedy, you don't want to give good lines only to the good. The devil deserves his due if you don't want to be dull or dogmatic. . . . There is more to making comedy than the values of the comedy writer."

And there is more to discovering influences on a writer than asking about the external pressures on his scripts—but that is the turf cut out for this book. For this reason, we have tried to place network television in a larger context that includes some advisory comments from talent on the ways they go about their craft. And, since a knowledge of the basics is necessary to evaluate social influences in general, we have included some explanatory material on the way things work in network television at the risk of treading familiar ground for sophisticated media watchers.

The producers and programmers quoted in this book, having answered a thousand questions from scholars on the ways in which their programs influence viewers, said that few had ever asked about the societal pressures that color programs before they hit the air—other than ratings and greed, as former NBC chairman and long-time producer Irwin Siegelstein put it.

We are concerned here with what values people in the industry profess personally and about what forces in government, business, technology, the press and the voluntary sector (i.e., pressure groups) challenge their values and presumably shape the content of their shows. Most people in the creative and network community told us they usually were questioned about the rare power they had to transmit their tastes and values to viewers. (Their answers, predictably, underscored the many "prosocial" messages that were crammed into their vehicles. Unlike those shows that were harmful to society, theirs fairly bristled with sensitivity and social concern . . . so some said.)

To assert our concerns for the forces acting ON the television community rather than forces coming FROM the community, we peppered television-makers with questions they were not used to answering:

• What things of a moral, social, political, economic or technological nature have influenced you, your plots and characterizations?

• Do you really let your values (liberal or conservative, religious or secular, moral or permissive) predominate in your scripts or do some of your characters speak with their own voices?

• And getting down to the press-worthy issues that concern most critics—sex, violence, ethnicity, gender, social philosophy and politics—what things do you avoid or self-censor in order to play the television game with networks, advertisers, pressure groups, the press and politicians?

Despite the unexpected angle, eliciting candid responses from creative people about society's influences upon their own work was surprisingly easy. References to various restrictions on their freedom helped trigger responses. For example, many were quick to react to the spit-and-polish morality of Rev. Donald Wildmon. They gave thoughtful responses to the possible influences of minority and racial groups, to feminists and gays.

Most, however, were loath to concede a willingness to play the censorship game with networks, much less consider some of the larger pressures from business or the press. The implications of self-censorship made them uncomfortable and the following questions were often dodged:

• Have you ever changed a storyline or a leading role because of what advertisers might think about the fallout?

• Had the networks standards departments "precensored" any storyline?

• Are you aware of the "indecency" rulings of the FCC and does this factor into your thinking?

• Do you follow newspaper polls in which viewers are asked about the levels of sex or violence on the tube?

• How sensitive are you to what leading print critics have to say about the content in your shows?

A few, like Arthur Price (former head of Mary Tyler Moore Productions and now an independent producer) were blunt. Price described a meeting he attended with the heads of Disney, Paramount, Fox, Universal, Lorimar and a few others with the CEO of NBC-television, Robert Wright. They were discussing the 1989 dismantling of the standards departments at CBS and NBC. Price remembers that Michael Eisner of Disney, almost as new as Wright in television programming, said that producers could handle standards problems themselves.

"I [Price] said, 'that's nonsense. There's not a producer in Hollywood who has not received notes from network programmers asking for more sex and violence. Now how can you resist these pressures unless the censors are in there pulling for the other side? The networks have the greatest system ever devised, an internal battle between programmers and standards. And it's worked for thirty years and kept Congress off our necks. Why ask for trouble?' "

Most of the television-makers, especially those who had to cover their backs at networks, were more cautious. Questions that seem to suggest a willingness to compromise freedom for program acceptance led some to counterattack, and rightly so. They wanted to know the authors' intentions and presuppositions. Where were we coming from?

We tried to be candid about the baggage we carry. All evaluations are tinctured to an unknown degree with the observers' own assumptions. In letters to those who did not already know us, we admitted that our minds were not empty of opinions, beliefs, leanings and angles of approach. To say so would posit a false objectivity. All we could promise was to be as fair as good journalists try to be.

It was trickier to explain that the authors brought different experiences into the study and therefore looked at television through widely differing lenses. Richard Gilbert had spent thirty years in and around networks and producers, both on staff at NBC-television and as a technical/story consultant to various writers and producers. He had been able to eavesdrop on the way networks wooed producers and the ways in which producers welcomed and resisted that tight embrace. Gilbert's experience made him suspicious of both researchers and watchdogs, particularly the experts who not only disagree among themselves but speak *ex cathedra* on the "legitimizing" effects of television on viewers. Gilbert admits to the insider's admiration for the entertainment game and for many of its players, albeit holding the firm conviction that networks are currently turning their backs on public responsibility.

Gary Selnow brought the academic perspective of social psychology into the analysis of television influence and an educator's suspicion of a saber-toothed industry. He respected the dramatic arts enough to know that in evaluating entertainment, you often kill the thing you count. But he had done enough content analysis on primetime programs to believe that dramatic content is never value-neutral and that entertainment is ever punctuated with education—good, bad and indifferent.

In one respect, however, Selnow found himself in partial agreement with Gilbert. As a result of his own research, Selnow had found a surprisingly high level of benign values in primetime programs. In situation comedy, the spiciest language could not hide the preponderance of Judeo-Christian values like tolerance, honesty and loving concern (e.g., "Roseanne"). Neither violence nor realistic situations had changed the familiar values of justice and freedom found in the police/detective genres (e.g., "Law and Order," "Top Cops"). More liberal and less commercial, Selnow brought a scientific method into the study that sought to balance previous assumptions with a commitment to the facts.

Both authors, however, wanted the creative people in primetime, network television to dwell on the forces in society which in their opinion conditioned to some extent what ultimately gets on the air. We hoped to take media students as well as general readers on a ride through the minds of writer-producers and network programmers with side visits to network brass, advertisers, pressure group leaders and technocrats. We especially wanted viewers to understand what outside elements in government and the public sector create the boundaries in which television-makers must work, boundaries that have been gradually extended by writers who "push the envelope" even as the envelope pushes back. The responsibility that networks have for setting boundaries with independent producers is a major subtheme of the book.

In 1993, network television is a face in which wrinkles have appeared. Previously it was a worry line over cable or a tic over cassettes. Today, a terrible frown has settled over the features of a once fat and happy face, and media moguls along Manhattan's Sixth Avenue regard a swarm of competitors with unconcealed horror. Viewers zap their commercials with "clickers" and government bodies intervene unpredictably. Above all, that nightly invitation to act as entertaining guest in every American home is up for grabs, no longer the automatic domain of the Big Three – ABC, CBS and NBC.

Time for change? The Greeks had two words for "time." One was *chronos*, for the space of time, the regularity we call the chronological. The other word, *kairos*, meant something indeterminate, symbolized by the time it took olives to ripen in season. No Greek knew exactly what day or week that would happen but when it did, the critical moment of *kairos* had arrived.

The networks and the creative teams they commission are facing their *kairos* moment. If our interviews are any criteria, that defining time in which television-makers must reexamine their nature and purpose has struck the industry. Licensed to serve the public but unleashed to make a profit, the players do not need our advice on money making. But with the words of the writers and producers ringing in our ears, we do presume to advise networks about their public responsibilities, a two-sided affair that involves both the public interest and the interested public.

Throughout the investigation, we tried to keep in mind another audience, the people who watch television not for instruction and "legitimation," but for entertainment. We remember the caution of H.L. Mencken, who said of puritanical critics that they suffered from the "awful haunting fear that someone somewhere might be enjoying himself."

Our sympathies lie with viewers who enjoy the national Thing, perhaps the only endeavor all Americans have in common. If that is anywhere near the truth — and perhaps a rueful one at that — we all have a stake in understanding what influences the values of those who daily influence us.

Much of what follows will have to do with the boundaries that *viewers* wish networks to maintain. Traditionally, when the public believes that a given medium has the power to shape its awareness and behavior, it immediately sets moral boundaries that limit that medium.

Looking back a few years, it's plain that the public has been consistent in demanding more of its most popular medium than from the less prominent ones. Thus, when the novel was number one in the public's heart, the public demanded that it respect generally accepted tastes and values. When movies replaced books as the favorite entertainment, they too were closely monitored for their moral and social effects.

But few people noticed that with the emergence of the film, the moral manacles on novels came unshackled. Today, none but extremists worry about the content of bestsellers on the *New York Times* booklist. Those who had predicted that the end of the Christian era would be hastened by "dirty books" turned their attention to the new moral menace, "dirty movies." From the Legion of Decency to the Hays Office to the institution of the film code, moral forces played on the public fear that 40 million people each week should not be looking at Douglas Fairbanks, Sr., bedding Gloria Swanson. Quickly, the ribald scenes of the early silents were replaced with careful proscriptions on sex, language and violence. However much we may smile at the puritanism of twin beds for married people, the truth was that the public, well represented by the pressure groups, demanded a cleaner moral slate for its most popular medium than for lesser media. Lost in the confusion, books were free to turn blue. A citizen's arrest of movies allowed books to make a clean getaway.

When radio surpassed the film industry's public impact by penetrating every home, shows were dissected for helpful or harmful effects on society, and a new set of boundaries sprang up. Almost unnoticed, once again, was the subsequent moral liberation of the "old" medium, motion pictures, from such massive scrutiny. Gradually, films pushed back the walls of self-regulation until the Motion Picture Association of America's ratings marked the virtual end of industry limitations.

Today, except for a few conservative voices, hardly anyone gets excited over "dirty films." Only rarely do pressure groups waste time claiming that R-rated films are subverting the morals of our nation or demeaning the images of minorities, a prominent exception being *The Last Temptation of Christ*, and even there, putting Jesus in bed with Mary Magdalene was no more than mildly provocative to the nation at large.

Finally, when television replaced radio as *the* home medium and replaced movies as *the* entertainer, it became the new medium of foremost public concern. Given television's ubiquity and appeal, few interest groups or politicians can hold a press conference without referring to the "awesome, legitimizing power of television." The public has agreed. It believes that nothing so influences the nation morally, socially and politically as does television—acting as a substitute parent, substitute teacher and, possibly, substitute preacher for America.

Only recently has it dawned on people that radio, no longer in the limelight, has shaken its moral bonds to pursue "topless radio," the explicit sexuality of Dr. Ruth, the vulgarities of Howard Stern, and the racist, sexist and violent language of hard rock "rap" songs. Aside from an occasional news item on truly nasty content, nobody says much anymore about "dirty radio."

The moral is: Quality control, or censorship if you like, is the sincerest form of flattery. Whatever medium the public is convinced has the greatest power to affect the greatest number of people is the one that the public monitors most vigorously. By contrast other channels of communication are treated more leniently. In short, the American people are less vigilant of the taste and values of minority media but demand that the most popular medium deliver both good entertainment and entertainment that is good—or at least not terribly harmful.

Further, the case for television boundaries has justifications other than those of popular opinion. Distinctions among media involving private homes (television, radio) and public locations (film) and visual properties (film, television) also affect the rigor of policing. Exploding body parts in the parlor *is* more traumatic than a sword fight in *Hamlet*. Free broadcasting isn't being picked on arbitrarily. It *is* different.

Is the public's attitude toward its ubiquitous home appliance far-fetched or unreasonable? The authors' attitude is popularist. The public, we think, believes that the power to influence almost all the people at least part of the time is too great a power to trust to the industry alone. Here, common sense is on the side of "the average reasonable viewer."

That viewer's common sense says that whatever you do a lot does a lot to you. If kids watch too much sex and violence, they will become too sexual and violent. If people hear words like "kike," "nigger," "fag," "Spic," "Jap," and see demeaning images of minorities and women, they will be poisoned by bigotry with resulting harm to vulnerable parties. If TV characters call the mentally ill "crazies" or the disabled "cripples" or the hearing-impaired "dummies," the same attitudes will break out in the lives of certain viewers. If good programs have the power to uplift, isn't it reasonable to suppose that bad programs have the power to drag down?

The public doesn't care if some scholars and critics seriously doubt a cause-and-effect relationship between viewing and behavior. The public doesn't care if the creative community insists that it is more the quality of an expression than its quantity that is significantly influential. The public doesn't care if sophisticated sorts see television as visual wallpaper, a mere backdrop that does not corrupt or improve but merely grinds on, creating short attention spans among kids, activating consumer lusts and acting as the national nervous system. And the public doesn't care if television executives are bleeding-heart liberals or bottom-line realists.

The public feels in its bones that whatever the home is exposed to seven hours a day and each individual is tuned into four hours a day is going to influence monumentally. They have bought the industry's own propaganda that tells advertisers that primetime is in the business of behavior modification, even if the net result is only that of getting John Q. Public to switch brands. Viewers don't see the distinction and do not exempt dramatic material from the behavior-modification business.

For that reason, most viewers will continue to regard network TV as the most powerful father figure in the land, setting the moral tone and the social agenda of America, ultimately giving sanction to conduct by saying, "That's the way it is." In this respect, audience pressure groups and special interest groups represent legitimate fragments of the nation's TV households. Together they communicate a more profound picture of the public's needs and desires than dozens of opinion polls.

To broadcasters, the people still say, "Yours is the power to shape lives!" By "yours" they mean the network broadcaster. Is it fair that cable and independents who use the same sets escape the public demand for boundaries? One reason is surely scope and penetration. Standard cable, with its news and weather channels, religious and sports channels, its superstations and MTV, is so fractional that it does not threaten consensus values. No one channel can substantially enlarge boundaries on sex, violence, ethnicity and the like.

Another reason for the public perception that "television" equals "networks" surely stems from heavy use of network reruns. (Quite possibly the public, accustomed to the fact that networks can still draw 100 million for a Super Bowl, has not digested the drop in share from 92 percent down to the upper fifties.)

There does seem to be evidence that the public draws a line between standard and extra-pay cable, the latter running uncut theatrical films whose moral impact on children is still considered the responsibility of parents. The line between limited and unlimited content is now drawn between standard cable and premium cable. (The jump in cable rates has probably done as much as anything to highlight the difference between free and pay television, particularly since ESPN, HBO and the others have been larding in commercials. Congress may reregulate cable, particularly in monopoly markets.)

Admittedly, it is not fair to burden networks with total responsibility for television content. Doubtless the public's attitude is lightly coated with ignorance. Nevertheless, when parents, political leaders and moralists are asked who is responsible for "television" programming, they invariably pinpoint network officials. Since the networks take such pride in still being the preeminent force, why shouldn't the moral accounting go the same way?

All of this really means that the public expectation of the boundary-setting responsibility of networks will persist until their power wanes and their purple mantles are assumed by some once and future king. Direct satellites? The fiber optics of AT&T? On that day the perception of legitimizing influence will pass to the new communicator who will also be expected to regulate his program content.

If the video writer and producer want the freedom granted film and other media, they have only to wait for television to lose its power, its prestige and its profitability—the very things that draw most of the talent to it. In that sense, censorship is the compliment paid to clout.

Meanwhile, the party closest to the tastes and values of the "average reasonable viewer" is the one most overlooked in the Hollywood/network scheme of things—the writer. The storyteller invents plots, characters and situations that have time-honored acceptance to ordinary people who crave entertainment. Heroes win and villains lose, Davids prevail and Goliaths bite the dust, honesty is celebrated and dishonesty condemned; from timeless days of old to last night's sitcom, most good stories turn out to be morally good.

2

The Writer-Producer and Network Boundaries

Of all the players in the television game—networks, advertisers, agents, press and writers—only one influences day-to-day programming substance in a major way. Most observers concede that content role to the networks on the theory that he who pays the piper calls the tune. Of course, the power and influence of network top management is considerable. It is sensitive to government regulation, to press reaction and to advertisers. But few networks actually create shows. As producer Grant Tinker says, the networks are only glorified middlemen between the supplier and the consumer. The point to remember is that networks think like distributors, not creators.

An argument can be made for the first-fiddle role of the agent. Without the agent, there is normally no deal, no script, no show. But the agent is essentially a link in the process of weeding out the creative competitors for network approval. Agents never create.

Advertisers pay the bills and call many of the shots, but does that extend to script control? No. They do establish boundaries in advance based on their experience with the negative or positive "environment" of a show as it bears upon their products. But again the advertising impact is indirect; it has more to do with what cannot be said or done on commercial television than with the actors' lines. Advertisers no longer create.

Press reaction, often stimulated by public interest protests or demands, has even less to do with the final content in a given program. In 1980 when the Moral Majority was decrying sex on the tube, the press generated so much heat that in 1981 and 1982 the networks reduced the "jiggles" while programming more "action." This backlash, however, did not affect the conventional ways of presenting sexual scenes.

Following the media protests on sex and violence in 1988, nothing really changed the trend of evolving permissiveness. Moralists screamed and the press roared but except for a "blanding" of the airways in 1989 and 1990, the 1991–1992 seasons reverted to the familiar game of extending the boundaries of taste. The 1992–1993 offerings feature younger casts doing younger things but the substance of television did not change. Critics do not create.

Surely the cardinal influence on television content is that of "programmers"? The answer is no. To be sure, the development executives at the networks (and to some extent at the major studios) determine what properties enter the sweepstakes for spots on the schedule. Without their judgment, nothing gets through the mixing machine; they cue talent on the network needs, and they make suggestions at every stage of development from treatment to script to casting to editing and finally to acceptance or rejection. But however much they may shape the dimensions of given shows, programmers do not compose the dialogue and action implicit in a program's values. Indeed, they tend to disappear once a series succeeds only to resurface when ratings drop. Programmers, in short, set the terms of content taste and values, but leave the implementation to others. The "developers" do not create.

Those who create are the writers. Writers may have less to do with setting boundaries, packaging programs and choosing the winners than any of the top powers, but they have the most influence on the final product. What we see and hear and evaluate according to its quality, its taste and its values is their product.

There may be 500 writers in Hollywood who make a fair living. The Writers Guild lists 4,000 who have credits, 2,000 of whom are actively pushing projects. However, only 100 to 150 make credits each year, and they tend to be the same names over and over. The odds shrink even further where the big money is concerned. Possibly fifty writers do 75 percent of the shows and consequently draw the lion's share of the fees. At any point, as few as ten names are "hot," and they get the megamoney. Major leaguers, their names are on the lips of development executives who want the busiest professionals for any new projects. The reason for sticking with writers with good track records is instructive.

When we interviewed network executives, each emphasized that primetime has an insatiable appetite for material, a hunger that must be appeased 365 days a year. From 8 P.M. to 11 P.M. alone that works out to 1,144 hours per year (22 hours per week, figuring in an extra hour Sunday evening). Multiplied by the Big Three, that comes to 3,432 hours per year. Add in Fox's seven nights for the 1992–1993 season to say nothing of made-for-TV movies at USA, HBO and others, and that brings the network primetime total of 4,576 hours per year. For comparison, figure that the most prolific film studios turn out less than forty hours of theater entertainment per year. How can anybody feed that incredible television maw with only fifty top writers?

Well, they can't. The market, however, finds a way. One solution is to promote writers to producers. Once a writer gets hot, he or she usually becomes a writer-producer. In almost all comedy shows, and in many dramas, the person credited with the title of executive producer is a glorified writer. He or she, in turn, hires other writers (or more often teams of two) who also get a variety of "associate" and "coproducer" titles. Sometimes a nonwriter like Fred Silverman will team up with a writer like Dean Hargrove and the two will share the executive producer title (e.g., on "Matlock"). These writer-producers are the most valuable players in the Hollywood league.

Because they supply the actual program material for the networks, the writer-producers are called suppliers. Naturally, the term they cherish is "creative community." Sometimes the team consists of several partners who combine writing, producing, pitching, administrating and financing talents. For our purposes, we will refer to the writer-producer/supplier as one person.

After developing and selling a show to a network, the supplier usually heads up a team composed of ten or more writers who collaborate on a given show week after week. If one of these writers is essential to the show, he or she may also receive some kind of producer credit, plus the guarantee of so many episodes written and paid for at the going rate. The others on the team are minor leaguers ranging from old pros (maybe a doddering forty-year old) to kids in the Grapefruit League with no credits or experience, hired as "staff" writers for a few weeks. Shortly, we will look at this overworked, overextended, incredibly pressured world of the team in action.

One of the nerves that animated this book was the irony that television is actually waterlogged with everyday, commonplace, American family values. But despite this heavy values content, television is perceived by its critics, its public and even its makers as a wasteland of values, a veritable swamp of sex, violence, bad language and negative stereotyping. Since the writers are most responsible for the final product, we sought to test our findings with those who turn out programming night after night.

In most of the interviews that follow, we asked writer-producers about the ingredients of storytelling. Is there something inherently moral in the genre? Our experience, both in network evaluation and content analysis, had led us to conclude that television stories may contain antisocial elements, but the perspective remains prosocial and high-minded.

One reason for thinking so is the nature of the fairy and folk tales that are precursors of television drama. In Vladimir Propp's pioneering work, *Morphology of the Folktale*,[1] only seven leading characters inhabit the stories—hero, villain, false hero, donor, dispatcher, princess and father.

In a typical adventure show like "Angel Street," "Top Cops" or "In the Heat of the Night," these leading characters appear with predictable regularity. The hero is the detective; the false hero is a bad cop or dishonest businessman; the donor (who does good deeds) is a doctor or kindhearted relative; the dispatcher (who sends the heroes and heroines out on the chase) is the crusty captain with a heart of gold; the princess is the victim (male or female) who needs rescuing; and the father is the grateful person who wants the princess rescued.

Given this formula, it is almost impossible for an adventure show to be immoral. From our content analyses we discovered that almost every television drama contains a principled point of view: namely, that goodness is better than badness; that courage is better than cowardice; that tolerance is better than intolerance; that the strong should help the weak; that laws should be obeyed despite their flouting by the powerful (who generally meet their match); that personal relationships should be suffused with caring, trust and sharing; and that, above all, honesty is the key to a good character.

This has been called the "altruism index" of American television. Given the wide circulation of the Gerbner Violence Index[2] and its preoccupation with atypical incidents, we wonder why there is not more equal treatment for the overwhelming substance of altruistic incidents.

One question we addressed to all the writer-producers concerned the deliberate salting of comedy and drama for exploitation and sensation. Do antisocial incidents serve only to season the moral perspectives of the show, or do they dominate the program? C.B. DeMille was the master of sex-and-violence seasoning in religious shows. Often accused of using the Ten Commandments as an incidental backdrop for battle scenes and scantily clad dancers, he was able to finesse the censorship boards in his day by pointing to the biblical nature of his films.

Nevertheless, from Aesop to Dickens and from Frank Capra to Gary David Goldberg, popular storytelling takes the side of the heroes against the villains, of the white hats against the dark hats, of human goodness against demonic evil.

Could it be otherwise? Try to imagine some of television's popular shows written from an immoral, antisocial perspective:

- On "Cosby," Dr. Huxtable encourages son Theo to cheat on an exam in order to get into law school. Meanwhile, wife Claire carries on a torrid affair with her law partner.

- On "L.A. Law," the women partners conspire to keep homosexual juniors from qualifying for promotion, resign any case that is not attracting big fees, and send the retarded Benny to *One Flew Over the Cuckoo's Nest*.

- In "Wonder Years," the young lead has his first sexual experience with a prostitute and discovers that using women as sex objects is fulfilling.

- In "Civil Wars," lying becomes the basis for personal relationships.

- "60 Minutes" does a segment on Champion Mills in North Carolina and concludes that polluting the Pigeon River is a small price to pay for corporate profits in a capitalistic society.

- On "Designing Women," Julia encourages Suzanne to lie about Anthony's parole behavior because what's one more "nigger" sent to jail?

- "Who's the Boss?" features verbal attacks on Jews, lesbians and the Pope.

- "Murphy Brown" aborts during her final trimester, saying that she's too busy to be a mother. (Little did she know that Vice President Quayle was on her case.)

- "Coach" throws a couple of games.
- "MacGyver" sells his scientific know-how to Libya so it can nuke Israel.

Quite apart from advertising and standards regulation, no writer would dream of such plotting. However much television writers may yearn for freedom from conventions, this is not the direction in which they would move. They might think, perhaps, of inventing wild characters who would put a reverse spin on moral attitudes. They might well portray the hypocrisy behind the facade of those who talk morality and live corruption. True, they punch up action shows with multiple car crashes and automatic weapons. Doubtless, they inject as much sexual tension as the boundaries permit and as much salty language as conventions now accept, but they would never endorse a life-style based on dishonesty, injustice, betrayal and criminal intent.

Occasionally a supplier as talented as a Steven Bochco will transcend the superficial morality of conventional police drama with a moral realism, or he will choreograph a "Cop Rock" a bit ahead of his time. But he is not going to endorse evil over good, wrong over right, lying over honesty, compromise over honor, hatred over love.

Would anybody? Lives there a television writer with a soul so dead that he or she would become the Sam Kinison of sexist comedy, or the Howard Stern of four-letter words, or the Peter Greenaway (his film, *The Cook, The Thief, His Wife and Her Lover*, has a little boy hung up on a wall and tortured) of sadomasochistic television?

If so, such writers would find themselves *hors de combat* with the network censor. Pay cable has dissolved boundaries, but in all other television, suppliers would run into a brick wall of public revulsion and viewer abandonment.

Our interviews with Norman Lear, Gary David Goldberg, Maurie Goodman, Steven Bochco and Bill D'Angelo explain just why radical content has never made it onto network television. They also give us a feel for the surprising influences of the public on their work.

VIEWS OF WRITER-PRODUCERS TOWARD TELEVISION CONTENT

Norman Lear

Norman Lear's office in Century City looks across Santa Monica Boulevard into the exclusive backyard of Beverly Hills. Golfers are seen in the background, shanking drives beyond the manicured fairways that are off limits to Jews among others. Casually attired in slacks and sweater, the creator of "All in the Family," "Maude," "Mary Hartman, Mary Hartman," "The Jeffersons," and several theatrical films (e.g., *The Princess Bride*, directed by Rob Reiner) is talking about his values.

I can't write without values shining through everything I do. To me, it's a matter of being serious. You separate the serious people in this business from those who are not. Either you are serious about your wife, your children, your religion, your work, your citizenship, or you are—what?—frivolous, cynical? I guess I'm serious, at least about the values I subscribe to.

How does that square with being a comedy writer and producer? Lear had said in a previous interview that he was at heart a jokewriter, not a missionary. His success in comedy, however, had given him a platform for his ideas. "Most comedy writers are very serious. Of course, we see life from the opposite end of the telescope, that is, the comedic perspective. I see the comic lining in the jacket of life—but that doesn't mean I'm not serious."

To illustrate, the writer launches into a description of two fifteen-minute shows he had hoped would make it on CBS after the 11 o'clock news. One of them features a woman who is a news writer and reporter on one of the new "infotainment" shows. When she gets home, her mother calls each night to get the news.

Why should she watch the news when her daughter can tell her about it? So the daughter (on camera alone with a phone) tells Mom what happens. Only it is her commentary on her own (on-air) commentary. Remember, this is live and she can really talk about what happened to the world that day.

Smiling at the freshness of this approach, Lear describes the second fifteen minutes. "It is completely different. Again, it's one person, sort of a Dabney Coleman type, who is outrageous, fatuous, ribald, and full of Sidney Sheldon stories into which he injects himself after much heavy breathing. This will offend people, but he makes me laugh."

This year, Lear has sold a comedy series in which he is again the head-writer to CBS. He calls it "Sunday Dinner," and the first episode had network brass laughing but scratching their heads.

"It's about a guy I should understand," he says, "who falls in love with a woman half his age and brings her home to meet his surprised and resentful family. As they gather for Sunday dinner he introduces this wonderful woman, an environmentalist with a spiritual concern for people and things, to his children who are her age but who represent quite different values." (Note: The show received fair ratings, but was canceled.)

Lear observes that one way of doing a good story is to satirize principles that represent the opposite of what you believe—like short-term profits in the American economy where instant returns war with long-term success and humane practices. Or like his satire on Washington, D.C., called "The Powers that Be."

What is he trying to say in his new series? As a liberal and a citizen, Lear has been the target of the religious right, which has called him a "secular humanist" and the "number-one enemy of the American family in our generation." Lear says that he answered the last accusation by becoming, with his wife Lyn, a parent for the fourth time, in his sixty-sixth year.

What he took aim at in "Sunday Dinner" was American values, which he finds in disarray. "Our culture celebrates the material and largely ignores the spiritual—greed is the order of the day—and many people rightly feel that the moral ground is crumbling beneath their feet." Why, he asks, should the devil have all the good tunes and the pietists on the right have exclusive rights to morality? This also holds, he feels, for the California crowd of New Age swamis and the "I'm OK, you're OK" ego boosters.

Lear deplores the fact that public schools are loath to deal with spiritual values. In the zeal to keep sectarian religion out of the schools, they have made it into a secular wasteland. Between the forces of religiosity on the one side and spiritual hollowness on the other, says Lear, he finds himself in the middle of the road, "where as Texans are wont to put it, you usually find nothing but a yellow streak and a dead armadillo."

To counter the absolutist extremes, Lear had his characters in "Sunday Dinner" examine the fundamentalists and narrow sectarians in order to promote what he called "the spiritual imagination." He also explained cracks in the bottom line of the business types, the "me" generation and the religious racketeers.

One of his characters for a 1992 series was invented for a talk to educators. This blue-collar theist put it this way:

> Hi. You can call me Bill. I'm what you call a working-class American. I've got a wife who works (I wish she didn't have to) and three grown kids—a couple of cars I keep up myself. . . . I got a house, a mortgage and bills that could choke a horse! . . . (but) something's really wrong. Inside I feel like an empty room—and here's the part that's tough to talk about: I'm thinkin' a lot lately about the G-word. You know, God. Damn, why is that so hard to say? . . . My kids turn off at the mention of the G-word. They think I'm talking God cause I'm gettin' on in years . . . no, it has to do with that question they made into a movie: What's it all about, Alfie? . . . I wish I had it to do all over again. We've talked about that round the dinner table.

Lear conceded that his team made some mistakes on "Sunday Dinner," but he is still projecting a dinner table that could make it into 30 million homes where comedy is cross-lit with common values, including the yearning for the transcendent, the otherness of life. Or as Lear put it, bringing the G-word back into American conversation. Now what will the conservatives have to say about those "family values"? As for the real secular humanists, they will be radically embarrassed by Lear's intentions to introduce God-talk into primetime.

Speaking of the "kids" on his shows who do the writing, Lear says that entirely too many of their counterparts in and out of the television networks know too little of life to write about it.

> Most of the kids you talk to in the entertainment industry have horizons no broader than the TV set itself. They were brought up on the tube, and it is from the tube that they get their values, their judgment, their sense of history. If it didn't happen on television, it is beyond their experience, certainly not worth programming on a network. They are prisoners of a sitcom mentality.

Lear believes in learning by your failures. One of his least successful shows was called "AKA Pablo." The world was not ready for it, least of all the Hispanic world that objected to the unvarnished portrayals. Lear notes that the young writers he works with simply do not know that sixteen-year-old girls don't jump up and down and say "oh mah God" when their mother announces lamb for dinner.

> That's why you see so few children on TV who act like children. The kid-programmers at the networks never knew any other kind except the ones already on television and they were unreal . . . it must be agonizing for experienced producers to take their ideas to twenty-four-year-old business school graduates who are comedy programmers at the network but who have never written a show, edited a film, produced a hit, acted in a series or worried about audience expectations.

The juvenile syndrome also infects writers. Lear tells why no new show can afford the best writers today.

> They all have their own shows or projects and are priced out of the supplier's market. So you make do with as many solid professionals as you can induce to join you plus some very young, potentially talented writers who have nothing to their credit but a few rejected scripts. Even when you hire them as staff writers, their agents want $5,000 a week. It simply does not make sense to produce a nine-show deal (when a network licenses nine shows for production with a commitment for a full season hanging fitfully by a thread) unless you can pay "scale," which is about $2,000 a week for a staff team. I know some young writers who are considered hot by a network on the basis of having had a small part in a near hit now off the air, and they are making million-dollar deals. It's madness. On the other hand it is even worse to realize that an agent, who does nothing more than represent somebody when a series is put together, can pull down $40,000 a week. That's more than the producer or the writers get all together and they do all the work.

The writer-interviewees did not agree on many things, but they were painfully consistent in their loathing of agents.

In a nice segue into the next conversation, Lear was asked what writers have the best sets of values in Hollywood. "Well, you have to start with Gary Goldberg. . . . "

Gary David Goldberg

In an interview conducted on Paramount's lot shortly before "Family Ties" closed, Goldberg sat in a typical studio office that looked more like a barracks building than the venue for one of the most successful producers in the industry. Sitting beneath a large picture of his black Lab,[3] Goldberg was asked to discuss his vision for the show.

> I don't think anybody ever conceived of a communications system that would come into every home, producing audiences of 100 million people. In a sense that is everybody,

and that's why we have always felt a particular concern for children. I don't want anything in "Family Ties" which would make me uncomfortable as a father. On the other hand, I think TV's influence is very benign. Family values will always be the strongest influence in a child's life and when they are solid and strong, it's very hard to rock that boat with any dramatic turbulence. It's very hard to knock it out of the water with entertainment material.

How unique is the Goldberg concern for humaneness on the air?

Sometimes critics assume that people who create TV are not also part of society . . . we have children . . . we go home . . . we vote . . . we care. That sets up some self-created boundaries. In writing, we might feel that creatively we should go in a boundary direction, but we can't do it because we live with and are happy to live with the fact that children watch the show in great numbers. I think [producer] David Milch is right here, that you must first let your writers be creative without restrictions, and then you must go back and self-edit. And if you don't, the network should.

Goldberg added that comedy, at least comedy between eight and nine P.M. has very different boundaries from later night drama, something like "Hill Street Blues" or "L.A. Law." These are going to push the envelope. "On our show, the younger people without children are much more willing to push that envelope, but the older ones are much more the guardians of traditional values. It's very odd for me. As one who was an outlaw in the sixties, I find myself a defender of traditional values. It's funny."

This sense of being an old person in a young person's profession was shared by Michael Ogiens, Bill D'Angelo, Steve Bochco and others who may be in their forties but look thirty. To them, however, the writers in their early twenties look sixteen and are in fact young enough to be their children. Writers share the irony of age with baseball players who, in their late thirties, are too old to play and too young to retire.

Goldberg discussed his relations with the editor/censor in the department of standards.

I saw a lot more of our standards editor than I did of anybody from the network program department. We work very closely with a family man whose instincts I trust. Now, I don't live in fear of critics or pressure groups. In fact, I'm willing to lose certain people as an audience. If upset, let them watch elsewhere. The danger (of legalistic boundaries) is that you never take a point of view about anything and end up with a nothing message. Take abortion, admittedly a volatile issue. And yet there is nothing more stupid on TV than a character who passionately gives both sides of that issue. You should be for it or against it. An audience must be capable of accepting that character's position, and the producer must be capable of fair-mindedness in the long run.

Reminded about an episode in "Family Ties" on sexual behavior, Goldberg recalled the angry letters he got from people who felt that he was encouraging premarital sex by talking about condoms.

The fact is that in families where sexual behavior is discussed, sexual activity is delayed. I can tell you that the show is very autobiographical. . . . My daughter is now fifteen . . . and some of the dialogue for a show comes out of our experience and out of seminars we attend. Believe me, moralistic sermons never stop anybody. Therefore there were two points of view in that show: One, sex is never a test of love. If you love somebody, forcing them to have sex is a loveless act. The one who does that reveals that he or she does not truly love. If somebody loves you, that person should respect your feelings.

Two, a parent is someone you can talk to about sex. All right, those are the two values, as you would call them, in the show. Now, who is the audience for this information? Not the ones who are strongly opposed to premarital sex. Not the ones who are sexually active and will continue to be. No, we wanted to talk to kids who had not made up their minds, who were perhaps confused and trying to figure it out for themselves.

Looking for all the world like the teacher he had intended to be, Goldberg said that the nation had better wake up to the fact that teenage sex is epidemic. Babies are having babies. "Family Ties" is advising them to wait, please wait. Do not have sex now.

But if you are going to, for God's sake, use birth control. But we got letters from parents who said they stayed up all night discussing with our teens the values on that show. Incidentally, one of the great things that standards does is reply to letters of complaint. Maurie Goodman [then NBC vice president of standards, West Coast] wrote beautiful letters to those who were upset, explaining the care with which they reviewed the show and affirming the principles we were trying to dramatize.

Since letters of complaint often miss the balance in a show and concentrate only on the portions that offend, what about the people who missed the "don't do it" message and heard only the word *condom*? And for that matter, do liberals — who make up most of the creative community — have the right to dramatize their messages that might seem antisocial to conservatives?

Goldberg conceded that television writers tend to be liberals, but he was unwilling to admit that conservative values seldom make it on the air.

When I think of all those years that I had to watch Jack Webb shows where he was standing for law and order over freedom, and all those FBI shows glorifying J. Edgar Hoover — shows out of all proportion to reality — well, that was pushing a certain ideology too. A lot of right-wing people found that reassuring. But I am a member of this society, and I have a right to present some of my points of view. I read, I support certain causes, I'm socially concerned. And you can't make a TV show without the characters having some point of view. By the way, Michael J. Fox's character, Alex, is just at much at odds with my point of view as Archie Bunker is from Norman Lear's.

Ideology aside, is there one value like honesty or justice or peace on earth that a Gary David Goldberg tries to dramatize in his shows?

If you ask me what one value I try to affirm uncompromisingly, it is just the family it-self. Someone wrote me that after watching our show, her whole family wanted to hug one another. On one show we had Alex, who is very flip about his sisters, go to bat for them because we wanted to say that no matter what the differences and the arguments, when push comes to shove, he loves them and they love him. He will step forward and take care of his sisters. Once an executive watched a cassette with me and he said, "If my son ever talked to me like Alex talks to his father, I would smack him." And I said, "Yeah and your son is going to leave home at seventeen and you'll never see him again because you are confusing order and control." The Keaton parents have control; you may not see order there, but they have the control based on love and respect. And that is not a liberal or conservative value but one that has been espoused and proved over the centuries.

One of the more difficult things to maintain, said Goldberg, is the consistency of characterization in a show. Children are going to grow. But the character in a comedy remains much the same, just more mature. That is what keeps the values or messages in a show from getting artificial. He was reminded of a priceless line uttered by the teenager Malory, who was born to shop. In her paper on the American Revolution, she wrote, "The British wore red; we dressed casual." It is not only funny, it defines the character.

The actors are very helpful. We did a show which touched on religion. I had written the last scene about death. What is God like? I said that God looks like Cary Grant. People wrote by the hundreds protesting that, but the actors felt very comfortable saying those lines. Often guys like Ralph Daniels [the VP for NBC Standards], whom I respect and love, will come to me and say, "Look at this line again, will you, and tell me if you think it should stand." I may say, "This is what we meant but if is not clear to your people, maybe we ought to write around it." We find ourselves being very careful with jokes on drugs. Sometimes you sacrifice humor because kids can take things the wrong way.

Goldberg said that he had never appealed a standards decision by going to the network president. "The important thing to me is that they are fans of the show. They are not arbitrary. The head man [Ralph Daniels] is the class of the network. His people look at the context of every line. And of course they look at it from their perspective, which is rightly different from mine. That's the creative and the critical out of which comes resolution."

What about stereotyping? Has "Family Ties" ever received any criticism for ta-boos on race or ethnicity?

We hear that we do not use enough blacks. We are also very careful about the charac-terization of women. I wanted to push that perception up a notch or two. And I also wanted to present a softer view of parenthood which does not control families by fear. That is what I have to say as a writer. That is part of my world view, and it represents the reason I became a writer . . . to get this out. And the miracle for me is that it goes out on world television and is validated by the acceptance level.

In one of the books on Hollywood, written by an author who was complaining about the antibusiness ideology on television, you and Norman Lear were accused of propagandizing your Jewish, secular views on the public air. Does that bother you?

> That's not a terrible thing to admit. It's not as if you called me a child molester. I am what I am. But we try to be very fair to other ideologies. I don't remember Jack Webb being nice to a liberal, secular Jewish type. Take Alex Keaton. We do not make him ridiculous, but very winning . . . young, very bright, energetic, popular, attractive. He is not some conservative nerd. Why should these values be mutually exclusive? A good comedy transcends that. Here's a family which holds values which counsel respect for parents, respect for sisters and brothers, respect for the views of others, respect for society. It glorifies education. The father does the dishes and the kids do chores. I hope it is subtle, but along with the laughs, you get a moral backdrop to the action.

One of Goldberg's favorite expressions is the "compact" he has with his audience. No matter what the uplift or the humanity, a show has to be entertaining.

> We are comedy. That's our compact with NBC and with America. We have sworn that each week we will deliver a half hour of humor. When I first started out, I wanted each show to address a major issue. But there was no audience for that . . . and we got bored with it. Now the best stories are the small ones that look so trite in *TV Guide* but which work because of the writing and characterization. The value orientation must come in subtly, by surprise, naturally, unforced.

Looking back, Goldberg referred to his first days as a staff writer for MTM Productions. Nobody on staff had a single credit, but

> Grant Tinker [then head of Mary Tyler Moore Productions] had this talent that looks deceptively easy. It's not. He always talked to us about why we came into the business. He had this faith in us which brings out the best. One of the talented writers on WKRP Cincinnati said, "Grant never wrote a single line, but his fingerprints are scattered all over the show." I think about that now with my young staff. And I remember the first time I brought him in something I thought was great. He gave me that charming smile and said, "I can get this from anybody. I want what can only come from you." Wow! You don't think that sends you flying?

Does Goldberg's point of view support our thesis that television is just as influenced by society as society is by television? Assuming that writer-producers are the principal architects of their series, the answer is yes. Goldberg's values are as shaped by viewers as his shows shape viewers. Writers, immersed in the prevailing values of America, feed back those meanings in the dramas they create. Social influence and television is a two-way street, or as Goldberg said, "we breathe in and breathe out the surrounding atmosphere."

David Milch

Another product of MTM Productions is David Milch. In 1990 he won critical praise for the series "Capital Newsroom," whose reporters and editors are thinly disguised workers at the *Washington Post*. At the time of this interview, Milch was wrapping up a short-lived spinoff from "Hill Street Blues," which he produced during its past two years following Steven Bochco's departure.

Sitting at his favorite table in the breakfast room of the venerable Beverly Hills Hotel, the former Yale poet and professor was ruminating about the sensitive relationship between a writer and a network censor. Called standards editors, these network executives review scripts for offense, accuracy, taste and values. Traditionally, the censor operates as an ombudsman for the viewer. Milch, an Emmy winner of philosophical bent, was saying:

> That conception of the editor as surrogate for the viewer is a curiously intriguing one but not without dangers. My first impulse is, let him help me by telling me what the viewer will like as opposed to what is good for him. On the other hand, I have to trust my own instincts at this point in the creative process as over against someone in authority. At the early point of development of a show, I am not sure what the editor should do. At this inchoate state, I know I want to shrink the network programmer. I don't want him around.
>
> Also, audience expectations and a show's continuity are quite tricky. Let's say that Gary David Goldberg wanted to make Michael Fox's character into a flaming liberal. The ombudsman for the viewer must object. The programmer goes crazy. But at that point of playing with an idea, you must abstain, suspend judgments. Even if you betray a show's franchise and alter the chemistry that made the show successful, you must go down that street of fancy. Maybe Alex Keaton falls in love with a liberal and you get the emotional beats from this all-consuming action. So you play with that for a while. You probably keep him somewhat consistent in the long run but a recurring character can be a combination of opposites, like Belker in "Hill Street." Otherwise the characters get all normalized, ground down and lose their eccentricities.
>
> So my sense is that the editor should stay with his values and audience expectations and leave my characters to grow. I can't isolate all the effects on content out of the mix but the adversarial nature of standards to creator should not be changed.

Milch's point bears repeating. The best system ever devised for protecting the writer's freedom *and* the responsibility to viewers is the rivalry between talent and editor. We asked Milch about the mentality of writers, the extent to which they referred consciously or unconsciously to their values and ideologies. He replied that most probably suspend their moral framework while considering the likes and dislikes of the viewer, the intentions and quality of an episode. The problem for the writer, and certainly for the editor, is that in returning to a value orientation, one might have to oppose 99 percent of what had already happened with the story. "The paradox for the editor, as Ralph Daniels [NBC standards chief] has refashioned him, is that after elevating oneself to the level of artistry and the total range of creative perceptions, one has to make judgments primarily on the moral aspects. But maybe one makes a better moral judgment for having gone through the crafting experience. I think Ralph would say that morality is a function of taste."

Would it be useful for a network to codify its system for evaluation, or at least to talk with writers about their own critical method?

> I don't think you can codify what you are describing. What we are talking about here is just as important, perhaps more so, for the programmers and top management to cope with than the censors alone. Why can't a network frame its own hermeneutics, its own critical philosophy? I would suggest to editors that they consider the very elusive process of understanding the intentions and fabric of a show as opposed to individual moments, determining what can and cannot be included. With the axing of the standards department, NBC is in danger of losing a very noble ambition. The way it's been done is by an ad hoc process, by individual case; the subtext, then, is for editors to be ever alert, responsive, to stay emotionally alive as they encounter things, because it is that, rather than the superimposition of censorial checkmarks, that strengthens a show. It's not this bad word or that violent action that they look for. If I understood Ralph Daniels, it is not hard and fast rules that count but the very air a program breathes. It gets away from the Orwellian and Kafka-esque perception of the network censor, but do you think GE [NBC's parent] will buy it? Will they understand or care?

While on that subject, we asked Milch about his reaction to the CBS method of transferring the standards task to the programming department and asking suppliers to be coresponsible for censorship.

> That's a mistake born of broadcasting ignorance. It's asking a person to wear two hats at the same time, and I don't know how he can do both honestly. The genius of the process is to incorporate the dimension of time . . . to allow seemingly mutually exclusive goals to cohabit by assigning them primacy at different moments of time. First the creative and then the critical. [Asking the program department to enforce standards] forces a programmer to do both simultaneously, and that is impossible unless the guy is a schizophrenic. I mistrust that. A certain kind of cynicism or duplicity would have to enter the process.

Thinking back to some of the battles over "Hill Street Blues," Milch described the script that led to Steven Bochco's favorite phrase, "pushing at the bindings." It was an episode called "Trial by Fury" in which Davenport (woman defense lawyer) and Furillo (precinct captain) were arguing. She says accusingly, "You threw the book out the window," and he replies, "I went by the book, but I just pushed a little hard at the bindings."

Milch is amused by the fact that everybody in Hollywood tries to psychoanalyze Steven Bochco, a tribute to his originality.

> My own impression is that he needs a true dialectic, an antithetical moment. Steven talks about pushing at the bindings because he truly needs the adversarial relationship with standards. It allows him to find out what he thinks, to make articulate his inten-

tions, and to crystallize his dramaturgical sense. But that kind of butting up against authority lies outside my own process of dramaturgy. The antitheses that I envision happens to be within the framework of the world of the work as opposed to the framework of the creative process of a show. It's just a different methodology. If that analysis is correct, I suspect that in the new CBS/NBC system Bochco would be distressed to have to play both moments of the dialectic. How would he ever get to the synthetic moment under those circumstances? The writer becomes a Janus-headed beast. If Steven no longer had Maurie Goodman to scream at, what would he do?

In a later chapter, David Milch offers his original perspective on the "influences — good and bad — of pressure groups on writers. Milch understands the collaborative game of television programming in which the writer pursues his "fancy" and the network provides him with feedback from the public. Both activities serve a purpose.

Maurie Goodman

David Milch's suspicions about the CBS of financial mogul Larry Tisch, and the NBC of General Electric, proved prophetic during the 1988–1989 season. Both virtually dismantled their standards departments. Maurie Goodman, together with every editor but two on the West Coast, was sent packing by NBC. His boss, Ralph Daniels, took early retirement and was replaced by "sales-oriented" executives. Undaunted, Goodman hung out his shingle as a writer and began to peddle his ideas, treatments and scripts around the studios and networks.

In that capacity, he is the typical professional writer, far more representative of what goes on developmentally than what occurs in the elite circles of Lear, Goldberg, Milch and Bochco.

Goodman has the body of a boxer, which he was, and the demeanor of a salesman, which he was, before joining NBC. Few people in the business know that he is also a world-class gambler, having participated in the World Series of Poker (by invitation only in Las Vegas) and in high-level blackjack in the casinos. One of his scripts, now making the rounds, is based on the exploits of a big-time gambler who uses his skills to bring down the corrupters and scam artists. After freelancing for two years, and selling a couple of scripts, Goodman has returned to the network side as the number-two man in standards at Fox. He describes the process of selling scripts from the ground up.

Unlike Norman Lear, I don't walk in to Stringer or Tisch [CEO and president, respectively, at CBS] and say, "Howard, Larry, I got this great idea on the back of an envelope and you're gonna love it, kiddo." Not long ago, I pitched a series to NBC about my professional gambler. They turned it down, not because it was about gambling but because it was not "way out." So I called Dan Philly, vice president for development at NBC and asked what they meant. He says, "Maurie, we're looking for off-the-wall stuff right now . . . you know, like a one-eyed autistic dwarf private eye." That was a big help to me.

Goodman, who still looks like he could go ten rounds, pauses to reflect on the irony: Networks churn out the same old thing but are always looking for the exotic. "Right now, Steven Bochco is running "Cop Rock," a musical about the police. When that word got out, NBC called Disney, which is developing a cop show for them, and I understand that Warren Littlefield[4] told them to make it a musical." (Note: "Cop Rock" was canceled after several weeks of disappointing ratings.)

Unlike most of the other writers interviewed, Goodman is not bothered by the developmental layer of the "kids" in network programming.

> Of course, we look back from our age levels and they do look like teenagers. But it's a youngster's game because age is not a factor in success. No, a writer like me has to go into a network with backup. First, you go to a major [studio] like Universal. Their development people will look at your idea, as they looked at mine, assign you to an established writer-producer and together you rework the idea and pitch it.

Writers across the board, like Goodman, share an impression of network programmers, whom they feel are "programmed" to say no. The minute they say yes, they stick their necks out and that can be dangerous. The exception, says Goodman, is walking in with an agent like Michael Ovitz, who will call the entertainment president and say he has an idea and a star to go with it. That improves chances. At least you get a fast decision.

> Very rarely do you see people like Brandon Tartikoff [formerly head of Paramount] who is not only decisive but who comes up with so many ideas himself. Brandon is probably responsible for at least two or three of the series for NBC that are really hot. He simply gives an idea to a producer like Michael Mann, and the supplier will develop it. Then, if Brandon likes it, you get a deal for a pilot and six [shows] or a pilot and eight. That's the way to fly in Hollywood.

Goodman says he went into one network with an Emmy-winning writer plus Dick Lindheim, who is in charge of all development at Universal Studios. They never got to talk with anyone who could actually make a decision. They had to pitch the idea to young programmers and depend on them to present that concept to the real decision makers. "No one," says Goodman, "can verbalize your idea like you can. Maybe you leave a one-page concept sheet [just the idea, log line and story progress] and a standard five-page treatment which plots out several shows. Then you wait and wait."

When he shifted from standards to writing, from "censoring" to "creating," did he make any conscious effort to get in a creative instead of an evaluative frame of mind? And what values, if any, does he try to incorporate in scripts?

> The writer thinks log lines—the one line I can throw at these people that they will remember. A good example is the producer of "Nasty Boys" [Dick Wolf] who walked in on Brandon with a picture about wall high of the hit team dressed up, in their black

leather ninja clothes, and they were all holding automatics. At the top of the poster it said, "Nasty Boys." At the bottom of the picture it said, "We make house calls." Wolf walked out with a commitment.

Wolf, says Goodman, threw him a welcome assignment to cowrite several scenes on another police show.

> They gave me a "beat sheet," which is divided into four acts. I get maybe one act which has six beats, like, "Sam enters the bar and sees the crook." That's one beat. Two, there is a shootout, three, the police show up and view the body. The job is very much like writing full treatment in which every part of a script is outlined for "moments" or "beats" which pull the action along.

Goodman notes that the life of a struggling writer is one of rejections and unreturned phone calls. By contrast, a helping hand evokes passionate gratitude. "Steven Bochco took time out of his incredible schedule to read one of my scripts and give me notes. He spends two hours with me saying this is great and this is lousy. You think that's not rare?"

Goodman was reminded that not many people get to see program content from the standards side *and* the writer's side, this adversarial arrangement so admired by Milch and Goldberg. After plowing through hundreds of scripts and appraising scores of pilots from the standpoint of taste and values, what is it like to start with the blank page?

> I really think that taste is the same from any side of the business. But whatever the problems of sex or violence, the writer is on a different track wondering if his dialogue will snap off the page and grab the people who are reading it. Are any of his characters so outstanding that the reader can visualize this person, what they call a breakaway character? Nobody knew in advance that Michael Fox's "Alex" would make that show, but that is what every writer prays for.

Putting back on his standards cap, Goodman stated that once a program is launched, a producer has more to do with censors than with the entertainment executives, who by this time are on to the next deal.

> What the programmers at NBC did was mostly to keep [Brandon] Tartikoff informed of a show's progress. They'd look at the "updates" [a sheet on each show on the air and in development] and say this actor is leaving or that writer will be hired. Brandon, as entertainment president, is the last word and the others are mostly filters. And that's what makes him as good as he is. He can look at a show and tell what works and what doesn't. Grant Tinker, on the other hand, was just one of those guys everyone instinctively wanted to please. He had a way of delivering bad news that the producer would end up thanking him profusely and feeling grateful. That's why he was the most successful network chief in history.

Maurie Goodman had already introduced Steven Bochco, who is arguably the most creative writer-producer since Norman Lear.

Steven Bochco

A surprisingly large proportion of the people visited on behalf of this book referred at one point or another to the creator of "Hill Street Blues," of "L.A. Law," and "Doogie Howser, M.D." We first interviewed Bochco before he contracted with CBS to do "Doogie" and several other shows. Sitting in a modest office, he pulled a baseball cap over salt-and-pepper hair, grabbed a bat, which he twirled about from time to time, and addressed one of his favorite themes—the intolerable interference of network standards. Unlike Milch, Goldberg and Goodman, Bochco is not a fan of network editing, whether adversarial and creative or bitter and divisive. He begins with the writer's credo.

> Since you ask about values, I think that mine grew out of anecdotes, stories so funny and wonderfully illustrative of the silliest and most noble aspects of life that I incorporate them in all my writing. But values are not hanging out like clothes on a line. There is a big difference between "L.A. Law" and "Nightrider." The difference is in intent, complexity, density, ideas, thematics. And that entitles me, I think, to respect.

Bochco said he objects to the very existence of network standards and the limitations they put on creative people. The problem he sees is the parent-child relationship. The network-parent tells the writer-child what he can and cannot do. Why? Because it has the authority.

> But if you have to have editors, they should all be like Frank Dowling [now at NBC programming]. You know that in life there are very very few gifted people, and then there is a fast middle ground of mediocre ranging from low mediocre to high mediocre. That is true of writers, artists, directors, shoemakers, whatever. In this particular area of standards, Frank is one of the rare gifted people. Aside from the fact that he simply works hard at the job, and by that I mean that he studies more, reads more, thinks about it more, agonizes, more . . . then if he likes something in my script he will fight for it harder and longer than anyone else. Now Ralph Daniels [then vice president for NBC Standards], I think he is one of the nicest, smartest, truest gentlemen I have ever encountered in twenty years of working at TV, but the bottom line is, I cause Ralph trouble. With all due respect, because I adore the guy, I know that if I were sitting with him outside the job, in twenty seconds he would be agreeing with me.

Thinking back to one of his struggles at NBC with "L.A. Law," Bochco latched onto a line that still rankles in his heart. He explained that a divorce attorney was showing a wife some compromising photos that had been taken of her philandering husband. The viewer does not see the pictures but the attorney describes them. Bochco, with rising anger, describes the scene:

The lawyer says that here is a photo of George and his honey doing some love-making in a hot tub. "They are engaged in a sex act that can best be described by a two digit number." That was it. And standards tells me that I cannot use the metaphor of 69 on the air. And I start screaming and saying that we never say the number, you idiots, and I'm using a euphemism and it's damned funny. It is a smart line. It comes out of my artistic sensibility . . . and I don't give a damn what anybody says, it is a delightful, nonoffensive line.

Is there anything that Bochco would have a network restrict, in language, sex, violence or stereotyping? The answer is nothing. "You leave people free to do shows their way, and if the audience is offended they can tune it out." Like many successful rhetoricians, Bochco is a master of the relative. He mentions the fact that Los Angeles television station KTLA aired a show that used every one of Carlin's dirty words and got away with it because they plastered the air with advisories (viewer warnings before and during shows thought to require parental guidance). And what about the film, *The Deerhunter*, which featured a Russian roulette sequence and evidently caused some borderline people to commit suicide the same way?

I was still doing "Hill Street," NBC was running "Miami Vice," which was the most graphically violent show on the air. At any given moment a cop or a perp would blow people out of the room, cut in half by submachine guns. I won't say if I would let my kids watch that show, but the decision would be my responsibility. Now, Gary David Goldberg chooses to do the kinds of family shows that he does so brilliantly but not because someone is standing over him with a club. So why should they stand over me and tell me what values I can stress? That is the worst kind of censorship because it is self-imposed. It begins to cut away at the edge of TV so as to make it by and large the crap that it is. You go out to the movies, and you see the worst kind of irresponsible story-telling, the most graphic violence, the most gratuitous, nonmotivated erotica. So what? Don't go.

Describing his own creative process, which is heavily collaborative, he says,

I am open to all kinds of creative input. Like baseball, this is a team sport. On one show we may have a team of ten writers. My job is to listen to each vision, each story, each contribution. We have a bunch of consultants on "L.A. Law" just as we did on "Hill Street." Two writers are also attorneys and we have a very bright guy who is a technical advisor from UCLA. It's the whole tapestry we are after, asking the right questions, seeing the right beats, finding the subplots and tying it all together.

What are Bochco's values? He mentions honesty and competence.

But I think I put the highest premium on courage, a very underrated word. You have to have courage in this part of the business if you are going to put the bolt in the hole week after week. And incidentally, I am not interested in film. TV is the most extraordinary medium in history. I feel responsible to it and for it. Video does not replace TV. When you get a movie, put it on cassette, it is no longer film but television. And don't worry anymore about size. A forty-five inch screen can give relatively the same experience that you get in a theater. And you will learn more by watching *Gone with the Wind* on cassette because you can back it up and study it. I love this medium, and that is why I get so crazy whenever the creative impulse is deadened.

Bochco wins some and loses some. In the 1991–1992 season, he managed to get Doogie Howser deflowered, at least off screen; at the other extreme his singing and dancing cops went the way of all ratings. Still, many people in the industry think that Steven Bochco deserves the top award for courage with his canceled series, "Cop Rock." Critic John Leonard of *New York* magazine called it the "bravest try of the year."

William D'Angelo

Bill D'Angelo is president of Grosso-Jacobson, a production house that operates out of New York and Canada. Their 1992 hit is "Top Cops." D'Angelo, like Bochco, is a casting director's idea of a producer—fortyish, graying about the temples, handsome and articulate. He has been a writer-producer-director on such hits as "Alice," "Flo," and "Webster," among others. When interviewed in 1991, he was trying to keep afloat a winter replacement with Robert Mitchum called "A Family for Joe." He allowed us to sit in on rehearsals and writing sessions with his team of eleven writers and writer-producers. What took place was typical of television's serial madness.

It was Tuesday night. The "punch-up" session was in progress. Working out of Grant Tinker's Culver City Studios, the writing team for "Joe" had just attended the cast walkthrough of their lines during the afternoon rehearsal. As D'Angelo put it, "You can never tell what's funny until you hear your words spoken by the actors. The same is true of 'unfunny.' What sounded hilarious in your mind, and what looked great on paper can collapse when you hear the characters say the lines, and you know you're dead."

At this session, the "punch-up" writer was on hand, a man who gets $5,000 for three hours' work one night a week. It is his job to react to the script-in-process and throw out a barrage of funny lines in the hope that four or five will hit. D'Angelo explains.

> He also keeps us loose. It's a spitball session and we need somebody to come in cold and keep the room lively. The punch-up writer improvises and associates words and ideas freely and pretty soon everybody joins in, and maybe nine out of ten things he says are useless, but that one is worth the enormous price. I had a guy on "Webster" who never wrote a word, but he was worth the $5,000 because he encouraged the others. I know guys on hit shows who are getting $15,000. Can you believe it? For one night's work!

In the room, the writers subdivided into teams of two. Generally, one partner is good "on the machine" while the other is "good in the room"; that is, one operates quietly in the privacy of an office while the other shines at verbal interaction in a group. True to this distinction, about half of the writers in the room said nothing, and the other half talked on top of each other all the time, shooting out ideas, jokes and straight lines. All too often the sessions are funnier than the scripts. Anything goes. The punch-up writer was working on an idea about a stamp collection for Joe. "He gets this Rachel Welch stamp, see. Like, you lick it on the front, not the back." (Appreciative laughter in the room but a no-no for the family time script.)

Another trade distinction: For a given script, one team is usually the writer of record and listed in the opening credits. In effect, they submit the basic idea, and once approved by D'Angelo, pound out the first draft. After one polish, Arnold Margolis, the head writer (and also executive producer) will assign various "beats" and scenes for rewrites according to ability and interest. With D'Angelo, Margolis hires the teams, sets their staff salaries at anything from scale on up and guarantees them at least one script of their own for which they will receive an additional $5,000 to $15,000.

Back in the writing room, the argument rages around what one or another character would say under certain circumstances. One of them is arguing for a scene where the high school boy has cheated on a test and made an "A." Joe, the foster grandfather, finds out about it. The writer wants Joe (Robert Mitchum) to administer another test on which the boy is made to study and draws a "C." D'Angelo argues against this. "You end up rewarding him for cheating on the test. He still gets an "A." First, we have to go back and write around this problem."

Later, D'Angelo is asked about his concern for values in the show. What does he really want out of the show? "I want twenty-two minutes that are funny, fit the concept of the show and the characters in it, that make the network happy enough to pick up the show and make us all rich."

With the grin of an Italian boy right out of the Bronx, he says that any honest writer-producer will tell you the same thing. But he adds,

> If you examine storytelling, you will generally – not always – find the same human qualities and principles. There have always been porn and violence but the best stories from the Greeks through the modern classics held up standards of courage, of honesty, of justice. Very few evildoers became heroes in works lasting through the centuries. Contrary to what scholars like Gerbner seem to think, you can do a very violent show from a transcendentally moral perspective.

Does that mean that writers consistently start with a message, an issue, an ideal like courage that they want to put in dramatic form?

> Most writers don't know how they start. It varies. I've done action and I've done comedy. With the latter, it's standard to start with something that struck you as funny, with a concept if you are creating a show, with a character if the show is already set. I doubt if many of us begin with an abstract principle like justice or some answer to the drug problem. But I have had the network ask me to do an antidrug episode. Really, you

can't separate the parts in the mix, but a writer must deal with some emotion, a vision, an anecdote, some peculiarity, some switch that will catch people's interest.

In the case of "Joe," the network was looking for a family show that could be co-produced with NBC Productions. So Arnold Margolis and I put together a simple concept, hardly new, but attractive, about four kids orphaned by a car accident killing both parents. Since the kids were afraid they were going to be split up, they went out and "hired" a grandfather, in this case a bum played by Robert Mitchum. So far it has won its time period but still hovers on the cusp for a share of audience . . . getting a 19 to 22 share when you need maybe a 25. Frankly, it's a shame because it is a nice show, Mitchum is the consummate professional, the kids are all good, and the people who see it think it's funny. The trouble is, we struck out on all kinds of publicity and it wasn't NBC's fault, just bad timing and the fact that Bob hates interviews and won't cooperate. He's a great guy but he is just as likely to tell the writer at *TV Guide* to go fuck himself.

D'Angelo says that the ultimate test of values lies in the hands of the audience.

They happen to want wholesome shows, at least in comedy, and at least on network and standard cable. Maybe that will change. It certainly has in film. But TV is different. During the times when the family is up and around, some of us men may want raw T&A. But you can't hide the set under your pillow like *Playboy*. You remember the old Nielsen diaries? They were flawed because people reported that they were watching "Masterpiece Theater" when they were actually tuning in "Three's Company." People aren't always prepared to admit what they like. So you get the raunchy movies on after midnight when your kids are asleep and your wife is asleep, and your mother is asleep.

Other writers echoed D'Angelo. They added that in sitcoms, the viewers like to have their own values reaffirmed. A twenty-three-year-old staff writer said, "Just add up the cliches, 'work hard, love God and get ahead,' or 'do unto others . . .' or 'I don't want to be rich, just happy,' and so on. I learned when I started writing not to laugh at the things that the everyday guy thinks are right or wrong. A good story can put those things in conflict and resolve in favor of what you have been calling universal values. So is that a crime?"

D'Angelo pointed out that once the concept of a show is established (e.g., in "Joe" everyone needs to keep up the pretense that this street character is the real grandfather), the rest has to do with keeping the characters authentic, consistent and growing. The concept controls the "situation," which in this case is a suburban family with kids from three years old to high school age, living with an ex-sailor-bum who comes to care for them despite his crustiness and irreverence. Then the characters and the setting and the circumstances of each episode are woven together with a plot based on family values.

All the writers agreed that the networks frequently want to have their cake and eat it too. They want the cake of uplifting messages and moral principles, but they also want the meal garnished with titillation and gunplay. One of them said,

Take "Miami Vice," for example. Sure, it had style, pastel colors, great rock, pace and density. And in the end good won out over evil. But along the way the good was damn near evil itself. Sexy guys and girls rolling around in bed, incredible violence, but the style of the show covered up the slop. Mann [Michael Mann the producer] was a genius at that. But I'll tell you a funny thing. None of those reverends out there ever protested "Miami Vice" because it had that aura of morality that comes from good guys chasing bad guys.

D'Angelo told a story that illustrated the craziness of the business as well as the writers' peeve against programmers.

Sometimes I think of all those thousands of students taking courses in communications and I wonder what the hell they are going to think when they find out the way it really is. Recently, I sent in a full treatment at the request of one of the networks. It was about four college guys who room together; I spent days delineating their characters, finding something interesting and unique in each. Together they take on all the jobs that make money in the school—laundry, typing, food—and I create some funny situations, but the whole idea is to do a piece on the kinds of kids who visit my son in college and who are different from any other generation. Well, the development executive, who is thirteen years old, and looks like his mother dresses him every morning for work, tells me that it's not funny enough as it is, and they want to send it out to two young writers for jokes. I try to explain that the humor comes in the interplay of the characters, because TV is not stand-up comedy. But no, they farm it out.

D'Angelo looks to heaven and swears that what he is about to describe is literally true.

I get this script back from two slimes with even less experience than some of you teenagers and here is their concept: Three guys live off campus and need a roommate. Lo and behold, a stunningly sexy woman walks in, announces that she is a professor at the college and wants to share a room starting now. Nothing wrong with that of course, so she goes in the bathroom to take a shower while the three guys work out ways to peep in. Meanwhile, one has an invention which lights up his hat whenever he's aroused, and that's the running gag for the entire thing. Now this was sent back to me with that network executive's rave about the "creativity" of these writers. I'm so furious I want to call the entertainment president and tell him to fire those incompetent slimes. I'm no puritan, but this was the most despicable kind of cheap, tawdry, sophomoric, behind-the-barn-door piece of shit. No network decision maker in his right mind would look at that crap for thirty seconds, but that is what the development executive thought was "high concept" and "off the wall" and "sharp-edged" and all the other euphemisms for trash.

Asked to comment on network editing or censorship, D'Angelo's writers took positions all the way from Gary David Goldberg's positive attitude toward standards to Steven Bochco's negative one. They agreed that Bochco—not unlike Bill D'Angelo—finds psychic satisfactions in battling the network. Standards provides a backboard for their carom shots into the net. They also respect Goldberg's "prosocial" ideas that suffuse his material. But they feel it is much easier to do comedy within the boundaries of commercial television (because the audience by and large prefers the values of a "Cosby" to a far-out "Simpsons") than it is to do drama within the constraints of sex and value standards, especially the subgenres of police, adventure, melodrama and docudrama.

CONCLUSION

Whatever boundaries the networks draw, it is the suppliers, a/k/a storytellers, who will have the last word. In *Three Blind Mice*,[5] Ken Auletta describes a visit made by Michael Eisner of Disney to an electronics exhibition held in Las Vegas. Eisner walks through the futuristic displays of technology, from AT&T's fiber optics to tiny window satellite dishes from England. He is overwhelmed by the instantly changing scene of high technology until he notices that every machine in every exhibit is playing a show written and produced in Hollywood. Auletta says that the light dawned on Eisner that "the future belongs to the product. All else is distribution."

In 1993, the distribution of product to the mass audience still belongs to the Big Three webs with a vigorous nod in the direction of Fox. But when new technology produces new hardware, the new distributors will still be forced to turn to the old talent. And as Grant Tinker said when he took up independent production again, "There ain't that much around. For mysterious reasons, the supply of good writers is always a finite thing."

That being true, the Lears, Goldbergs, Bochcos and D'Angelos and their small band of storytellers will continue to invent the content that supposedly inculcates tastes and values in the public, while at the same time drinking in the very values that they transform into stories.

No doubt the "Three Blind Mice" will one day be devoured by some vertically integrated, worldwide cat like Time/Warner, which owns studios, newspapers, cable channels, satellites, television stations and a network. When that corporate day dawns, some slightly mad version of a Milch or D'Angelo will charge into the new executive suite and purr, "Swifty, have I got a log line for you!"

Grant Tinker, interviewed at length in the next chapter, and referred to by talent as the ideal network executive, describes the future this way: "Network television is the business of retailing the wares of others. Ours is an ornamental art; it makes us laugh and its pleasurability is undeniable. But no matter what happens in New York City, most of what television does between eight and eleven is storytelling. . . . If you don't get that, you don't get anything."

With that idea in mind, we turn to the retailers, the network programmers, who are paid to elicit the ornamental from writers and producers.

NOTES

1. For a discussion of Vladimir Propp's work, see Sarah Ruth Kozloff, "Narrative Theory and Television," in *Channels of Discourse*, ed. Robert C. Allen (Chapel Hill: University of North Carolina Press, 1987), pp. 47–50.

2. The Cultural Indicators project at the Annenberg School of Communication at the University of Pennsylvania reports annual violent-content profiles for primetime network television. These findings are reported in the *Journal of Communication* and other academic journals.

3. American viewers know the Lab as "Ubu," as in the line at the end of every "Family Ties" episode, "Sit, Ubu. Sit."

4. Warren Littlefield is president of NBC's Entertainment Division, having succeeded Tartikoff in 1991.

5. Ken Auletta, *Three Blind Mice: How the TV Networks Lost Their Way* (New York: Random House, 1991).

3

The Network Programmers

Each year, in a frenzied atmosphere not unlike that faced by General Eisenhower the week before D-Day, a tiny clique of network bosses meets to decide the fate of each pilot developed by the programmers and their suppliers. This is the moment of truth for "the kids" in the entertainment division. They are betting their jobs that the writer-producer they have been working with for a year or more will turn in pilots that make the final cut. During that spring period, the brass evaluates the upcoming series and places them into four categories:

- Accepted for the fall
- Postponed for introduction during the second season and/or used as replacements for immediate failures
- Rejected for the regular schedule but approved for summer fill-ins
- Rejected ("passed" is the network euphemism)

Although the network decision structures differ, the final cut in the selection process generally belongs to a brain trust composed of the CEO and network president, the entertainment president (who manages the program department), the vice president for sales, the president of affiliate relations, and a handful of top business, research or legal aides to the CEO.

The decision-making mentality is itself a product of many forces, both creative and corporate. At this tense moment of truth the beads of sweat on executive brows reveal the unspoken: that no one really knows what is going to succeed and what is going to sputter and die.

A great deal more enters into the fate of prospective shows than the mere audience appeal of the material itself. Some producers build into pilots more sex, violence and spicy language than they know will be retained once a series hits the air. Of course, the more adult the content the tougher the network's problem. Will the public put up with the latest limits-testing shows? Will advertisers defect? Will audiences prefer "tried and true" to "off the wall"?

Years ago when ABC and NBC rejected "All in the Family," it was the corporate mentality at work balancing the novel with the prudential. When ABC pulled "Cop Rock," a musical police show, novelty gave way to formula. More enters into the selective guidelines than the winsomeness, much less the worth of the material itself. There is definitely a programmers' mentality, a point of view that tempers and shapes not only program ideas but the actual content—the point of view, the values, the boundaries for language action, romance and characterizations.

THE ECOLOGY OF INFLUENCE

The day-to-day shaping of program content occurs at every level within the network and in outside production houses. In fact, the process of getting comedic or dramatic material on the air is ecological. Each party to the arrangement affects every other. Writers bring ideas to producers who, attempting to read the network mood, negotiate deals (abetted by agents pushing stars) with network programmers. They in turn answer to top management that makes the final cut in light of sales and advertising considerations, with a nod in the direction of public interest and federal regulation.

Although this chapter focuses on the programmer's relationship with suppliers, it is hopelessly artificial to treat the eight parties separately. Each member of the video family constantly interacts with the others because television is the most collaborative of all the popular arts—some would say the most incestuous.

The network is in the business of providing audiences for advertisers. But the business is federally regulated and that means having to abide by (or finesse) guidelines from the FCC and that in turn necessitates a "standards" policy that protects the network and the advertiser but often annoys writers and producers.

In the previous chapter we listened to that lonely hired gun, the writer-producer. Everyone in show business will tell you that the writer is the most important element in the creation of program material. Studios and networks are forever decrying the dearth of talented pens. One might think, therefore, that good writers would command the greatest respect in Hollywood. Actually, the reverse is true—with the exception of a few "hot" writing teams. The person with the greatest influence on subject matter has the least power in television. The writer has the least power in the selling process, and the agent has the most. The writer has little control over the acceptance of shows and no power over cancellations, that being a network decision.

Because writers "get no respect" in the Rodney Dangerfield sense, the successful ones instantly become writer-producers, which at least entitles them to select a staff. Although the credits on a show will normally feature the names of the executive producer, the associate producers and line producers, the chances are that most of these are writer-producers (not staff writers) who have a piece of the show's profits. And that last, profits, is the writer-producer's revenge. After two network runs, the residuals are mostly theirs.

Because the network and supplier view the same landscape from widely differing perspectives, we have separated the "network programmer" chapter from the "writer-producer" chapter, despite the constant overlapping of their concerns.

AGENTS

The other end of the power scale resembles an inverted pyramid. Those who often have the greatest influence on selling a show to the network have the least influence on program content. These powerbrokers, popularized in 1990 by the "Amazing Teddy Z" and the scrofulous character Al Roth, are the handful of major agents.

Their power derives from the ability to speed up the developmental process by bringing together a writer (whom they might represent) with a star (whom they most surely represent) with a producer or studio (where they have a percentage deal) and sell the combination to the network.[1] They operate something like advertising account executives who simply sell the efforts of the creative team to the sponsor. Agentry, however, is a good metaphor for the ecology of television marketing since these middlemen can bring together in different configurations those parties that make primetime work. This includes the network management, their programmers, the producers, studios, the talent and the writers who crank out the episodes. As sponsors, advertisers pay for it all in order to hold on to their share of the product market. Such symbiosis is the ecology of show business, television style.

PROGRAMMING AND MANAGEMENT

A network influences program content broadly and narrowly. Top management looks at material through wide-angle corporate lenses, which take in all network operations but specifically the concerns of advertisers, affiliates, regulators and public interest forces. That broad perspective is revealed in the following chapter. The programming department scrutinizes a pilot through the closeup lenses of audience interest, scheduling and demographics; in short, ratings.

These multiple interests within the network are not always compatible and sometimes are polarized by the business mentality of New York and the program mentality of Hollywood. By whatever structure, the inner wheels are geared to serve management's aim of arriving at the highest ratings with the youngest audiences (18–38) and with the least amount of public furor and advertiser resistance.

THE NETWORK PROGRAMMING EXECUTIVES

Network programmers exist to develop hit programs. They buy for the network. Suppliers (writer-producers) sell to the network.[2] Executives who work in network programming (lodged in entertainment divisions) must, therefore, be uniquely sensitive to their relationships with producers, particularly those with recent track records. Obviously, a good programmer will also know the Hollywood scene of agents, talent and writers.

Almost with one voice, however, suppliers trying to promote their shows to the networks complain that the low-level programmers, who act as filters for the thousands of ideas that bombard the networks, are too young, too inexperienced and often too arrogant for the system to work fairly and creatively. We will look at both sides of that complaint.

From the network perspective, the problem is based on the shortage of time and money. At least 2,000 ideas, treatments, deals and proposals[3] will be pitched to the program department each year. Of these, one hundred or more will be put in development and listed in the project book.[4] That means that roughly 1,900 will be rejected. Of the one hundred or so ideas that make it past the treatment stage—a treatment being anything from the back of an envelope (from big names such as Marcy Carsey and Brandon Tartikoff) to a hundred-page backgrounder called a bible—perhaps eighty will be immediately commissioned as scripts at a cost of $10,000 to $50,000 or even more, all out of the network pocket. Very few will go directly into production as a pilot. The remaining twenty or so may linger for months.

Consider the odds. Of 2,000 pitches to programmers, one hundred are developed as scripts. From these, maybe twenty or thirty pilots (production samples) will be ordered (at a network cost of $250,000 to $1 million or more), and of these pilots, maybe eight will make the regular season. Of these eight, the network will be ecstatic if two are hits and four win the ratings in their time slots. Two hits out of 2,000 proposals from studios and independent producers—those are odds of 1,000 to 1.

The odds, the inevitability of supplier rejections and the enormous amount of time it takes to go through the weaning process account for much of the tension between programming and suppliers. The expense has caused CBS and NBC to order fewer pilots and more visual storyboards that might consist of a few scenes instead of a thirty- or sixty-minute production. In the following interviews, we asked programmers and ex-programmers to comment on:

- The complaints about the outer ring of inexperienced programmers, the "kids" as Norman Lear calls them, whose entire frame of reference is television itself

- The process of development

- How they influence content.

GRANT TINKER

- Former chairman—NBC
- Independent producer

For a man who has been called the most successful executive in the history of television, Tinker is promiscuously available. Asked about his accessibility, the former CEO at NBC-TV replied, "I guess I just have round heels where appointments are concerned. One of these days I'll learn not to return phone calls promptly."

Asked about his method of operating a network, Tinker said, "I really did exactly what I did at MTM Enterprises. My idea was, you don't spend your waking hours listening to people pitch great projects, because it is not the project that works but the people. Therefore, find the Goldbergs and Bochcos, the Cannells and the Manns, develop the Susan Harrises and the Marcy Carseys,[5] and then go off for three months. When you return you will find wall-to-wall winners. At least that was the theory. Give them enough money to make them reasonably happy, lock them in a room with a typewriter and just wait."

We asked Tinker about a staff meeting at NBC-TV some years back in which he was holding one of his many "tell-Grant-what's-wrong-with-management" meetings. One young woman asked him why more shows were not filled with feminist values. "Why not tell the writers to sit down with feminist thinkers and translate their ideas into scripts?" Tinker answered, "Shows just don't work that way. They start with somebody's passion, with ideas that mesh with emotions, and they soon take on their own life or they die aborning."

Tinker looked puzzled. "Did I say that? It sounds awful moralistic." Told that his former standards chief Ralph Daniels confirmed it, the producer said:

If Ralph says so, it must be true. But I'll tell you something, shows don't start with a moral. Television is performance not persuasion. And not everything that suits my taste or principles accords with the public appetite. People often want enjoyable but instantly forgettable fare. And what is good, after all? Once we turned Jim Brooks loose, and he came back with a funny show. This is the same Brooks who did so many Mary shows ["Mary Tyler Moore"] and is now intriguing people with "The Simpsons" on Fox. But if you ask critics what they consider the all-time worst show ever on television, they would put at the top of the list "My Mother the Car." Well, I liked it. Jerry Van Dyke was funny and it had some great lines in it.

Tinker leaned back in his pink sweatshirt with "WIOU" written on it. On him it looked like cashmere. With a knowing look, he continued.

But people then and people now say it was the world's worst. Was it? I'll bet you that 99 percent of the critics never saw the show. It's like some of my recent projects. The tree falls in the forest beyond human earshot. Did it make a noise? My show "WIOU" toppled without anyone ever hearing of it. So I think it's unwise for a network to set content in advance even for good causes. Trust the writers and wait. They know what the standards are in networks, and if they don't I would rather let standards correct them after the inspiration, if any. I guess the point I'm trying to make is that shows are what writers want to write and not what people tell them to write.

Tinker went on to say that to "save money network programmers are taking their ideas to top writers and asking for a script. This is quite different from listening to original stuff from independent producers." Tinker continued:

At NBC I think you're beginning to see signs of trouble. Programmers are supposed to stay out of the way of talent. One of the things I worked on with Brandon [Tartikoff— then president of NBC entertainment][6] was giving the new writers a chance while sewing up as many of the top performers with deals. But programmers are human. As soon as some of the young ones especially see their names on an NBC check, they begin to identify with NBC; indeed, think they are NBC, and that their judgment is superior to the producers and talent who make the shows. They swarm all over people and drive away many of the best ones. I have the impression that a lot of folks are gravitating to Jeff [Sagansky] at CBS.[7] He announced when he came in that he was going to do the very same thing we did at NBC with writers and their development. You know, pay 'em and let 'em alone.

We talked for a minute about a previous interview with a writer-producer who was complaining about the kids at network programming. The producer had pointed to NBC's director of comedy,[8] Jamie Tarses, as typical of people in her position at all three networks: She is very bright, very pretty, very well educated, very young and very inexperienced. The fact that she had never written or produced anything did not, however, keep her from telling producers with a pocketful of credits what was right or wrong with their ideas.

Tinker laughed. "Yeah, that's the crime frequently committed by all networks. But that's funny because her father, Jay Tarses, is one of the most outspoken critics of the network programmers. Jay still rants and raves if Brandon [Tartikoff] or Jeff [Sagansky] or any of their staff presumes to criticize his work. Too bad he never made that point at home."

Since the "kids" are so universally condemned by suppliers, Tinker was asked why it is necessary to put young, inexperienced people in these roles. Are all these filters and buffers for the top decision makers in the entertainment divisions really needed?

What else can you do? People at the top can entertain just so many ideas per day, and with thousands coming in every year, they have to have somebody there to cull out and evaluate. But it is also the job of the CEO and the inner circle to train those young programmers in tact, sensitivity, patience and openness. The geese that lay those golden eggs do not work for the network. I'm afraid that too many top people just run for the bank each week and forget the need to encourage and stimulate and nurture. Still, it ain't easy.

The conversation with Tinker shifted to writers again. What about the fact that networks seem to deal in talent extremes? As network chief, did he seek either young writers of great potential, who have never done anything, or the hot writers who have just done megahits? And what about the condition of the more mature professionals, especially "old folks" of thirty-five or forty, who are in between?

Tinker, who is over sixty but looks a dashing forty, shook his head. "Yeah, thirty is pretty old in this business. But that's probably true. Networks figure that the journeymen will stay journeymen. After five years, if you're really talented, you should be visible. At the same time, television is such a ravenous machine that you have to rely on the old pros to give you a certain reliable segment of your programming."

When it comes to selecting from a host of pilots—that final time when you need to announce the next season—is that done with advice from all parts of the network or do the decisions reside with five or six top executives?

"Everybody gets some say on the deals but a few say more than others," Tinker said. "You'll hear from research, business affairs, law, standards, and of course from all the senior programmers. But in the final count, top management will make the decisions. The air is always thick with confusion; these meetings left me older but none the wiser."

Gesturing with a bottle of spring water, Tinker mused about the evaluative process of predicting hits and misses.

> Nobody can really tell a ratings winner from a loser. But it's really not hard to tell the good quality from the mediocre, and the mediocre from the bad. Each year of my tenure, we always had a handful that any idiot could appreciate. You launch scores of scripts and pilots and what comes back are four or five decent shows at best. It is easy to sort out the awful ones. They stand out embarrassingly to all. More difficult is deciding between the pretty good and the not quite mediocre. Then you wonder what shows might win their time period even if Tom Shales doesn't approve. Curiously, no one ever runs down the list of great films or great books in a given season to ask how many of *them* are really good? Compared with our resources, films have the money, and books supposedly have the talent, but both generate a ton of trash.

Tinker was reminded of his recent remarks in speeches to broadcasters about the industry's responsibility to "give back" a little something to a public that has made networks and stations unbelievably rich over the years. He noted that the traditional belief in over-the-air broadcasting as a public trust as well as a profit-making business is being challenged.

> The present owners talk about the terrible competitive situation in networking today and therefore the new need for a level playing field and lower standards. This may be true when it comes to the financial interest rules—the solution being for networks to pay producers more on the front end and enjoy more on the back end of syndication. But I think using competition and diminishing profits as an excuse to lessen responsibility is shortsighted. Also networks don't do so bad financially, even recently. Don't forget the revenue from owned stations. Any pullback on public interest simply shows that the new leaders of the networks are not broadcasters and do not stand in that tradition. We have to drop a little of the money on the way to the bank.
>
> Let me give you an example. At a screening once, the [NBC West Coast] standards vice president, a tough, combative guy named Maurie Goodman, left the theater after a certain scene. I went outside and found him crying. He was crying tears of anger and remorse because Universal had lied to him about taking out a certain violent scene, and

he was embarrassed to let us see it. Now can you see anybody in standards today who would care that much about some gratuitous violence or excessive sex?

Asked what his immediate plans were, Tinker said he was undecided as we spoke. "I may just decide to sit back and watch the grass grow, or if temporarily deranged, I may go back into producing."

Tinker referred to a 1992 meeting of producers, directors and writers in which everybody was deploring the fact that independent suppliers were shrinking as the networks used only the top ten who had the money to stay in the game.

> I'm doing a show for a network [don't say which one] that costs me a million four [$1.4 million] an episode. They're paying me $900,000. That's a half a million down each week! Maybe you get $200,000 abroad, but this show doesn't travel [sell overseas] as well as one with bathing suits and car crashes. So let's say that after a couple of seasons, I sell it for syndication at $300,000 an episode. Forget the cost of the money up front. I mean, we will have done all that work just to break even. Obviously, the answer is, this is a nonbusiness.

Why would anyone go in it? Tinker pointed out that the attraction was the same as going to Las Vegas. You do it in the hope that you might hit it big, as with a "Cosby."

How, then, can the writer-producer survive in the environment of deficit financing? Tinker repeated the formula, based on the congressional willingness to modify the Financial Interest and Syndication (fin-syn) rules. "Let networks put more up front and share in the back end. Let them pay independents about what it costs and then realize any profits when episodes are sold for syndication. That's the only way I think our business, based on the creativity of many suppliers, can survive."

SUSAN BAERWALD

- Former vice president for miniseries, NBC
- Producer for NBC Productions

Susan Baerwald has been a top programmer at NBC where she was vice president for miniseries. Recently she took on a new role, working the other side of the street (literally across the parking lot in Burbank) for NBC as a producer for NBC Productions.

Looking back on her years with the "long forms" of movies and miniseries, including a detailed knowledge of all areas of programming, Baerwald quickly rejected the complaints that writers and producers make about the impossibility of access to the network decision makers. Noting the huge number of projects pitched, Baerwald made it clear that nobody at the top could entertain them all, and therefore younger people (with smaller salaries) were needed to filter the proposals. Besides which, she said, the good ideas and the talented people have a way of rising to the top despite all the cries of network roadblocks and interference. Some of the complaints, she stated, were due to the natural, human response to rejection, which "is a daily reality in this business. There is more supply than demand."

As a new, in-house producer at NBC, she is more concerned with the matter of program content dealing with questions of value and message. She has a carefully thought-out position on the relationship between the business of supplying 2,000 hours of programming each year and the responsibility of doing quality shows. She describes quality as social as well as artistic merit.

> I think we end up with loads of prosocial entertainment on prime time because that basically is what the audience is interested in. When critics from academia . . . dismiss television as uninvolved in social issues or valueless in content, they speak out of ignorance. Parenthetically, consider the press critics who speak out of the other side of their mouths, taking us to task for all the "disease of the week" shows, which, of course, are issue shows. Remember, this is business. We are there to get viewers, not for altruistic reasons. Nevertheless, people want reassurance that their values are sound ones. They like these values reaffirmed in drama. Are you going to tell me that shows like "Family Ties" aren't filled with universal values?

Baerwald concedes, however, that many stories seem to have a different orientation. "Take the movie we made from the book *Blind Faith*," she said. "Here is a sociopath who does terrible things to his family and to his children. This man was the perfect neighbor, but he could display horrible, pathological behavior. How can that be moral? He showed the coincidence of good and evil. Yet, despite the evil, the man's children became survivors, not imitators of their father's values."

Baerwald said that what one deals with in miniseries and movies is the unusual and the unique. They are different from the moral behavior one sees on "Cosby" and the family sitcoms.

> I remember when we optioned[9] the bestseller about Gary Gilmore, called *The Executioner's Song*. Grant Tinker (then CEO at NBC) called me up and asked, "Why would you want to do this?" Well, that's always a responsible question. To justify doing Mailer's story, even a Pulitzer Prize-winner, on television you have to find a moral point of view. It seemed to us that Gilmore became his own punishment, his own retribution. Never in the Gilmore story, *Blind Faith* or *Fatal Vision* did we glorify the crime. Rather we let the audience feel the horror and disgust at the prospect of certain antisocial acts committed by "people next door." One of the lessons was, don't take everybody at face value.

Asked about the academic evaluations that find little morally uplifting in television, she pointed again to audience tastes and expectations. "People don't turn on their sets in the hope of being uplifted. They want to be transported, delighted if possible, and at least diverted. What's so immoral about entertainment that just entertains? It may not be a sermon, but it has the power to take viewers away from the problems of the day and into worlds they seldom visit. We don't apologize for such programming. If the fastidious critics object, so be it."

What about the complaints about gratuitous violence? The Gerbner violence index and others show that thousands of such acts occur on the screen each year. Can that be justified?

Smiling, Baerwald said that she has been labeled in the trades as the "Queen of Crime."

> That does not mean favoring violence. But how can you have action and adventure stories without it? The key word is "gratuitous." Is it unseemly, inappropriate, unnecessary to carry the action? Network standards oversees this. My job is to interest people. A great deal of what we do is escapist. Viewers do not think the cop chase is reality. They know the conventions. In romance novels, the reader escapes, even from school and church.

Like other network executives, Baerwald alluded to the need for variety in program content.

> I know critics don't believe it, but most shows are awash in morality. When years ago the Fonz took out a library card, there was a rush on public libraries all over the nation. Today Marcy Carsey and Tom Werner are putting moral and social principles in the mouths of all their characters. This kind of programming, bought and developed by the networks, has tremendous power. But networks are not going to be credited with it by the so-called critics, who, incidentally, are paid to put us down.

Baerwald was asked how networks directly influence program content? What directions, if any, do they give to writers when they start a film or a series?

> I always told my staff to read Aristotle. Read the *Poetics*. Aristotle said stories must have rising action, sympathetic heroes, someone to identify with, climax, resolution . . . it's all there. A good story has these qualities whether fiction like "Miami Vice," or a docudrama like "Wallenberg." When I sit with young writers, that is the point I make. I never say, "give me moral values or a prosocial point of view." But good stories incorporate those values—at least most of the time, whether directly or indirectly. I can't remember a story in which the audience was left with an evil lesson.

One of Baerwald's own values is the responsibility that women in television have for the medium. She and other highly placed executives meet regularly to trade ideas on what can be done to improve the record of social responsibility, and incidentally, the opportunities for women executives.

> At one time, we thought that all three networks were buying more exploitative material than we, as women, were interested in producing. We met with officials to determine what could be done, especially with those sponsors who wanted better quality. This

was not a feminist point of view but the feeling that television does not speak enough to women and with a feminine sensibility. Women are still one level below that of top management. We are now in the middle of the highest level but not yet decisive.

Her executives' group, however, is not sympathetic to those who are forever complaining about the dearth of female role models. "Those who talk that way never look at TV. What about Elise on "Family Ties," who was an architect and a homemaker? What about the female doctors on "St. Elsewhere" and the four lawyers on "L.A. Law" and on and on. Many of the network critics, whether academic or pressure group, have their own stereotypes of the networks, and they are just as unfair to us as they claim we are to them."

Can network influence be carried too far? She feels that networks are damned if they do and damned if they don't. On the one hand, that influence is very slight if thought of as the ability to brainwash viewers, or convert them to certain values that the network endorses, or to make them like what they don't like.

Those who accuse Hollywood and New York of keeping the audience fat and happy so advertisers can sell them are crazy. We cannot dictate audience tastes. They tell you every time they go "click" with their remotes what they want and don't want. The critics who think we can spoonfeed them, either philosophically or dramatically, just don't understand the business. Do you think a writer or a programmer ever asks what the establishment wants to say in a show? No, we try like hell to sense what the people want to see.

Baerwald was bothered by another complaint:

We criticize ourselves for pandering, for giving viewers what we think they want — regardless of worth or value — just because of the ratings pressure of the system. When we do that — too much of that — we are doing so much less than we as creative people can accomplish, which is to give people what they don't yet know they want but once recognized becomes a step up in quality. We can talk down to audiences or we can talk up to them, but ultimately, there is no way they are going to accept what they don't like and don't approve. To my way of thinking, the critics and the intellectuals do not give the audiences the respect they deserve. At least we try to think like them, not for them. We are not their moral instructors. We are entertainers whose shows typically reflect common values but sometimes depict and display material which would better play on cable.

As a final thought about content values, Baerwald spoke of her admiration for Gary David Goldberg (producer of "Family Ties") and Steven Bochco (producer of "Hill Street Blues," "L.A. Law," and "Civil Wars").

Goldberg is the master of moral comedy, the prosocial values disguised as very funny entertainment. Steven, however, is a master of the conflict of values, sometimes the conflict of antisocial things. He resolves things dramatically while leaving the conflicting ideas up in the air. He delights in the gray. If values have to be couched in black and white—which they don't—the artist is in trouble. As a result Steven gets about as close to reality as you can come in a popular arts medium.

COMEDY DEVELOPMENT

Michael Ogiens

- Vice president, daytime and children's programs—CBS
- Vice president, comedy development—CBS
- Vice president, CBS Entertainment—New York
- Producer

Michael Ogiens was, until recently, vice president of comedy, CBS. Previously he had been vice president of the entertainment division, CBS, New York, and before that, vice president for daytime and children's programs. Today he and Josh Kane (who had been a vice president with both NBC and CBS) work as producers, their latest vehicle being the western, "The Young Riders." Physically the two probably make up the handsomest partnership in Hollywood.

Reflecting on his job as head of network comedy development, Ogiens said that his first job was to discover talent.

> I began to look for writers. What I wanted was a script with a solid subtext, one with an emotional engine driving it.
>
> About the way a comedy programmer influences content . . . "Kate and Allie" is a good example. Let me walk you through it. Our job in New York was to complement what was going on out on the Coast. "Kate and Allie" fit the bill. It was good writing, had a dramatic foundation with an interesting subtext—single parenting—that was just surfacing as a social phenomenon at the time. We hoped we could tap into that.
>
> In this case, the writer came to us. (Josh was working with me.) She was relatively new to the half-hour form but had credentials in other areas. She had a good production house behind her and we both liked the concept, and the people she had in mind for it. So we made a script deal, I think in those days the price was $25,000. When it came back, we recommended it for pilot along with a few others. Obviously a lot of projects come in from staff and each programmer lobbies strongly for his own favorites. However, not everybody can win, and in this case the "Kate and Allie" script was turned down in favor of another one on our list.

Ogiens said that the other show was piloted but did not make the fall schedule.

> We were determined to get something on the air that season and the "Kate and Allie" concept just wouldn't leave our minds. So I put the idea to Susan St. James and Jane Curtin together. I got them the script with the help of CAA [an agency] and we met in New York with Susan, Jane and the agents. Josh and I spent an hour pitching the project to them. They were not enthusiastic. Both had other things in mind. We said we

won't let up . . . you two will be terrific together. Finally, they said yes, we cleared it with my boss, Harvey Shepherd, and never even made a pilot. We just assembled a terrific writing staff and ordered six shows then and there. It became a hit and everybody looked like geniuses.

Ogiens described the sheer magnitude of the search for comedy properties. In one year, a colleague on staff counted all the pitches that were made to them in their department alone. "We were amazed to find that 980 different deals were presented over the seven months' development period, and that season we probably ordered fifty or sixty scripts. I think that resulted in a dozen pilots, a pretty good season as it turned out because six got on the air."

One of the comedy hits of the 1990 season, "Designing Women," was also developed by Ogiens. "I tell you about it because it just shows how shows can develop in different ways." Normally, things go from pitch to script deal to pilot to commitment for several shows. "In this case, Linda Bloodworth came in and pitched an idea about four women in Atlanta played by actresses who, I agreed, would produce a remarkable chemistry. The idea was undeveloped, just a basic concept with very little substance. But I knew these ladies would fit in together and that Linda was a sensational writer."

Excited by the idea, Ogiens called up his boss who headed the Entertainment Division and said, " 'You've got to come into my office. I want you to hear something.' Harvey (Shepherd) came over, listened to the idea, and said, 'I guess you want a pilot.' I said, 'Yes.' Harvey, who was a great guy to work for, very experienced and decisive, said, 'You got it.' I swear, the whole thing took all of five minutes."

What about the values in "Designing Women"? Week after week, the show takes on one taboo, one hot issue after another from lesbianism to corporate greed, so much so that it has been called not only prosocial but sermonic.

"That," said Ogiens, "comes right out of Linda Bloodworth. She is just a very talented writer who finds significant things to say, and I'm sure that the network is pleased to let her take on social issues."

Another writer whose early promises became apparent to Ogiens and Kane was Diane English, the eventual creator of "Murphy Brown." She wrote a two-hour movie for CBS but had never written half-hour comedy. When the programmers saw her work and met her, they determined to give her a script as part of their talent nurturing. "We just wanted to give her a deal. When I talked with the network, I kept repeating, 'talent, talent, talent.' Soon she had a blind deal that resulted in 'Foley Square.' After that, she produced 'My Sister Sam' and then 'Murphy.' You never know."

Noting that he and Kane had enjoyed a fair amount of success in four years as independent producers, he described their method as one that did not try to inundate the network entertainment divisions with ideas in the hope that one or two would pay off. Rather, they waited until the right one came along, one they felt good about, and then they selected the network whose scheduling need they could best fill. Sometimes they call a writer and ask if he or she wishes to kick around a concept, and afterward they may decide to flesh it out and make the pitch to the network.

"We may spend a few weeks or a few months before it's ready for the marketplace. Everything has to be nailed down, concept, the plot, story springboards,[10] the relationship between characters, and what Ogiens had called the engine for the show.[11]

What about the messages put into scripts?

"I don't know if anybody, even Linda [Bloodworth] starts with values as such. Generally the reason you watch a series is simple: you find something in a character or group of characters that makes you empathize with them. It could be— and I suppose often is—a point of view that you agree with, but mostly it's that rare emotional chord that is struck. Then again, it may be that your show is just a little more entertaining than the guy's across the street. For my money, it's a matter of well-drawn characters, artfully tied together, who grow continually."

MADE-FOR-TV MOVIES

Frank Dowling

* Director of films, NBC

Frank Dowling, director of films for NBC-TV, came to the network entertainment division by way of the standards department after a short stint in NBC business affairs. Dowling is an ex-Jesuit priest (the mystery series, "Father Dowling," is not based on his life), and in a profession where twenty-nine is old, Dowling will never see thirty again. Tieless and jacketless, he peers professorially over thick spectacles, and describes the multimillion dollar turf over which he presides.

"Our department of three executives and our boss, Tony Masucci, entertain about 5,000 pitches, ideas, treatments, outlines, scripts each year. We get calls from writers, producers, agents, and all say they have this incredible idea and can they come over in a couple of days and discuss it?"

With a pained expression that is common to program developers at the networks, Dowling said that it's impossible to meet with everyone. He and his colleagues, therefore, try to screen as many as they can over the phone.

> Maybe I'll hear one concept that is similar to what we already have. That happens more than you think. Or I may be able to save that producer's time by pointing out that we are just not in the market for that kind of an idea this year, and then I mention what our needs are.
>
> I average maybe six pitches a day, I supervise my share of the forty movies we are shooting at NBC each year, each of which has to be overseen for progress on scripts or

dailies. Then I keep an eye on the 150 or so projects that are being developed but not yet approved.

Is this the reason that networks are forced to put a lot of young and inexperienced programmers on staff to filter out the incredible number of proposals?

"You age quickly out here. But sure, especially in comedy and drama, where Brandon [Tartikoff] and the top people have the entire network fare to administer, you simply must have the sieve, the filters and screeners. Time is the problem. It's a killing job."

Dowling made the point that unlike comedy and drama series, the content of NBC movies differs in essence. Movies have no built-in audience, no word of mouth with which to build audiences, not even the traditional audience that used to tune in NBC out of habit.

That means that you have to have a promotable story, one with a great log line [where a concept is easily described for quick appeal]. In one or two sentences that fit into *TV Guide*, a movie must grab the viewer's attention and win him over from alternative offerings. If a story line is soft, you can't do that. You're out of luck. This argues, therefore, for "higher profile" shows, ones that may have owned some press previously or come by way of a bestseller.

Does scheduling play a part in the things you will accept?

You bet. We do movies on Sunday and Monday nights at 9 P.M. That's it. Not Thursdays, not Tuesdays. Now what happens those nights? Monday, of course, we go up against NFL football. That means we look for a high-profile show that will appeal to women, maybe it will be about some young woman in jeopardy, a person something is happening to that makes you say, "that could happen to me." Maybe somebody in a psychological pressure cooker, someone who triumphs against great odds. That's the hard-edged material we look for as opposed to softer, romantic, low-key tales which may have great charm. On Sundays, we can go for a broader audience but even then, ESPN will be doing football, and Fox is taking a bite with "Married with Children." The aim is to win our time period, at least.

Dowling spent a good hour "walking through" the process of film development:

For example, he said, let's say a writer-producer comes in with an intriguing idea. He will take it to Tony Masucci,[12] kick it around and possibly get an okay for a script deal. The supplier is told the good news plus any advisory comments. Maybe there is some question about a writer who has done comedy but not an action show. Or another has failed to deliver four times. Why take a chance with so much money and so little time riding on it?

The next step is to agree on terms for the script. Something around the $50,000 mark, although Dowling is not involved in these negotiations directly. He will talk with an agent and remind him that if the writer gets $55,000, then the next one wants $60,000 and a hotter writer demands $75,000 and multiply this by 150 scripts and you're talking an average of $3.75 million.

Agents will scream at you. Some call Tony and say, "I just read the first draft, and it's the best thing I've seen in thirty-five years." And Tony will call me and ask why he has never heard of this masterpiece and I say, "Cause it's a piece of shit, that's why . . . and so on.

Once a first draft (two hours of action equals about 120 pages, roughly a minute a page) is in, Dowling reads it and discusses it with Masucci. There may be legal problems or standards limits. That frequently occurs when a piece is fact-based. If Dowling feels that the network is in danger of incurring legal or pressure group troubles, he may recommend that the docudrama be transformed into thinly disguised fiction.

Whenever I make a ninety-degree turn, however, I must go to Tony. He sees the whole picture and may have had something else in his mind — often a show that fits the overall blend he has planned for the year. Occasionally we will see too many problems. Then I have to break the sad news to the supplier. The odds are about one in three that a script deal will go to film. Sometimes we like a thing so much that it kicks around for two or three years, looking for the right ingredients.

Changes, however, are expensive. On a script deal, all NBC is entitled to is a first draft with two revisions and a polish. To make one more complete pass at the script, the writer must be paid additional money, often another $5,000 to $10,000. Sometimes other writers are brought in, and they must be paid extra.

Once approved for shooting, Dowling tells the happy producer and joins the negotiations.

Let's say the budget is 3.2 million. NBC says to the supplier, "We'll give you 2.7, and you deficit the rest." Where does he get half a million difference? Well, once we sign a deal, he can sell it in Canada and overseas. Sometimes a distributor will take it off his hands, make up the difference and give him a $700,000 profit. Those "back in" profits can add up. If the producer takes a chance on waiting for distribution profits outside the USA, he can make a lot more or a lot less. Of course, he has to do well because unlike a successful series, he can't make a ton on reruns since most films do not become evergreen or perennials [shows that can run in syndication over and over again, e.g., M*A*S*H). We get the rights to one rerun and that's it.

After discussing casting and location with NBC (possibly a change to a state that has a right-to-work law so as to reduce union costs), the producer begins shooting. As the dailies (results of daily shooting) come in, the programmers watch carefully, sometimes critically, especially when a star is performing. (Television movies do better with television stars, not film stars, and certainly not unknowns. An actor like Ted Danson will insure success because home viewers are primed for him.)

Dowling underlined the feelings of others we have interviewed who said that television is a business of rejections. "I try to tell people no in the same way that Grant Tinker did. He was famous for giving people bad news in such a way that producers would go away walking on air, saying, 'Grant really cared.' But that's not easy."

How do programmers tell good from bad? Dowling, like every producer or network executive interviewed, had nothing but contempt for critics. He alluded to the *Caddyshacks* and the *Teenage Mutant Ninja Turtles* and to all the marginal printed output, and concluded that the emergence of quality shows like "An Early Frost" should be occasions for rejoicing while the cotton-candy productions should not be a cause of despair. Talent is a sometime thing.

> Writers are like the ten guys in a bar. Nine will say this incredible thing happened to them and everybody yawns. Then one guy will say, "I got out of bed this morning and put on the wrong shoe, then . . ." and you laugh your head off. Now what causes that? What makes one movie send the audience off to bed with a smile or a tear or a sense of uplift?

We asked, "What influence does network programming bring to bear on the ideas, values and issues in movies?"

Having dealt with moral values and ethics and with social values in his former position as a standards executive, Dowling was slow to answer. "How do you deal with a question like that? With the exception of those few projects we originate or that NBC Productions generates, our role is bound to be reactive. I would love to say about a concept, 'yeah, this is so significant, we should take a chance on it.' "

Dowling described at length a movie he just completed on Down's Syndrome.

> The parents gave up on the child at birth; an older couple fell in love with the child and asked the parents to join in "reclaiming one soul." The parents refused, and the couple wound up taking custody and giving new life to one human being. Naturally we love a story like that.
>
> I'm working on one now called "Decoration Day" based on a novella published by the University of Arkansas Press. It's headed for Hallmark Playhouse, and I just hope we can do justice to the novel. If we do, you'll see that rare thing in television or any other medium: an exciting story which just breathes morality and humanity.
>
> I think most great stories have moral themes. I worked a lot with Steven Bochco who came at values indirectly, sometimes negatively, especially in subplots. Still, his point of view was very humane, very real, very honest. Does that mean that his value orientation paid off in ratings? Not even Bochco can bring it off every time. Remember "Bay City Blues"?

Although reluctant to speak about the standards situation at NBC, where so much controversial change has occurred since his time, Dowling spoke generally about the fact that all three networks are returning to a position in which the censors fulfill the public responsibility mandate. "I don't think that Brandon Tartikoff here or Jeff Sagansky and Robert Iger[13] over at CBS and ABC want to fill that role, not that I spend a lot of time with those guys. Certainly programmers and producers do better to concentrate on the creative and not the critical, the cautionary."

Overall, network programmers agree that suppliers get as much access to networks as is financially and temporally possible. They speak with one voice about critics whom they see as competitors in a print medium who can't see the forest of values for the occasional trees of sex, violence and negative stereotyping. They recognize their own power. They see how suppliers write and produce to meet the needs and the boundaries which the network sets, or has to set because of government strictures. They agree that it is best to separate the standards department's critical, evaluative role from the programmer's developmental role.

NOTES

1. For an enjoyable insight into the Hollywood "art form" called The Deal, see Todd Gitlin's book *Inside Prime Time* (New York: Pantheon Books, 1983).

2. The FCC limits the number of programming hours per week networks can produce themselves. These usually are developed through a separate division called Network Productions. Even so, half of the NBC Productions, for example, are coproduced with independent suppliers, and although allowed by the FCC, are not accomplished entirely in-house. At ABC, Brandon Stoddard launched a motion picture studio to produce theatrical films and Brandon Tartikoff while at NBC began a similar venture.

3. A treatment is a minutely precise and well-developed paper of five or six pages that describes the essential aspects of a proposed show—the idea, the characters, the setting and a plot example. A deal is a verbal, sometimes written, declaration of the network's intent to buy a script, a pilot or a series, and is preparatory to a contract. A proposal is an idea, a treatment or a script that is presented to a network by its originator in the hope of getting a commitment to proceed in its development.

4. A project book, sometimes called a status book, is a list of each idea, script, treatment or pilot that is being developed by the network, usually one-page long with the concept, the producers, writers and a brief description of the progress of the development.

5. Marcy Carsey and Tom Werner produced "The Cosby Show."

6. Brandon Tartikoff, then president of NBC Entertainment Division, headed Paramount until quitting in November 1992 to be with his family.

7. Jeff Sagansky is president of ABC Entertainment Division.

8. The director of comedy is responsible for procurement of all comedy shows purchased by the network.

9. An option is a fee paid to hold a literary property exclusively for a period of time at the end of which a decision is made to continue the option, drop it or go ahead with the development.

10. A springboard is a moment or incident in a story that pushes along the action; for example, a chase, a misunderstanding or a twist in the plot.

11. The basis of a script is the "story," which in turn has an "engine" that drives the story along. The engine is the moving force of the story.

12. Anthony Masucci is vice president, NBC Motion Pictures for Television.

13. Robert Iger is president of ABC Entertainment Division.

4

Suits and Censors: Senior Network Executives and Standards Editors

In Hollywood, the word "suits" is a nasty metaphor for the top executives in New York who run the network. The word is used by writer-producers in their designer jeans and programmers in their casual wear bought for outrageous prices along Rodeo Drive. Each is making a statement. The idea is to set oneself apart from those Brooks Brothers bean counters who do not belong to the creative fraternity. Whether on the set or dining in the studio commissary, the costume one wears instantly reveals one's function and rank. For example, big-shot directors affect safari wear. Agents sport $400 Italian silk shirts with monograms. Stars wear shades and heavy make-up. Studio heads make do with $4,000 Armani imports. God forbid that one be mistaken for an East Coast executive, a suit no less. Thus among the mature personalities in television who resent uniformity, the uniform is everything.

If the term "suit" carries with it the faint odor of gray flannel conformity, the word "censor" is calculated to wound deeply. The image conjured up is that of a white male with narrow flinty features, suspicious eyes glancing left to right in habitual frowns, casting gloom over the land of palm trees and hibiscus. Those so called understandably resent the term and insist on the euphemism of editor or standards executive. They have a point, although usage is against them. After all, as standards people remind you tirelessly, much of what they do is exactly what editors at the *New York Times* do when blue-penciling anything that does not conform with "all the news that's fit to print." In the entertainment industry, however, accuracy is sacrificed to nastiness every time.

Interestingly, these editor/censors dress somewhere between the suits and the creative types, generally affecting a blazer, soft slacks, loafers and open-necked shirts. The senior vice presidents, presidents and CEOs stick with their pinstripes and ties, mainly because they always look a little silly dressing down. The only executive ever to beat the rap was the classy Tinker, who was born to wear cashmeres and sneakers.

Uniforms aside, the suits in television set the broad parameters for program content and the censors implement these parameters show by show. It is these interlocking roles that we describe next.

THE SUITS: SENIOR NETWORK EXECUTIVES

The Payer and the Piper

In network television, it is not quite accurate to say that he who pays the piper calls the tune. A better musical analogy draws on the royal patronage in the time of J.S. Bach. While nobody would deny that Bach composed his own music, just as writers write their own scripts, it is also true that Bach's patrons influenced the music he wrote. If they didn't like his form or substance—what, another sonata when I ordered a Mass!—they could refuse payment. They were forever complaining about his production and stipend. All of this made for a delicate balance. Johann Sebastian Bach wrote the music but patrons set the parameters. The fact that this master composer died penniless gives one the idea that the power of patronage belonged to the payer and not the piper of the tune.

That same balance prevails in television commissions. Networks don't write scripts but the suits in charge deeply influence content by setting the coordinates by which the writing is judged and programs are licensed for payment. Straying too far beyond the boundaries can result in a no payment. Measuring how far "too far" is is the job of the censor.

In the previous chapter, we discussed network programmers working with writers in what is called the development process. That process, however, gets its direction from the top down, from what might be called the "mentality" of those New York executives who work with advertisers, lobby in Washington, deal with pressure groups, relate to affiliate stations, fence with the press, worry about overhead and ponder the inscrutable ways of shareholders and market shares. Strange as it may seem to outsiders, the directions that the suits give their own programmers often conflict with the directions they give the censors. Thus they ask networks programmers to encourage writer-producers to "push the envelope" of taste and values while instructing the censors to keep programmers and producers well within the boundaries. Whether this polarity makes for civil war or a wise, dialectical tension—that is an unsolved problem in networking today.

Out of this clash of forces and interests comes the "givens" for program development. At the level of top management (i.e., the CEO, the president, the senior vice presidents for sales, public relations, affiliates, finance) the suits establish the "culture" of the network And it is here that the brass and their advisers pound out the social responsibility of networks as it touches upon ratings and earnings.

How do corporate managers and standards editors influence program content? Like Bach's patrons, the suits never tell suppliers what to write, exactly, but they do provide generalized guidelines (e.g., "tried and true is dead and buried").

Similarly, censors don't have anything to do with original concepts but once they see a script, they make particular suggestions (e.g., "no four-letter words, no bare breasts, no gouging of eyeballs, and no calling African Americans "niggers").

In this way the suits broadly determine what kinds of programs their own programmers develop with suppliers (as we have seen in the previous chapter) and more, how their own censors deal with the ongoing scripts of writer-producers. Before Marcy Carsey and her staff put one word on paper, she knows that senior network officials have both the economic power (the purse-strings with which to license shows) and a conferred legal power (derived from the Communications Act) to set the standards that are enforced by editor/censors. On the other hand, as Carsey/Werner brings in hit after hit, their power increases commensurately.

Very successful writers are known to tell the press piously, "I only write for myself; if I like it, my instincts tell me the public will." Fine, but deep down, a little voice is forever reminding them that in this business there are certain givens, however fluid, confusing and unspoken.

Networks announce that they want quality shows, then often buy cotton candy. They call for originality, then buy formula. They want writers to be free of interference but raise hell when advertisers defect from a boundary busting show. The suits tell the programmers to tell the writers to put in more romance and action (i.e., sex and violence) and the suits tell the censors to tell the writers not to go over the line. Well, nobody ever said that guidelines for content had to be clear.

Nevertheless, to put the programmatic mentality of networks in clearer perspective, we look at the setting of parameters at the top and the policing of those boundaries in broadcast standards. What is the thinking of top management in New York and how do they translate that notion of "quality control" into action? In TV jargon, what do the suits and censors do?

The Double Mandate: Profitability and Responsibility

Broadly speaking, the business of broadcasting grows out of a federal mandate that gave local stations (and on their behalf the networks) the right and power to set the boundaries for the programs they air. Patrolling these boundaries on a day-to-day basis are the censors or editors in broadcast standards. Their scope and power, however, are defined by top management.

Curiously, the so-called creative community (which includes both the producers and the network programmers who hope to become producers) wears blinders when it comes to the economic clout and the legal mandate by which networks set content boundaries.

The Power to Set Boundaries

The Hollywood community, although as money-mad as Wall Street, preens itself on the product it creates — which is entertainment — but often deludes itself on the controlling aspects of the advertising dollar.

Back in New York, the suits do not indulge that sentiment. They never forget that the most important term in "show biz" is "biz." Whereas the operating assumption of those who create product is to tell a better story, the operating assumption of the suits is to make a better sale. Their mentality is "distributional"—buying the product cheaply enough to sell it to advertisers for the widest possible dispersion.

Does the business mentality of these senior network executives affect the tastes and values in a script? Did the suppliers for Wal-Mart listen to Sam Walton? And did Sam Walton, probably the most successful merchant of this generation, enforce his standards by sending messages down the line?

Dollars and Censors

Some years back, one of the authors hosted a seminar held by ABC-TV for its executives in programming and standards. Understand that the executives who develop programs and the executives who review them for standards enjoy an adversarial relationship within the network.[1] From concept to answer print,[2] the programmers seek greater freedom, particularly in sex, violence and language, whereas the censors in standards aim for public responsibility, corporate propriety and quality control. (The "kids" in programming also want to curry favor with the studios and hot writers who may employ them in the not-too-distant future.) Caught in the middle are the writers, who hear the programmers call for lower moral standards and the censors call for higher ones.

When the ABC seminar opened in the lush surroundings of the Century City Hotel, the youthful program executives with dreams of becoming top producers gave vent to righteous indignation over in-house censorship. (Two who worked in comedy were Marcy Carsey and Tom Werner, who later brought in the "Cosby Show.") Programmer after programmer, clothed in their genres of comedy, drama, soaps, and specials, made impassioned speeches in behalf of freedom of expression. Typical was one woman who asked: "Why should the network give censors the power of life and death over material? This denies First Amendment freedom to the creative community. By what right do people in administration presume to tell the artist what he can and cannot write?"

Tony Thomopoulos, then the successful president of ABC Entertainment, had an answer: "Because, Roxanne, it's our candy shop. If suppliers want to exhibit on our shelves, they'd damn well better conform to our standards. If they won't, they have the freedom to shop other networks, write a play, produce a movie or hire a band. That's why the work of our standards editors is called self-regulation and not censorship."

Congress Creates the Double Mandate

Thomopoulos had it right, at least in the legal sense. Back in the twenties, the Congress decided that the broadcasting "candy shop" would belong to the stations (and by extension, to the networks). As trustees of those exclusive channels, the shop owners were responsible for the product. That product had to meet certain minimal standards, or the license (and channel slot) of a given station could be revoked and given to another trustee.

The Network, Not the Supplier, Enjoys Free Speech

That being true, the only party with First Amendment rights of free expression (more limited than print, however) is the station/network, not the hired talent. The distributor not the supplier, the publisher not the writer, has the right to free speech uncensored by government. The broadcasters' programs are "protected speech" under the Constitution, which means that with very few exceptions (obscenity is never protected speech and indecency can be regulated by the FCC) broadcasters are free to run whatever material is attractive to audiences, the only limitation being their mandate to serve the public interest.

Just as important, broadcasters/networks are free to reject anything submitted by producers and writers. To repeat, that is their editorial right and not an act of censorship. The "creative community" finds this hard to swallow.

This point is so crucial to an understanding of the network's influence on program content that one wonders why it is so little understood. When writer-producers complain about their "right" to free expression, they speak out of constitutional ignorance. Just as the *New York Times* has the right to edit or reject anything its writers and contributors submit, so the broadcaster has the legal right to edit or reject anything a producer submits. (It really sticks in the craw of the networks to be accused of censorship when newspapers do the same thing and are never called by this odious term, and, of course, the editors in standards prefer racial epithets to being called a censor.) If that's censorship (and legally speaking it is not) writers must make the most of it, or as Thomopoulos said, go somewhere else to ply their trade.

By Any Other Name, Isn't Editing Really Censorship?

Networks can call their standards people editors but aren't they in fact censors as the word is commonly understood? That's just the trouble. Censorship carries both an repressive, un-American meaning ("the only obscenity is censorship itself" according to First Amendment absolutists) and a milder meaning of any limitation, line drawing or quality control.

Most dictionaries draw a distinction between official censorship (curbing the press in time of war or scissoring the letters soldiers write home) and unofficial censorship (a film board set up voluntarily by an industry to self-regulate its products). Dictionaries also distinguish between censorship that is repressive and that which is critical in the literary or editorial sense. The former is censorious, fault-finding and condemning while the latter is a discernment of the merits or failings from a sympathetic point of view. The critic A.C. Benson speaks of the "high intellectual pleasure" of having a "tete-à-tete with a man of similar tastes, who is just and yet sympathetic, critical yet appreciative. . . ."

In show biz, however, success is equated with absolute, individual freedom of expression, a strange concept in this most collegial of all arts. Critical, evaluative scrutiny, no matter how just, sympathetic or appreciative, is regarded as insult.

That's why any limitation on the expressions of TV-makers will be seen by Hollywood narcissists as ironclad censorship. It's one way creative types define themselves against the Philistines. And that is the ultimate reason why the censor's life, like that of the policemen in *The Pirates of Penzance*, "is not a happy one."

On April 29, 1990, C-Span broadcast a lengthy debate on the FCC's right to oversee the broadcaster's self-regulation. It was called "What's Indecent? Who Decides?" and featured the usual polarities from the American Family Association to poet Allen Ginsberg. At issue was Ginsberg's "spanking" poem, which used the F-word repeatedly in alluding to sadomasochistic sex.

A First Amendment lawyer saw no reason such an artistic creation should not play on over-the-air television. A Morality In Media spokesman read the federal statute that makes such on-air talk a crime punishable by jail and/or fines. FCC Commissioner James H. Quello said the Supreme Court had supported the FCC's right to hold broadcasters to decency standards, however hard to judge.

But no one made the point that the broadcaster-buyer has the clear right to reject the Ginsberg material without violating that poet's right of free expression. In light of the muddled conventional thinking on free speech and its limitations, one can hardly blame producers whose stock in trade is creative liberty. Justifiably, they regard each show as their own property, not that of the network. That is technically true. Suppliers do not really sell a program to networks; they lend it for two airings, after which it reverts to them as producers with full rights to syndicate as they please.[3]

Nevertheless, the networks are responsible for that program the minute it hits the airwaves, despite the fact that producers own the material afterward. If public umbrage results, letters fly and congressmen mount their soapboxes, it is not the writer, producer, actor or director who takes the heat. It is the network. In these days of watchdog boycotts, the advertiser is the one who loses money while the producer remains unscathed. And since the buck stops (and starts) with the broadcaster, the network finds it hypocritical for those with no risk, no responsibility and no constitutional right of access to demand unlimited creative control. Which brings us back to the "biz" in showbiz. Just what kind of business do the network suits think they are in and how does that affect the content of shows written in Hollywood?

The Legalized Profit Motive in a Licensed Business

If Hollywood has a hard time understanding censorship, the academic orthodoxy that interprets television has a hard time choking down the entrepreneurial nature of broadcasting.

The Thomopoulos metaphor of "our candy shop" is accurate insofar as the supplier is concerned. Like McDonald's, the network shop is franchised. It happens to be, however, the most benevolent franchise arrangement in the history of capitalism. The corporate McDonald's would never agree to a deal in which the store-franchisee kept all the profits, subject only to a few health ordinances and the promise not to poison the customers.

But that is precisely the deal that the government made with stations when radio went national in the late 1920s.[4] All the group pressure and political rhetoric about the "public air" misses the original and ongoing intent of Congress. That body decided in 1927 that the best way radio could entertain and inform the American people would be for the government to license entrepreneurs. The best interests of the people at large would be served by businessmen trying to earn money within the constraints of federal regulation and public responsibility.

The intent of profit making has often been forgotten by the social critics and the intent of trusteeship has often been ignored by the suits. Are these two principles at war? What does it mean to the manager who is asked to run a private business that is publicly licensed?

The Communications Act of 1934 (updated from radio to television) makes profit-oriented entrepreneurs responsible for the information and entertainment needs of the nation.[5] Congress put the most public medium into the hands of the most private entrepreneurs. They entrusted the public interest to private parties intent on making a profit. There was one catch: the companies had to operate as trustees of the air, not as the owners. Theoretically, they had to program "in the public interest, necessity and convenience."

Was this a sell-out? Should the public's airwaves belong directly to the public and should use of these airwaves be administered by the trusted hands of government?

Many educators and media critics regret Congress' choice. They believe that network preoccupation with profits was flawed from the beginning, growing out of the capitalistic philosophies of President Hoover and his Congress, which decided that the American system of broadcasting, for better or worse, would never take the path of state ownership as did the British and most Europeans. Evidently Congress believed that business motives would ultimately produce better information and entertainment than would state control.

Today, in a mixed market economy, the Hill is betting that free enterprise will offer a greater variety and quality of broadcasting services than one controlled directly by the government. The fact that American television sells many times the number of programs abroad as it imports would seem to support that gamble. If sheer entertainment is seen as part of the public interest — as it is by most politicians — then the system surely works. At any rate, there seems to be reasonable public support for the concept of profit-minded trustees.

Television, therefore, should not be expected to be any less bottom-line oriented than a local utility, which is also licensed to private companies who make profits (guaranteed profits, unlike those of networks, which can go broke). By the same token, ABC, NBC, CBS and Fox are no less publicly mandated to be responsible than a local utility. Indeed, the Communications Act was a watered-down version of the utility concept by which a private company is licensed to make money by serving the public good.

The business of broadcasting in this country is meant to be a profit-oriented enterprise run as competitively as possible within the boundaries of public responsibility and service to the viewer. But what does that mean for program content? How does this double mandate affect the writer-producer? Oversimplified, it means that the suits in top management delegate to the programmers the money-making function and delegate to the censors the public responsibility function. These are different goals; polar, almost always incommensurate, sometimes conflicting head on.

In the past, this adversarial relationship between program and standards departments has been healthy. Writer-producers know that they must please two parties: the programmers who want ratings and the censors who want boundaries. What they may not know is that the suits must adjudicate conflicts between the programmers and the censors. (And since the entertainment president is a suit in New York City but part of the creative community in Hollywood, he becomes a powerful advocate against the standards vice president, which is why, traditionally, standards has reported to the president or CEO, not the entertainment division.) It is no easy choice when it comes to ratings versus responsibility. Cynics are not aware that networks, both in the commercials and the entertainment they edit, have shown consistent courage in subordinating the interests of Hollywood "artistes" to that of the general interest, the best examples being the measures taken to avoid offending minorities.

In the early days of "Hill Street Blues," most of those arrested for street crimes were black or Latino, a true reflection of inner-city reality. Standards, however, pointed out that viewers could draw the wrong social and moral conclusion. Instead of perceiving that most street criminals in ethnic communities are black or Hispanic, they would probably assume that most blacks and Hispanics are criminals. Unlike the film from which "Hill Street" was derived, *Fort Apache, The Bronx*, television could not afford to influence 30 million people of all ages, races and background, week after week with that dangerous perception. Despite Bochco's understandable wrath over having his artistic instincts overruled by moral standards, it was done. And the reason was not fear of pressure groups but the desire to be socially responsible. It made the show less realistic but more ethical, and the portrayals of more whites as criminals did not water down the sense of real life.

Such internal struggles at networks underscore the often conflicting nature of ratings versus responsibility, of success versus integrity. Most sitcoms, with the exception of those that exploit sex, can live happily with the core values of American society. But in action shows and docudramas, the schizoid mentality of networks is evident. Insiders know that the network body, like Jimmy Carter, has lust in its heart but purity in its soul. Both mammon and Yahweh must be appeased. Unfortunately for public responsibility in the nineties, the drop in money has precipitated a drop in standards.

When the suits lose their shirts, what happens to public responsibility?

Until the mid-eighties, the double mandate of broadcasting was no problem. If you owned a TV station, you had a license, if not to steal, at least to prosper without fear. The government restricted anyone else's access to your channel, the networks supplied your entertainment and informational needs, the networks fulfilled most of your public service functions, and all you had to do was turn on the switch and stagger to the bank.

Keep in mind the fact that the most lucrative local stations belong to the networks. They have always owned the best stations in the largest markets (called Network O&Os – owned and operated stations), which have been the true profit centers, bringing in far better returns than the networking side of the business, which gambles on the huge costs of Hollywood production.

Since affiliate stations have always been the most sensitive to local protests by offended parties, they have been the most loyal advocates of tighter control by network standards departments. Their attitude: don't rock the boat and don't jeopardize the franchise. Whenever the flack flies, the network division of owned stations finds itself siding with the affiliates against the excesses of the entertainment division. It all comes down to the trusteeship of money.

Collectively the broadcasting industry has made billions of dollars each year in what was a protected market and a semimonopoly. All the networks were required to do was to serve the viewer's interests in entertainment (which they did gleefully) while also serving the public interest through news, specials, information, research, standards and community concern (which they did with self-congratulatory ease).

The beauty was, the suits earned enough from entertainment activities to spend millions covering election campaigns, wars, assassinations and space shots, which they did magnificently, and enough to afford large staffs in areas like standards and law, which were not profit centers. Then came cable.

Cutting Back on Standards and Public Service

With profits declining as audiences bought the alternatives, broadcasters began to fret about all that public service largesse. New network and local station owners with no experience in the traditions of broadcasting but with a bottom-line mentality blanched at the idea of "inflated staffs" working in areas that were patently nonprofit centers. Fresh from his success as landlord, theater-chain owner and investor, Larry Tisch led the way at CBS, cutting his standards department in half. He was followed eagerly by Robert Wright at NBC, whose varied career with General Electric had to do mostly with acquisitions, finance and plastics. One of the first questions Wright asked at NBC was, "Why do we need censors when cable doesn't?" Only at Capital Cities, the buyer of ABC, was there local broadcasting experience and therefore some understanding of the basic mandate given broadcasters.

All three networks, however, spent the first year pruning staffs. They called it "delayering," a euphemism for large-scale firings in areas not making direct revenue-generating contributions. They cut their news departments, eliminated most documentaries, gutted their standards (ABC excepted), research and community service departments and prepared for a market-oriented product. They still spoke about responsibility to the public but their actions suggested what they really meant by public interest was an interested public . . . only.

In the face of this new posture, public interest groups accused the networks and the stations of abdicating the viewers' "interest, necessity and convenience." There were a number of other strong reactions by advertisers and the government. Resistance to outside regulation went hand in hand with the dismantling of the self-regulatory apparatus. The same executives who had promised the FCC and congressional committees that they had not taken over the networks to change anything in the responsibility area began to change everything.

In great agony, they proclaimed that competitive pressures had altered the business climate that now required them to seek a "level playing field" with cable, video and film industries.

As they saw it, the networks could no longer live with the costly scrutiny of each program for possible offenses or with the restrictive boundaries that allowed R-rated cable movies to siphon off viewers from free television. Scores of lobbyists soaked the carpets of Congress with their tears. They forgot to mention that the standards departments cost about $3 million annually out of revenues in the billions. Still, the new suits at CBS and NBC felt they could not afford the old censors.

Looking to Congress for Protection

For the moment, Congress stands at the crossroads. A few senators have said that the networks and stations can't have it both ways. If broadcasters don't wish to give back anything for the privilege of using protected public channels, then Congress can open up these channels to the highest bidder and let the market truly decide. Broadcasters have not warmed up to that radically free market concept. They want deregulation *and* a privileged status.

With one exception, they got their way during the Reagan years. Led by Reagan FCC appointees, the oversight of the FCC was radically reduced. Both stations and networks were freed to pursue a bottom-line course that steered around the obstacles of public interest. Their greatest failure, however, was President Reagan's refusal to go along with the FCC recommendations on financial interest and syndication rules,[6] the result being a loss of potential profits on reruns that ran into the billions. Unfairly, in the authors' opinion, the President sided with his old friends in Hollywood and left the networks dangling in the wind.

The Loss to Low-Income Viewers

No one need shed tears for the networks. But that particular juncture, when networks were denied access to syndication in the eighties, marked the beginning of a sorry pilgrimage of sports and specials from "free" television to pay TV. The blue-collar worker who used to get championship sports events on one of the networks without paying extra soon discovered that pay-per-view was willing to rob him of up to forty bucks for what used to be free, to say nothing of the installation and carrying charges for his basic cable. Not even the Olympics would be spared. Who needs the mass of low-income viewers when a million times forty dollars will outbid the networks for almost any sports event? (Even though NBC lost money on its cable coverage in Barcelona, you can bet on pay-per-view in Atlanta for the 1996 Olympics.)

Today, the viewer is being asked to pay for an increasing number of baseball, football and basketball games plus the privilege of seeing commercials on channels that were supposed to be ad free. Interestingly, none of the religious or academic establishments with their professed concern for the poor testified in Washington on behalf of over-the-air service. Of course, the networks and independent broadcasters were not willing to offer Congress any trade-offs. No one knows what would have happened if the networks had presented the administration with a plan to step up their sports, news, standards and public interest programs in return for a compromise on financial interest and syndication. The network monopoly was transformed into cable monopolies, with a great deal less regulation than even the FCC had required of networks.

The Federal Communications Commission: A Paper Tiger

Even in the early days of television, broadcasters were not kept on a tight rein by the FCC. Having so much more on its plate than broadcasting and living with the ambiguity of the "interest, necessity and convenience" provisions, the FCC has had to rely on the integrity of broadcasters. Most stations, and all three networks, have traditionally accepted this gentle self-regulation as a small price to pay for the substantial returns. That is what Grant Tinker meant when he spoke of dropping off a little of the money on the way to the bank.

Insofar as the FCC's direct regulatory zeal has been concerned, that agency has always been a paper tiger, made even more toothless by Reagan's deregulation. At least the roar of the tiger at licensing time made owners (including the networks as the richest owners) think twice. Instead of stonewalling this pressure group or demeaning that ethnic representative or running those offensive commercials, the suits gave the censors the power to curb the excesses. But today, when stations are bought and sold like any other commodity without waiting periods or promises of public service, even that power is meaningless. From time to time, Congress will jawbone the industry. Since a disproportionate number of congressmen own stations or stock in stations, and all are partly beholden to local home stations for favorable political coverage, their actions seldom go further than words. Many members of Congress have bought into the ideology that says that the only public interest they owe is that of attracting an interested public, certified by high ratings.

One of the important points raised in chapter 5 is the surprising ideology of the deeply conservative Herbert Hoover, who endorsed the idea that the rights of the public outweigh the rights of the broadcasters. This meant that the service of trustees was to stand before profits. Today the industry would not welcome Hoover and his radical views.

Suits and Credos

Earlier we posed a rhetorical question: Did the suppliers of goods to Wal-Mart bear in mind the expectations of owner Sam Walton? The fact is that Walton's standards traveled quickly down the line to his vendors. He didn't tell them how to make an appliance but he did expect them to make the best product at the most reasonable price. That is what they will try to do. On the other hand, if the CEO is willing to stick shoppers with a shoddier product, the suppliers get that message as well and lower their standards.

That is exactly the ethical dynamics of network television. If the CEO, like a Grant Tinker, aims high, then writer-producers like Gary David Goldberg get the message and craft their work accordingly. If CEOs, like Tisch of CBS and Welch of GE/NBC, aim low, then people like Geraldo Rivera get that message and act accordingly.

That is why corporate credos, if enforced from the top as part of a company's culture, are so important. Some thirty years ago, many American corporations, led by the nonprofit Conference Board, began to embrace public responsibility as a coordinate of profitability. The best known and most radical creed was that of Johnson & Johnson, the drug manufacturer. Instead of embracing the traditional laissez-faire stance of economist Milton Friedman, who claimed that the only thing corporations owed the public was the best return to shareholders, J&J put profit making last in their credo. First, they said, we will serve the buyer with the best product at the fairest price based on rigorous quality control; next we will offer our employees just wages in the best working conditions; next we will fulfill our responsibilities in plant communities and finally our obligations as national and world citizens. Then, and only then, we will return to shareholders a profit that grows out of the principles that manifest our business. (And when Tylenol was tampered with, the management of J&J put its money where its mouth was; $100 million was gambled against that credo. And just like a sitcom, virtue was rewarded with public support for their product. But the point remains that they stood ready to take a $100 million bath by taking Tylenol off the shelves and re-funding money.)

In the 1970s the Conference Board reported that 60 percent of the CEOs in the Fortune 500 sent similar messages down the line, namely that public responsibility and vigorous profits are two sides of the same coin.

Then came the Reagan administration with its robber-baron philosophy and deregulatory zeal, building upon the waves of Harvard MBA graduates who were taught to quantify everything and honor nothing. The Milkens and the S&L bandits, who stole from the poor to give to the rich, were given a national benediction.

Today, the pendulum seems to be swinging back to public responsibility and quality control—at least in many American corporations. Network brass and the station owners they represent must decide what direction they wish to take. The fishbowl environment in which television lives means that the networks will have to decide very publicly what messages they wish to send down the line to writer-producers; and more to the point, what expectations they will enforce internally with the programmers who develop the shows and the editor/censors who set the boundaries for the content in shows. With that in mind, we turn to the censors themselves and look at the equivocal conditions under which standards executives have had to work in the last five years and hazard a guess as to the future of standards in a business that is "mature," a euphemism for losing customers.

THE CENSORS: NETWORK STANDARDS EXECUTIVES

The Censors AKA Editors at the Standards Departments

Traditionally the standards departments at all three networks have personified the roles of ombudsman, referee and self-regulator. Then in 1987, CBS signaled the new corporate ethos of those who had bought control of the networks from traditional broadcasters by cutting staff and watering down the authority of editors over shows. The suits decided that the quality control responsibility could be shared with the audience-pleasing executives in programming and with the suppliers themselves. This is tantamount to letting Peter Rabbit guard the cabbage patch.

In 1988 NBC followed suit, and the adversarial process within the network in which standards editors were free to contend and negotiate with programming executives was lost in the transfer of power. Indeed, the man who succeeded Ralph Daniels as NBC censor sought ways of making the editing process a "profit center," and subsequently took his finely honed discriminations to the Home Shopping Network. (Although ABC was slow to accept the transfer of standards power to programming, it had to loosen control in order to compete for top producers who wanted complete autonomy over their work.)

In the seasons of 1987, 1988 and 1989, there was an element of poetic justice in the fact that even the ethics of the marketplace were higher than those at 30 Rock (NBC) and Black Rock (CBS). So much sleaze slipped through that the advertisers began to demand stricter content review and in many cases, set up their own watchdogs to filter out offensive material. Following the 1989 season, in which it was stung by such criticisms and public outcry, NBC had to beef up its gutted standards department.

At least on paper, the power of quality control and public representation was returned at both CBS and NBC. However, real power—which means access by standards to the CEO and his delegated authority to take on the programming department—has not been restored. Until that happens at NBC and CBS, the editorial responsibility and power of those chosen to represent the public will be subordinated to the audience concerns of the entertainment presidents. And ABC will be forced to compete against the lowered standards at the other networks.

Happily, there is reason to think that the program departments, to say nothing of the suppliers, are sick of the censorship role they have been asked to play, a role that strokes against their grain of creativity. Should that happen, the proper relationship between censors, suppliers and programmers will be restored. That relationship, which goes to the heart of network influence on program content, was personified by Ralph Daniels, senior vice president for Standards and Practices, at NBC during his fifteen years on the job.

The Standards Departments—the Once and Future Editors

The questions are: What is the influence of censors on what writers write? How ought they to carry out the "quality control" function in the future?

It is no exaggeration to say that the executives in broadcast standards make value judgments that affect not only writer-producers, but also every part of the television business. The lines editors draw between the acceptable and the unacceptable affect the suppliers, the men and women in network sales, the programmers, the researchers, the people in law and public relations, the affiliates, the ad agencies and the rival media. Like the ripple created by a rock dropped into the middle of a lake, editorial decisions at the networks affect almost everybody sooner or later.

In light of this comprehensive influence, one would think the networks would monitor their jobs carefully and interpret to the rest of the industry the proper place and role of standards editors. This is not the case. Very little information exists on the nature of their work, particularly how it ties in with programming, the law, top management, and above all, the nature of their relationships with writer-producers.

According to the popular wisdom of Hollywood, censors operate with a rack of cast-iron values on which each television program by whatever tortuous stretching, wrenching or hacking must be fit. As some suppliers see it, censors make no effort to judge a work by its own intentions, possibilities or effects, make no effort to assess its appropriateness—just strip it of bumps and lumps and make it conform to the network mold.

In the C-Span hearing cited earlier, one of the anticensors said that the prevailing mentality of the network editors is, "When in doubt, take it out." Interestingly, there was such a sign placed on the desk of an NBC censor who worked on the West Coast a generation ago. No one has seen it since.

The myth of network censorship, whether thought of as a standards department or as top management cowering before the protests of advertisers and watchdogs, is fed by horror stories that pervade the industry. A few years ago, a story appeared in the *New York Times* about a young comedian who had complained to the reporter, "I've found that on network TV there is very little freedom of speech. When I did David Letterman, I was told that I couldn't bring up the Pope, the Catholic Church, Ronald Reagan or drugs. I'll hit all those things in my night-club act on Saturday."[7]

Neither the comic nor the reporter saw fit to mention that each of the "taboo" themes had already played on "Late Night With David Letterman," or that the very day the comic was exercising his First Amendment rights (chez cabaret), "Saturday Night Live" was taking on the Pope, Ronald Reagan and several salty themes.

Still, the censor myth persists. As echoed in the interviews with both writer-producers and network executives, attitudes toward the role of standards vary from the hostility exemplified by Steven Bochco to the begrudging admiration for the adversarial process exemplified by Arthur Price, who headed up MTM Enterprises Inc. after Tinker left.

Why is it that a good many producers and even writers like David Milch find the limitations protective and prudential? They take some delight in the give-and-take of the creator versus the critic and save their raw energy for the talent that has to be assembled in teams, nurtured and administered.

Price said in his interview:

The auteur theory of the lonely creative artist battling against the "suits" at the networks is bullshit. Most of what we do is mediocre by the very nature of the demands on time, talent and money. Occasionally something comes along that is not only entertaining and commercial but has aesthetic and even ethical value. That has very little to do with network systems of quality control. I remember sitting around a table with Bob Wright of NBC and several studio heads when the subject of a cutback in standards was brought up. Bob wanted to know why the producers and programmers couldn't self-regulate. Michael Eisner [CEO at Disney] said he thought they could. I was appalled and said so. I told them the standards system was the greatest process ever invented to protect us from Congress and the crazies. Besides, what does programming want? There was not a producer around that table who had not had programming notes asking for more sex and violence. Now you want that same programmer to also play the censor and ask for less? Give me a break! No, those are opposite, polar roles. And without standards in the adversarial position, you are asking for a regulatory Congress. I'll tell you what standards does. It gets Brandon and Jeff and Bob and all the entertainment guys off the hook. The censors take the rap. It simply is unrealistic to ask Bochco to define his own boundaries. And what about the guys who do not have Steven's talent and just like to write dirty words on the wall? Well, thank God, they are beginning to reverse all that and now I see that NBC has had to hire back a bunch of editors. Well, high time.

From these exchanges, it is evident that the standards editors are stuck with the pejorative word censor even though it ill defines their day-to-day work. Ironically, the editors in New York City who ride herd on *commercial* copy and blue-pencil the creative efforts of ad writers are not called censors. They are lauded by the same libertarians who think dramatic copy should be limit-free but that commercial copy should be severely curbed.

What Do Standards Editors Actually Do?

What Grant Tinker was to network management, Ralph Daniels was to standards. A navy jet pilot during the Korean War, manager of CBS-owned stations in Los Angeles and New York City, and president of CBS Owned Stations, Daniels brought to his standards role a rich background of broadcasting experience. As one vice president at NBC put it, "When you talk about what television owes the viewer, you think of Ralph. He's the class act of our industry. Whether testifying before Congress or hassling with producers, the guy's competence and integrity stand in vivid contrast to much of what you see in this world."

A tall, aristocratic Californian, Daniels was asked to comment on the need for what he calls quality control at the network:

> When writers ask, "Who the hell are you to decide what viewers' tastes and values are?" I sometimes come back with my own questions: When scripts come into the network in which characters refer to one another as "Guineas," "A-rabs," "fags," "Polacks" and "Krauts," just to use the milder terms, should anyone raise the question of demeaning language and negative stereotypes? When in an advertisement a drug manufacturer claims that "nine out of ten" doctors endorse a given product, should anyone look into this claim to see if it's misleading or dangerous? When some agency wants to play the Hallelujah Chorus during a deodorant ad, should anyone represent the people who will be deeply offended by such tastelessness? When a late-night show insults Billy Graham, Jesse Jackson, the president, the Pope, the Girl Scouts of America and motherhood, should the network have the right to raise questions about programs which it buys for its own air, for its own advertisers who pay the bills and its own audiences who share values and tastes? Or when a writer wants to use four-letter words in a cop show, should anyone point out that network television is still considered family entertainment by most viewers and that such words on the public air are still against the law?

During Daniels' regime at NBC, his department refined the "contextual" approach to editing. The decisions by censors became situational, not ironclad. The key phrase used was quality control. Judgments were rendered in response to the quality of a script, the genre it represented and the experience it evoked. Instead of a legalistic approach, this system required consultation and negotiation with writer-producers before decisions were rendered.

Daniels again:

> A 10 P.M. action show is treated differently from an 8 P.M. comedy. A fantasy like the old "A-Team" is edited differently from a realistic piece like "L.A. Law," or a surreal piece like "Miami Vice" or a "Twin Peaks." This show-by-show approach calls for stages of review from the initial concept to the script to the finished program. At each stage the editor has the right to order changes. Working closely with producers, the editors try to balance the creative spark of program makers against the expectations of a vast national audience.

That is a richer assignment than deleting damns, hells and a few lustier epithets. The step-by-step process described by Daniels differs from editor to editor.

With old hands, it is so instinctive that the editor is hard put to describe what happens. Certain things are constant: A three-way understanding unfolds simultaneously in the editor's mind when he or she reads a script contextually. The first is appreciative, the second is technical and the third is evaluative.

When a Censor Is Not a Censor: Editorial Guidelines

The Daniels school brought what writer, David Milch, called "contextual editing" to its maturity. How does it work? Appreciatively, the editor approaches each script just as expectantly as the viewer who sinks back into an armchair, food and drink nearby, and an "amuse me" look in the eye. It's very important that the editor never become too jaded to review works on this uncritical level. (Remember the comments of Goldberg who said of the standards staff that they were fans of the show and of Bochco who said that his favorite editor appreciated the artistry.) How else can the editor truly stand in for viewers? How else can one get inside the mind of the writer who faces a blank page and reveals his abilities and passions to public scrutiny? Experiencing a work appreciatively is the sine qua non of taste and the precondition of good judgment. Parenthetically, this is the impulse that is so often missing among print critics who are jaded and who find it almost impossible to identify with Daniels' "average reasonable viewer." Does this affect editing? Theoretically no, but a dull show will get a tight edit.

Technically, the editor is attentive to style, structure, substance and story. If there is a mental shift in the editor's mind from appreciative to technical, it is the switch from the unconscious region of the right-brain to the logical zones of the left-brain. Having read a thousand scripts and seen hundreds of pilots, the editor is familiar with the tools of the trade—with characterizations, plotting, plausibility, length, pace and overall theme. For that reason, experienced editors find it harder to deal with superior shows than with what Aaron Spelling calls "fast-food entertainment." Formula shows can be formula edited. But when a good piece of pop art makes its appearance, the editor is faced with material that is surprising, sometimes shocking. On balance, an editor will be kind to risk-taking shows because the craft and intentions are superior. Even when every red light on the standards dashboard is flashing, editors may be enjoying the ride. When that happens, appreciative taste meets technical understanding, and the editor does indeed become a fan.

Evaluatively, the editor approaches a script on ethical grounds. Even while laughing at a joke and commending a writer's style, a voice begins to ask at whose expense the humor is employed. Is there a value problem?

Evaluation is an exercise in the logic of responsibility and expectations, where themes and characterizations are questioned but not arbitrarily branded as taboo. Such editing rests upon the assumption that most Americans share such top values as honesty, fairness, freedom, caring, love, courage, order and respect for life itself. When these values are ultimately denied in a show, the editor wants to know why. If there is no artistic reason for depicting "disvalues," the editor raises a flag. If a program promulgates evil—which is very different from presenting the faces of evil — the editor would like to know why dishonesty, injustice, slavery, selfishness, greed or environmental pollution is being recommended.

Rules of Thumb

Whoever reviews the final product submitted by suppliers, whether it is the editor-censor in an area called standards and practices, or a top programming executive or a vice president in the law department, some things never change. Rules hold up and suppliers follow the rules or they sell to another candy shop. Thus, the disabled must not be ridiculed; dramatizations of the news must not be confused with the actual news; the use of drugs is not to be depicted as socially acceptable or glamorous; gambling must be presented discreetly; hypnosis and impersonations are carefully previewed for harm; professionals in dramas are expected to comply with professional standards; trade-name references in drama are not accepted where the intent or effect is to promote a product and pseudosciences like mind-reading and astrology are not to be legitimated.

These and other guidelines are widely accepted, seldom breached and will continue to act as primetime boundaries even if every auteur writer-producer in Hollywood protests all the way to the Supreme Court.

The Review Process

What happens when producers cannot live with a censor's decision? They have the right of appeal at all networks, the option to go over standards' head and seek a reversal from the CEO. In practice, most problems are ironed out between the producer and the editor. Less often, a sit-down meeting will be held that adds to this mix of supplier and censor the program executive and/or higher-ups. Before Larry Tisch took over CBS and GE bought NBC, it was rare for a producer to take complaints to the top simply because the CEOs backed the standards system and did not want to waste time arguing with guardhouse lawyers.

When standards departments were "delayered," two things happened. One, there were fewer line editors working shows script by script. Thus, more things could slip through. Two, the word came down that permissiveness was in. That cut the nerve of editing, which was the authority to make a judgment stand. Working with no protection, let alone understanding from the CEO, only a very brave, job-gambling editor could take on a programmer or a writer-producer and say, "write around this or that."

Predictably, this loss of integrity at the top led to the "sleaze season" of 1988–1989 in which NBC, closely followed by CBS, was ridiculed in the press, castigated by public interest groups, rebuked by advertisers and sent threatening messages by Congress.

A standards executive, speaking anonymously, told us of an incident on "Saturday Night Live," in which the late comic Sam Kinison wanted to do a skit about two homosexuals who suddenly died and "awoke" alongside one another in the same tomb. Wow! What a concept! With the taste for which Sexist Sam was renowned, he recognized the inherently humorous possibilities in necrophilia.

Even though Daniels had been replaced at NBC by a man with the kind of permissiveness that GE demanded, the "SNL" censor told Kinison, "Hell no, that will never fly." Incensed with this moralistic interference, producer Lorne Michaels went over the editor's head to the president. That gentleman said he saw no real problem, especially if they tested it out in the live run-through. (When the skit bombed with the studio audience, it was cut.) Elated with his First Amendment victory, Michaels swung into action with even more creative material.

The censor wasn't through, however. Knowing what second-guessing awaited him, he simply inundated the president's desk with every dirty word and problematical scene that appeared in daily scripts. Whereupon the word came back, "Please handle things your way from now on. I'm too busy." Score one for the little people.

Who knows? There may be hope that good management, if not high principles, will reanoint the standards departments by backing editors against narcissistic producers whose loyalties reflect their pocketbooks more than the public interest.

Having talked at length with writers, programmers and managers (the latter anonymously), we second the views of Arthur Price, Grant Tinker and David Milch, who question the wisdom of asking wild ones to edit themselves. What will programmers, with their interest in future employment, tell the producers whose shows they jointly develop? Out of one side of their mouths they must encourage writers to be fresh, bold, innovative and brave, and out of the other side of their mouths they must caution the writer to watch this or that, add balance and remember taste.

Putting the creative and the evaluative together can be done, of course, but it's as awkward as rubbing the stomach and patting the head simultaneously. Administratively, it seems wise for networks to preserve the dialectical tension between standards and programming. To be sure, programmers are aware of viewers' values and editors are (as we suggested in the three-step editing process) aware of entertainment values. It is nonetheless true that program executives need to concentrate their energies on serving viewers' desires (i.e., hit shows) and editors need to concentrate on serving viewers' desirables (i.e., taste and values).

It would be ideal if both management and suppliers stopped fighting over the semantics and took a fresh look at the review process. Were that to happen, we are convinced that the editor would be given a new mandate based on daily requirements that are as challenging as they are comprehensive. The job description calls for a loyal employee who exercises quality control for the company; a negotiator who knows how and where to draw lines with producers; a situationalist whose decisions grow out of such variables as theme, plot, characterization, genre, audience expectations, scheduling and product quality; and finally an ombudsman who is, as it were, black, Hispanic, Polish, Asian, Irish and Native

American, and who is parent, child, disabled, aged, WASP, straight, gay, rich, unemployed, homemaker, homeless, urban, suburban, rural, religious and secular, feminist and traditionalist.

As suggested earlier, the editorial mentality is akin to that of professional umpires. First Amendment absolutists are forever saying how impossible it is to draw lines between that which is gratuitous or excessive and that which is not. Really? A football official draws such lines between acceptable and gratuitous violence each game. Some do it better than others but all do it instantly and under enormous pressure.

Red Smith, the sports reporter for the old *New York Herald Tribune*, once said that the only people who truly love the game are the umpires because they alone want it played fairly. Their value judgments are rendered for the good of the game. All others, from the players and coaches to the fans and owners, are prejudiced observers.

Editor-censors share that same ethic. They draw lines between the acceptable and the unacceptable; they love the game; they want it played fairly; and the only way to do that is to maintain some control and enforce some boundaries. Otherwise, it's chaos.

One day, editing may borrow a leaf from the elegance of literary interpretation. It will be seen as the contextual use of logical skills and cultivated taste in the evaluation of programs. If one had to use one term for the quality control function of networks it would be "principled taste." At the moment, the most problematical issue before the networks is not sex or violence but whether or not top management has the integrity to accept its traditional role as broadcaster in the public interest with full responsibility for program content.

CONCLUSION

As this book goes to press, networks are ambivalent about their sense of public trust. It is not reassuring to hear Jack Welch, NBC's chairman, compare the social responsibility of a network whose ideas reach "everybody" during a given week with the trust he owes G.E. shareholders in the manufacture of nuclear facilities. Strangely, Welch puts a higher premium on the quality control of his appliances than he does on his network. But who is there to challenge his thinking on behalf of the common cause?

Not interest groups. Shortly we will see how the fractional nature of powerful national organizations limits their ability to speak for the people as a whole. Meanwhile, the networks are so busy singing the blues over their audience erosion that they are loath to balance the duty of entertaining the public against the duty of serving the "interest, necessity and convenience" of the public. That moral and social responsibility will be left to the people and to those government leaders who wish to take on the mission.

At the moment, network decision makers are held accountable only by their fear that advertisers will defect from shows that exceed the boundaries of tastes and values. Tied into that threat is the ongoing fear of bad press that inflames the public and arouses pressure groups. Prudence dictates that they stay away from controversial material.

Meanwhile the producers and programmers are put in the awkward position of drawing their own lines. Arthur Price, speaking out of thirty years of experience as a studio head, told the authors that the best protection both producers and networks ever had was the adversarial relationship between network programmers and network censors. With a wry smile, Price admitted that he used to play the game:

> I used to rail at the (standards) censors and scream every time anything was challenged on "Hill Street" or "St. Elsewhere." But I knew in my heart that this was the way to do business. I think I told you when we talked on the phone that no producer in Hollywood has been free of notes from the programming departments asking for more sex and violence in shows. But as long as standards was there to balance the programmers and those producers who wanted to test the boundaries, the system worked. Now, with standards diluted, we are leaving ourselves open to every Rev. Wildmon type who wants to capitalize on the excesses of the medium.

In that adversarial area between those who want more "action and romance" and those who want less, somebody must mediate. It is the network entertainment president who usually argues the case for material he thinks will increase ratings and pacify hot producers, and it is often the sales VP together with the chief legal officer who give prudential advice to the network head on the necessity to "protect the franchise and pacify the critics."

In the past, the standards vice presidents at all three networks had considerable power to veto any material. Only at ABC is that power partly retained. In one sense, it makes no difference who assumes the editorial role at a network. Somebody has to play critic to the creator. Standards, insulated from pressures in sales and programming, seems best suited to play the adversary.

But ultimately, the network cannot afford to ignore the boundaries. That means that someone – the entertainment president and his staff of programmers, the producers themselves or, as in the past, the censors – make those calls. No one doubts that the networks are caught between a rock and a hard place. They desperately want to hold on to the family audiences but just as fervently want to retake the generation of young adults who have drifted to cable and video for spicier fare. The dilemma is real: Whenever the network programs edge beyond the normal boundaries, they draw criticism from Washington, the advertisers, the pressure groups – happily promoted by the print media.

Worse, they contribute to the defection of family audiences to the morally impeccable reruns on independent stations. When they pull back (rehiring censors and beefing up depleted standards departments) the producers scream about freedom of expression and the print critics complain about the cowardly blandness of the new season. Meanwhile the share of primetime audience continues its decline from the 90 percentiles down to the sixties, with a frequent dip into the fifties.

Power over program content—the final cut and the standards responsibility that goes with it—rests with top management. The suppliers must answer to the buyers, to those who pay the piper.

As we have seen, entertainment is a business and business is based on profit. The lust for profit is tempered only by the more immediate threats of advertising defections. And there is a still the fear, as Arthur Price noted, of government re-regulation, public outcry and interest group pressures.

In short, a market mentality is the driving force behind program decisions affecting prime time entertainment in America. But the irony is that network officials, searching for that level playing field with cable and video, may discover that unlicensed freedom will result in greater "reverse" pressures from outside the network on program content than exist today.

As for writer-producers, they keep turning out the music in the hope that their patrons will not let them die penniless.

NOTES

1. Or used to before standards departments at NBC and CBS were emasculated and part of the censoring responsibility was shifted to programmers and producers. In 1990, however, following a disastrous season of sleaze and protest, NBC reinstituted its editors.

2. An answer print is the final step in the program development process in which the tape to be run on air is delivered by the producer to the network.

3. The financial and syndication rule (fin-syn) is a sore point with networks since they pay most of the budget for each show, hit or miss, but derive none of the profits (back door) when successful series go into syndication.

4. For an in-depth treatment of the process by which regulation progressed from radio to television, see chapter 10.

5. Networks are not licensed, only individual stations. However, since networks own the best stations and program for another 200, the FCC considers them coresponsible for the local mandate.

6. See chapter 10 for a detailed explanation of the rules.

7. Steven Holden, "Where the Laughs Are: Comedy Is King on City Stages," *New York Times*, December 5, 1986, p. C1.

5

Government Influence on Television Content

The history of broadcast regulation reads like a script from the Keystone Kops. Radio started out orderly enough when harbor masters used the airwaves to contact incoming ship captains. The discovery of radio's commercial value, however, changed the medium overnight into a chain of pile-ups. Broadcasters charged in, operating at any frequency and at any power setting they wished. Listeners bought radios by the thousands, only to find so many stations at the same place on the dial that they couldn't hear any of them. In came government regulators — the Keystone Kops — to sort it all out, and from the look of things, they used the billy clubs more on themselves than on the perpetrators.

Early problems arose from the government's reluctance to get involved in what many officials saw essentially as a private marketplace arrangement between the seller and the buyer of goods — the broadcaster and the listener. It soon became obvious even to the most ardent hands-off advocates that the distribution system, the airwaves, were different from most commodities and really did require some regulating.

Still, the government avoided a heavy regulatory hand, particularly when it came to content control. Over the years its policies affected content, but direct limitations have been few; prior censorship is nonexistent; and most regulatory influences have proven to affect more the agenda of broadcasting than the substance of programming content. This is an important distinction we will make throughout the chapter.

Overt attempts to alter content have been confined to children's television. Heavy doses of violence and advertising aimed at young viewers have inspired interest groups such as Action for Children's Television and the Parent-Teachers Association to beckon government intervention. The industry draws fire from interest groups and from Congress for some of its sex and violence during primetime hours as well, but most of that pressure comes from parents worried about the early evening when children are still watching.

The most sweeping content agenda provision, the Fairness Doctrine, which for thirty years has compelled balance in the presentation of controversial issues, had, in the late 1980s, been tossed in the dustbins. The Equal Time Provision for political discourse affects narrow content matter. Although it, too, is under fire, it is less vulnerable to challenges than is the Fairness Doctrine.

In this chapter we have several goals. First, we will review the events in broadcasting history that help explain the relationship that exists among federal regulators, the industry and the audience. This is a story of government tightrope walking. Fall to one side and you abuse the broadcasters' First Amendment and other free speech guarantees; fall to the other and you deprive American citizens of their right to hear a range of views.

Second, in this investigation we will examine the principal legislative acts and the doctrines that impact broadcasting content, even subtly. While government players are important in any discussion of regulation, they are particularly important in broadcasting where the national visibility associated with broadcasting attracts keen public attention. The Federal Communications Commission, the White House, the Congress and the courts each contribute to the regulatory process. We will take a brief look at their responsibilities and their involvement.

A BRIEF HISTORY OF BROADCAST
CONTENT REGULATION

A Flavor of the Times

The earliest broadcasting regulation was written quietly into the books as a means of coordinating ship-to-ship and ship-to-shore radio communication. Congress and the industry recognized a need for radio traffic controls, and so a pair of inconspicuous bills was enacted in 1910 (the Wireless Ship Act) and 1912 (the Radio Act) to manage maritime broadcasting operations.

This uneventful beginning was hardly a portent of how regulated the industry later would become. By the early 1920s, far-sighted entrepreneurs recognized the commercial potential in this wireless technology. To Secretary of Commerce Herbert Hoover, though, it was nothing but trouble. Just months out of the gate, radio faced problems of serious interference and confusion. Unregulated stations operated without restraint and without traffic control, at any power setting and at any frequency they chose. With no clear legal authority, Hoover sought to use the Radio Act of 1912 as a justification for the control of power, frequency usage and hours of operation. But his authority was tenuous and his efforts yielded nothing.

Driven by pressure from broadcasters and some in government to improvise his authority,[1] the future president assigned 833 kHz as the commercial broadcast frequency and stipulated in 1921 that only one station at a time in each area could use the frequency. A year later, in order to accommodate growing usage, Hoover added a second frequency—750 kHz. It was a pathetic stopgap. He was up against more than he could possibly imagine.

The next several years were filled with nightmares for broadcasters, the government and certainly the listeners. Regulating was tried and failed, but the sale of receivers continued to climb, and new broadcasters, thrilled by the chance to get in on an exciting medium, jumped into the crowding pool. The growing popularity imposed yet more confusion, which brought further cries for government control.

Not until 1927 did Capitol Hill move to break the logjam, but only after President Calvin Coolidge's plea, growing public outcries about the continuing confusion and congestion, and persistent industry drumbeats over what was becoming a choking economic problem. The Republican House and the Democratic Senate had different agendas (Krasnow, Longley and Terry, 1982). The House wanted the secretary of commerce to issue licenses and the Federal Radio Commission to serve as an appeals board. The Senate wanted to invest all the power in an independent radio commission and thereby prevent undue influence by the Republican House and the executive.

With battle lines drawn, the two chambers sparred for nearly a year; the House passing one version, the Senate preferring another. Finally a compromise bill, the Radio Act of 1927, called for an awkward arrangement between the secretary of commerce and a new, temporary Federal Radio Commission (FRC). Under this provision the Department of Commerce would receive all applications and renewals, which it would forward to the FRC where the power of action resided. The secretary of commerce would designate operator qualifications, assign call letters and examine station broadcast equipment.

It mattered little how acceptable this hard-fought arrangement might have been because it was scheduled to last only one year. This sunset provision would transfer all responsibilities to the secretary of commerce, making the FRC a part-time agency serving only as an appellate board.

Not only did FRC regulators have to deal with Congress's Rube Goldberg provisions, but they also had almost no staff, no funding and little legislative support. Such impossible conditions are not unknown when lawmakers reluctantly become involved in legislation, and when each side suspects the other of palming an ace. From the outset, broadcast legislation has been molasses thick with politics.

For government regulators, this decade-old industry was an unending source of grief. Many of the original and powerful broadcasters continued to support the general concept of government intervention—for newcomers—but opposed its application to them personally. They wanted to be grandfathered out of the new rules. Thus, efforts of the FRC to start afresh with new allocations for everyone ran into problems that undercut its most aggressive and possibly most effective remedies.

Even though the FRC never actually shriveled as planned to a mere appellate board after the first year—its enabling legislation continued from year to year—

its members routinely found themselves standing hat in hand before Congress to receive renewed authorization. It was a vulnerable position that invited congressional tinkering. For the next few years, Congress granted a string of temporary lives to the FRC but always used the annual occasions to putter with the activities of broadcast regulation (Barnouw, 1966).

As the years passed, congressional involvement continued, Hoover became president, radio was becoming entrenched in American life and the FRC's temporary status continued to undermine its regulatory authority to sort out the grisly industry mess. It was not until 1933, under an order from Franklin Roosevelt, that things began to break loose. Roosevelt established the Roper Committee, named after its chairman, Secretary of Commerce Daniel C. Roper, to recommend changes that would strengthen the government's regulatory role in broadcast communications.

The Communications Act of 1934

Congress, moved by the Roper Committee Report and by ongoing public disgruntlement with government handling of these matters, passed the Communications Act of 1934. This document was almost a carbon copy of the Radio Act of 1927, but it included a few additional items that mattered.

First, it made a permanent Federal Communications Commission (FCC). The commission had seven members rather than the FRC's five, and its mission was more clearly defined. Its authority was broader, covering all telecommunications, and it assumed an advocacy responsibility to examine innovative uses of radio and to promote new applications of the medium. The 1934 legislation did not solve all the problems, but it did meet immediate needs to resolve the chaos, and it set in motion thinking about how government could facilitate future growth of the medium.

Some scholars believe that the most notable provision of the 1934 legislation— a carryover from the 1927 act—is contained in a small but significant clause stating: "the Commission, *if public convenience, interest or necessity will be served* thereby, subject to the limitations of this Act, shall grant to any applicant therefore a station license provided for by this Act" (Communications Act of 1934, Section 7(a)) [ital. ours]. This element becomes critical in our later discussions of government content control.

The important philosophical underpinning for this provision is found in the words of Secretary Hoover, who expressed his concerns for public interests during his four radio conferences between 1922 and 1925:

> The dominant element for consideration in the radio field is, and always will be, the great body of the listening public, millions in number, countrywide in distribution. There is no proper line of conflict between the broadcaster and the listener, nor would I attempt to array one against the other. Their interests are mutual, for without the one the other could not exist.

There have been few developments in industrial history to equal the speed and efficiency with which genius and capital have joined to meet radio needs. The great majority of station owners today recognize the burden of service and gladly assume it. Whatever other motive may exist for broadcasting, the pleasing of the listener is always the primary purpose. . . .

The greatest public interest must be the deciding factor. I presume that few will dissent as to the correctness of this principle, for all will agree that *public good must ever balance private desire*; but its acceptance leads to important and far-reaching practical effects, as to which there may not be the same unanimity, but from which, nevertheless, there is no logical escape. (Report and Statement of Policy re: Commission en banc Programming Inquiry, FCC 60-70 [1960]) [ital. ours].

Tall oaks from little acorns grow. Embedded in the "public interest" provision is a statutory justification for government influence over broadcaster responsibility and, by extension, a context for content intervention. Based on this, defenders of government involvement postulate that a broadcaster must serve the public interest as a precondition for a license to use the public airwaves. As we will see later, this assumption serves as in important preface to more activist positions on broadcast content management by government.

At the time of enactment, however, the Communications Act of 1934 successfully served as a remedy for the most conspicuous ills confronting radio. More of the broadcast spectrum was opened up and parceled out to a growing number of stations. This unsnarled stubborn broadcasting traffic jams and restored relative order to the industry. Radio was now well established and on its way to becoming a national institution.

Radio with Pictures—The Emergence of Television

Commercial television appeared as a novelty around 1930 and made occasional news splashes throughout that decade, but it did not become a serious medium until after World War II. Even in the late 1940s there were skeptics who believed television was a flash in the pan. Viewers, they thought, would get over their initial flirtation with radio-with-pictures and return to their true love. No one has ever been so wrong.

In 1946 the television industry entered an eight-year period of fits and starts. During that year, the FCC issued dozens of station licenses, and it settled a debate over color transmission standards by selecting the RCA over the CBS format.[2] Although the quality of CBS color was superior, RCA color transmissions were compatible with original black-and-white signals, thus allowing continued use of the original black-and-white sets already in American homes.[3] This early decision standardized the hardware and avoided the hazards of incompatible systems.

In 1948, however, interference problems caused the FCC to freeze television development for several years. The hiatus allowed interest in television to well up like flood water behind a dam. When licensing resumed in 1952, stations poured onto the market and the American public rushed to buy new receivers. The rapid adoption rate for television is among the highest of any innovation; 172,000 sets were in operation in 1948 — there were 42 million a decade later (Folkerts and Teeter, 1989).

By the early 1950s, most of the significant technical issues were settled. New standards allowed many additional stations to begin transmission. Resolution of technical problems also enabled a nation of viewers to purchase television sets confident that rigid engineering guidelines would ensure continued receiver-signal compatibility and relatively uncontaminated transmissions.

In the years that followed, research and development efforts focused on improved reception, better color and miniaturized circuitry. It was not until the mid-1970s that this technology-driven industry experienced another surge of innovations that changed dramatically its usage, economics, programming and regulation. The most significant has been the vast expansion of programming options. Adding channels benefited viewers, but it also changed the industry in two ways: First, programming economics was altered, permitting entry by a larger number of broadcasters. It became less expensive to establish a new cable channel, find an audience and make a reasonable profit. This changed the calculus that once allowed the domination of three networks. Second, on the legal side, as additional broadcasters set up shop, the scarce-resource argument began losing its wallop. Many observers believe that an increase in programming outlets calls for a decrease in regulation. Indeed, the marketplace of recreation — if not of ideas — is becoming a richer and more varied place.

Seeing so many colors in the broadcasting spectrum, many advocates of deregulation say that the expansion of viewing options argues for dismantling of the seventy-year-old regulatory structure. Why not start over? After all, scarce resources led to necessary regulations half a century ago but are anachronistic today.

Before we deal with this argument, we must understand what *regulatory* forces are actually at work within the broadcasting industry.

Government Control of Television

Broadcast regulation is a stewpot of activity. The end result — which is a set of laws, guidelines and directions for broadcast station operations — is a function of formal rule making, deals, historical precedent, political wrangling, smoke-filled rooms, and gambler's luck. The formal components of rule making have traceable lines on a flow chart; the informal elements may never be entirely known. They include political and economic considerations, the brokering of favors and chits, and other horse-trading. As former FCC Chairman Lee Loevinger noted, it is unrealistic to talk about "government regulation; there is only regulation by government officials" (Loevinger, 1968). Despite a formal appearance of regulatory procedures, the officials involved are humans subject to the best and worst of human diversions. It is this human component that inspires the warning: there are two things you want to know nothing about: the making of sausage and the making of law.

That's our caveat. Beware the clean operating room claimed for government regulatory activities. The real conditions are messier, murkier and more byzantine.

Another warning about government broadcast intervention: There are few absolutes — regulatory, statutory or constitutional. For instance, Section 326 of the Communications Act[4] expressly forbids the FCC to censor broadcast material. That would interfere with the station's right of free speech ensured by the First Amendment: "Congress shall make no law . . . abridging the freedom of speech, or of the press . . ." (U.S. Constitution, Article I). Yet the government has allowed restraints on broadcast content (citing scarce frequencies as its reason) even though it has steadfastly avoided such interference for print media (Robinson and Gellhorn, 1974).

Conflict between two legitimate principles is sometimes resolved with reference to a reasonable and intuitively appealing compromise. In the case of broadcast content restraints, regulators have attempted to strike a balance between the rights of broadcasters and the rights of the public by expressing the need to ensure an opportunity for all voices to be heard — broadcasters and the public alike. As we shall see, such a noble goal is easy to support in theory but in reality more difficult to achieve.

The FCC's decision to require the airing of many sides in controversial issues was supported by the Supreme Court in 1969. The Court found that accommodating opposing viewpoints under the Fairness Doctrine served a compelling need for the public to have available diverse opinions on controversial issues. The Court, therefore, permitted government intervention. Ironically, the logic of this nearly quarter-century-old decision has been applied by the FCC in the enriched programming environment of the 1980s and yielded the opposite conclusion (Syracuse Peace Council, 2 FCC Rcd 5043 [1987]). More on this later.

Problems also arise when legislative and regulatory directions are not clear. The greater the ambiguity, the greater the likelihood of controversy, since loose descriptions invite individual interpretations consistent with one's self-interests, and competing self-interests lead naturally to conflict in an adversarial system.

One conspicuous instance of such ambiguity is found in the Communications Act of 1934. The act states that when granting a license "the licensing authority should determine that the public interest, convenience, or necessity would be served . . ." (Communications Act of 1934, Section 309 [a]). Over time the provision became a matter of increasing controversy as the FCC began applying this principle in broadcast license renewal cases. Among other criteria for license renewal, the government associates the granting of a license with the responsibility of a radio station to serve the public interest. In theory there is little to quibble about. In practice a problem arises over the meaning of "public interest." Which public? What interests? How much service is enough? How must this be accomplished?

Broadcast regulation, then, is a blend of formal and informal activities. There are clashes in the system among the many rights of participants. Laws rarely have mathematical precision, and the ambiguity of language ensures controversy and debate. Despite all this, the regulatory process has been reasonably effective in providing order to an inherently disorderly industry. Furthermore, against all odds, the process has balanced the rights of broadcast participants and of the public, and, as we shall see, it has done so with reasonable adherence to democratic principles.

In the next section we will summarize the formal roles of four government participants in broadcast regulation. Even though many government agencies are drawn into matters that affect broadcast content, four play the dominant roles: the FCC, the Congress, the courts and the White House.

THE FEDERAL COMMUNICATIONS COMMISSION

The Federal Communications Commission was established by the Communications Act of 1934 as an independent regulatory agency that reports directly to Congress. Over the years all three branches of government have asserted their influence on FCC matters, yet the commission retains its independent status.

The president appoints the commissioners with the consent of the Senate. Originally there were seven members, but in the spirit of deregulation in 1982 the commission was reorganized as a five-member body. Each term lasts five years (formerly seven), and the chairman is named by the president to serve as chief executive officer of the commission.

The FCC is responsible for an enormous range of activity. Robinson and Gellhorn describe some of the commission's activities:

> The FCC regulates all private broadcasting: television, both commercial and education, AM and FM radio, and cable television (CATV), as well as aviation, shipboard, amateur, and various forms of business and citizens radio services. It passes on applications for construction permits and licenses for all classes of non-federal government radio stations. It assigns frequencies, sets operating power, designates call signs, inspects and regulates the use of transmitting equipment. . . . The FCC is also in charge of domestic administration of the telecommunications provisions of treaties and international agreements. . . . It licenses United States radio and cable circuits to foreign points and regulates the companies operating the circuits. Radio stations on American planes and ships are also licensed by the Commission. Finally, the FCC has jurisdiction over interstate common carrier communications: telephone, telegraph, cable, microwave, and satellite communication. . . . (Robinson and Gellhorn, 1974)

In addition to these maintenance responsibilities, the FCC also must promote the industry it regulates and facilitate the availability of broadcast services to all regions of the country. Moreover, it has been charged to ensure that licensed stations serve the "public interest."

Broadcasters view government involvement in anything other than technical matters as meddlesome in their business affairs and threatening to their First Amendment rights. Over the years the commission has had many battles with industry over usage policies, and these often are settled in the courts.

As an independent regulatory body, the FCC has responsibilities that span lawmaking, judicial and enforcement roles. In its legislative capacity, it develops administrative rules following standard procedures observed by all government agencies. In its judicial capacity, it hears cases on a wide variety of issues including license applications and challenges to license applications and renewals. The FCC may sit in judgment on regulatory issues and violations and, although rare, it also may hear cases involving license revocations.

Finally, the FCC enforces broadcast legislation passed by Congress and enforces its own rules under the authority granted by Congress. Broadcast deregulation—begun in the Carter administration and continued with particular enthusiasm under Reagan and Bush—has provided for greater flexibility and independence in the industry, but has also opened the door to owners who, lusting for private gain only, thumb their noses at the public good.

Some of the more important deregulatory changes include a reduction in documentation and paperwork at license renewal time, less frequent renewals, fewer commissioners and other administrative items. Most significantly for these discussions, deregulation has resulted in the abandonment of the Fairness Doctrine on the one hand and the instituting of decency rules, on the other. We will examine this paradox later.

CONGRESSIONAL INPUT

Although the FCC technically is independent, its responsibilities and activities are not immune from legislative review and political intervention. The Communications Act of 1934 compels the commission to report to Congress, which also controls the purse strings through the power of appropriations.

The means by which Congress uses this influence are both "routine" and "provisional." Routine procedures, which allow for periodic examination of FCC affairs, keep the congressional hand on the broadcasting pulse. Provisional intervention occurs when congressional interest is stirred by industry events, FCC actions or initiatives or other events that may arise from within Congress itself. An example would be hearings on violence and crime. In these cases Congress may conduct committee reviews of FCC activities or investigations that often accompany controversial issues.

Congressional input also may take informal courses such as the personal intervention of individual members who express a particular interest in some action or issue within the commission's purview. Oversight committee chairmen hold particular sway with the FCC because of the inherent power of their positions and broadcasters worry about their jawboning.

Finally, Congress retains the power to enact legislation related to FCC operations. Although Congress rarely has chosen to exercise such authority—allowing general provisions of the Communications Act to set forth the broad direction—it occasionally has become involved with such legislation. For instance, in 1991, it passed legislation on children's television. Similar congressional attention has been given to legislation related to the Fairness Doctrine discarded by the FCC.[5]

Seen in action, Congress has a variety of means to exercise its oversight function and to provide direct input to broadcast regulation. The extent of this intervention is a function of the political climate, industry events, the introduction of innovative technologies that impose new conditions on the market and initiatives arising from the commission. Moreover, much is determined by individual interests of congressional members who, for personal or singular political reasons, decide to invest their time and efforts in broadcasting matters. On the whole, Congress has maintained an active interest in commission activities, a concern that has not diminished in this era of broadcast deregulation.

THE COURTS

The FCC's relationship with the courts is considerably different from its relationship with Congress. With the courts it's all business. Everything takes place on the record, in full view, according to the rules. Judges reviewing broadcast regulation obtain all their information during formal court proceedings. Unlike the climate on Capitol Hill, there are few occasions for ex parte or out of court discussions and bartering. Moreover, while lower court decisions can be appealed, there are no provisions for jawboning as there are with rulings of other bodies. Consequently, because of the isolation of their deliberations and the finality of their judgments, the courts' responsibilities are viewed with particular reverence.

Although judicial involvement is guarded, influences on the judiciary still exist; several are worth noting. For one, the appointment of judges is awash in politics. Through the advise and consent procedure, the Congress can influence appointments to the bench. Presidents often seek the nomination of judges from lawmakers, and this along with other features of the appointment process introduces the opportunity for political intervention. One assumes that the ideologies held by judges before nomination will be manifest, if ever so subtly, in the spirit of their rulings after appointment.

Political convulsions over the confirmation of Clarence Thomas, and before him the failed nominations of Robert Bork and Douglas Ginsburg, demonstrate some of the intense passion associated with the confirmation process. Such concerns grow out of the impact of a nominee's philosophy on later decisions. Although Supreme Court nominations draw considerable public and legislative attention, similar conflict is evident, although less celebrated, for lower positions on the federal bench.

Networks, station owners and the National Association of Broadcasters keep a close watch on the courts, especially the Supreme Court, which has consistently backed the FCC's power of oversight while assuring the stations' rights of free speech.

THE EXECUTIVE BRANCH

Influence by the executive branch is often less formal and direct than it is for other regulatory participants. Nonetheless, the power of the presidency should not be underestimated. During the 1980s the conservative philosophy of Ronald Reagan established an environment in Washington that induced profound change throughout government, including matters of broadcast regulation. Force of personality and the command of public attention become potent presidential tools.

Generally the president and the executive branch staff affect the process in four ways. First, the president, by virtue of his high office, has command of the American media, and therefore the capacity to affect materially the public agenda. We offer again the example of Ronald Reagan, who was well known to assert his philosophy opposing taxes. Even in the face of a monumental national debt under Bush, the public continues to embrace the antitax lessons Reagan taught during his presidency. His distaste for government regulation also became a factor in the considerable changes of broadcast policy. Changes in licensing requirements, station ownership rules and abandonment of Fairness Doctrine requirements demonstrate the point.

The executive also can affect broadcast regulation through the appointment of FCC commissioners and appellate judges. Although the president's nominees require Senate approval, most are appointed without much difficulty. Through the power of appointment, the executive can fill key government positions with ideological soulmates who likely will support administration views on broadcast matters. While there are examples of appointees who, once in position, have not supported the president's outlook, most often the views of nominees become accurate predictors of decisions they later will make on the job.

The executive also can establish advisory commissions that come under direct control of the White House. These commissions provide the president with direct input on matters affecting government broadcasting policy. Although they are created solely to advise the president on broadcast issues, they are seen by some critics to tread on the FCC's authority.

Finally, the president retains a veto power over legislation. Although exercise of the veto varies by administration, presidents can erect this stonewall into which much legislation has crashed over the years. In 1988, legislation resulting from a long and hard-fought battle over children's television (reviewed later in this chapter), cleared both houses of Congress but was pocket vetoed by President Reagan. President Bush, well known for his unbroken string of successful vetoes, never had occasion to pass judgment on broadcast matters. The history, background and structure in place, we now focus on the government's influence on television content.

THE DEBATE OVER GOVERNMENT CONTROL OF
BROADCAST CONTENT

It was not long after the Federal Radio Commission began correcting the "maintenance" problems of radio, sorting out frequency assignments and power outputs, that it took on early "utility" problems. Even in the late 1920s, the FRC had to deal with broadcasters who used their stations as platforms for staging personal doctrines. In 1929 the radio commission finally took on one of the offenders—The Great Lakes Broadcasting Company—by denying license renewal for three of the company's stations. The FRC's ruling set the tone for subsequent cases dealing with broadcasting content concerns:

> Broadcasting stations are licensed to serve the public, and not for the purpose of furthering the private or selfish interests of individuals or groups of individuals. The standard of public interest, convenience or necessity means nothing if it does not mean this.
>
> In so far as a program consists of discussion of public questions, public interest requires ample play for the free and fair competition of opposing views, and the commission believes that the principle applies . . . to all discussions of issues of importance to the public.
>
> In such a scheme there is no room for the operation of broadcasting stations exclusively by or in the private interests of individuals or groups so far as the nature of the programs is concerned. . . . (Great Lakes Broadcasting Co., 3 FRC An. Rep. 32-34 [1929])

During the 1930s the commission confronted a number of station owners who, it said, used the public resources for private ambitions. In many cases the offending owners were denied licenses at renewal time. Less serious offenders were warned against such practices, then monitored to ensure compliance.

Even in these early days—before content matters became more celebrated through intervention by the courts, the FCC and Congress—several key principles were forming. On the side *opposing* government intervention in broadcasting content:

- The First Amendment. "Congress shall make no law respecting an establishment of religion, or prohibiting the free exercise thereof; *or abridging the freedom of speech, or of the press*; or the right of the people peaceably to assemble, and to petition the Government for a redress of grievances" (U.S. Constitution, Article I) [italics ours].

- Section 326 of the Communications Act. "Nothing in this Act shall be understood or construed to give the Commission the power of censorship over the radio communication or signals transmitted by any radio station, and no regulation or condition shall be promulgated or fixed by the Commission which shall interfere with the right of free speech by means of radio communications."

It is difficult to see how one could adhere to the letter and spirit of these provisions and at the same time control broadcast content. The First Amendment is firm about the government's intrusion on the right of free speech and free press, and the Communication Act is serious about its prohibitions against censorship of broadcast communications.

Nevertheless, opposing these provisions are two viewpoints commonly offered in *defense* of content controls.

- The Communications Act of 1934, Section 7(a): In granting station licenses, the Commission should determine "if (the) public convenience, interest, or necessity will be served . . ."

- Radio is a scarce and public resource. This principle is articulated in early Congressional debates: ". . . there must be a limitation upon the number of broadcasting stations and . . . licenses should be issued only to those stations whose operations would render a benefit to the public, are necessary in the public interest or would contribute to the development of the art. . . . If enacted into law, the broadcasting privilege will not be a right of selfishness. It will rest upon an assurance of public interest to be served." (Stated by Maine Congressman Wallace H. White, Jr., 67 Cong. Rec. 5479, March 12, 1926.)

Based solely on these provisions one might conclude that the government remains within its legal authority to impose at least some level of content control. It would need to have available such authority to ensure that broadcasters serve the public interest as they make a profit with a borrowed public resource.

So provisions of the First Amendment and censorship proscriptions of the Communications Act were poised against the public interest measure and the scarce public resources argument to provide the stuff of great legal debate. It was late in the 1930s, as radio matured and the industry explored new and innovative programming applications, that conflicts became more serious. The issue that opened a decade of debate over the content question—which would end with articulation of the Fairness Doctrine—concerned the editorial policies of radio station WAAB of Boston.

In 1941 the Mayflower Broadcasting Company challenged the license renewal of Boston radio station owner John Shepard, of the Yankee and Colonial Networks. Mayflower contended that Shepard presented one-sided opinions on a range of political issues and never attempted to provide alternative positions or to allow other views from the community. Ultimately the FCC granted the relicensing of WAAB, but in its review admonished WAAB for its restrictive practices. The commission's statement portends a position it would develop more fully by the end of the decade:

Radio can serve as an instrument of democracy only when devoted to the communication of information and the exchange of ideas fairly and objectively presented. A truly free radio cannot be used to advocate the causes of the licensee. It cannot be used to support the candidacies of his friends. It cannot be devoted to the support of principles he happens to regard most favorably. In brief, the broadcaster cannot be an advocate.

Freedom of speech on the radio must be broad enough to provide full and equal opportunity for the presentation to the public of all sides of public issues. Indeed, as one licensed to operate in a public domain the licensee has assumed the obligations of presenting all sides of important public questions, fairly, objectively and without bias. *The public interest — not the private — is paramount.* (In the Matter of the Mayflower Broadcasting Corporation, and The Yankee Network, Inc. [WAAB] 8 FCC 333, 340) [italics ours].

Two years later, in *NBC v. U.S. 319 U.S. 190*, the Supreme Court affirmed the FCC's authority to go beyond its maintenance role (assigning frequencies and power settings) to assume a utility function (how the spectrum is used by licensees). In this case the commission found that network practices throttled the options of local stations and, among other remedies, ordered NBC to divest itself of one of its two operating networks. As a result of this case the FCC developed the "Chain Broadcast Regulations" governing many network practices. Although this case did not deal with content regulation directly, it was important as a foundation for subsequent arguments over the commission's wider responsibilities within the broadcast industry.

In 1946 the FCC published the "Public Service Responsibilities of Broadcast Licenses" (more commonly known as the "Blue Book"), wherein it spelled out its position on the obligations of broadcasters to serve the public interest. Publication of the document immediately received comments from throughout the broadcasting community; praise from many legislators and interest groups, complaints from the industry.

Three years later, after public hearings, the commission issued a second, more thorough document titled the "Report on Editorializing by Broadcast Licensees" — the Fairness Doctrine we will discuss in a moment. (*In the Matter of Editorializing by Broadcast Licensees*, 13 FCC 1246, June 1, 1949.) Members were particularly concerned about clarification of criteria by which it evaluated public interest requirements of licensees. Adding to the pressure at the time of the document's release was the volatile Richards case, which focused the commission's attention on control questions.[6]

The "Report on Editorializing" was more than a list of dos and don'ts. By design, vague wording of the Communications Act prevented any such handbook of standards. Instead the commission set forth a philosophy justifying its obligations to consider the public interest in its licensing decisions. In so doing, it presented the legal arguments for its position, but it also offered a more general discussion of the logic for having broadcasters observe balanced programming.

From the legal viewpoint the report cited the intentions of Congress and the concurrence of the courts to observe balanced content:

The legislative history of the Communications Act and its predecessor, the Radio Act of 1927, shows . . . that Congress intended that radio stations should not be used for the private interest, whims, or caprices of the particular persons who have been granted licenses, but in a manner which will serve the community generally and the various groups which make up the community. And the courts have consistently upheld Commission action giving recognition to and fulfilling that intent of Congress. KFKB Broadcasting Association v. Federal Radio Commission, 47. 2d 670; Trinity Methodist Church, South v. Federal Radio Commission, 62 F. 2d 850, certiorari denied, 288 U.S. 599. (*In the Matter of Editorializing by Broadcast Licensees*, 13 FCC 1246, June 1, 1949, 5)

Its rational arguments offer more intuitive reasons for a need to recognize the public claims in broadcasting:

It is axiomatic that one of the most vital questions of mass communication in a democracy is the development of an informed public opinion through the public dissemination of news and ideas concerning the vital public issues of the day. Basically, it is in recognition of the great contribution which radio can make in the advancement of this purpose that portions of the radio spectrum are allocated to that form of radio communications known as radio broadcasting. Unquestionably, then, *the standard of public interest, convenience and necessity* as applied to radio broadcasting must be interpreted in the light of this basic purpose. (*In the Matter of Editorializing by Broadcast Licensees*, 13 FCC 1246, June 1, 1949, 6) [italics ours].

The commission further discusses the airing of public events programming along with the balanced presentation of ideas:

And the Commission has made clear that in such presentation of news and comment the public interest requires that the licensee must operate on a basis of overall fairness, making his facilities available for the expression of the contrasting views of all responsible elements in the community on the various issues which arise. . . . *These concepts, of course, do restrict the licensee's freedom to utilize his station in whatever manner he chooses but they do so in order to make possible the maintenance of radio as a medium of freedom of speech for the general public. (In the Matter of Editorializing by Broadcast Licensees*, 13 FCC 1246, June 1, 1949, 7) [italics ours].

The freedom of speech theme runs throughout debates on the content regulation of broadcasting. Licensees argue that any content directions violate their First Amendment or freedom of speech guarantees. The government, including the Supreme Court, has said that balanced presentations ensure the public's right to freedom of speech. Broadcasters see content controls as an abridgement of their free-speech rights; public defenders see the absence of such controls as contributing to an abridgement of public free-speech rights. A concluding portion of the FCC document deals further with this decisive issue:

It would be strange indeed, however, if the grave concern for freedom of the press which prompted adoption of the first amendment should be read as a command that the Government was without power to protect that freedom. . . . That amendment rests on the assumption that the *widest possible dissemination of information from diverse and antagonistic sources is essential to the welfare of the public*, that a free press is a condition of free society. Surely a command that the Government itself shall not impede the free flow of ideas does not afford nongovernment combinations a refuge if they impose restraints upon that constitutionally guaranteed freedom. . . . (*In the Matter of Editorializing by Broadcast Licensees*, 13 FCC 1246, June 1, 1949, Section 19) [italics ours]

This 1949 report generally reversed a previous position that restricted editorializing by licensees. Now the FCC said the desirable approach to encourage balance and to brew the richest broth of ideas was not to silence one viewpoint but to expand the opportunity for airing of many viewpoints. This adopted position, then, encouraged the presentation of controversial topics. But it further specified these presentations should include a more comprehensive account of the arguments involved in such matters. Clearly, the stated purpose was not to restrict discussion but to encourage a more open and robust treatment of issues. Many disagree about whether these means achieve the desired end.[7]

The Fairness Doctrine guided the industry through the 1950s although its legitimacy always has been a matter of some dispute. These positions established by the FCC never have been codified through legislation, and many in the industry opposed to its provisions believed that it was vulnerable to legal challenge. While Congress never boldly endorsed the Fairness Doctrine described in the 1949 FCC Report, in 1959 it tipped its hat to the general concepts the doctrine embraced. The matter began with congressional consideration of a different concern (equal broadcast time for political candidates) and by the time it was over involved at least a tacit recognition of the legitimacy of the Fairness Doctrine.

The Fairness Doctrine drew continuous broadcaster and regulator attention since its inception, but it was not until 1984, amid the era of deregulation, that it began a serious unravelling. In this year, the FCC issued a Notice of Inquiry "to reassess the wisdom of applying general Fairness Doctrine obligations to broadcast licensees."[8] Its reexamination of fairness doctrine issues considered the 1949 *Report on Editorializing* in light of contemporary market conditions. Not quite a year and a half later the commission completed its study, concluding that the Fairness Doctrine no longer served the public good. The commission even suggested it might be unconstitutional. Despite this ruling, the FCC said it recognized congressional concerns for these matters and therefore decided to continue enforcing provisions of the doctrine. The commission acted with more force in 1987 when it was ordered by the appeals court to consider fairness doctrine issues in *Meredith* v. *FCC*. Its final ruling on that case found the doctrine to be unconstitutional and contrary to the public interest. The FCC found "that in the order to administer and enforce the doctrine, it is necessarily required to intervene in the editorial process and second-guess the judgement of broadcasters" (FCC Report No. MM-263, Aug. 4, 1987). This time, the commission forwarded to Congress a report that argued against retention of the Fairness Doctrine, largely on First Amendment grounds, but offered a number of measures as an alternative to complete dismantling, which it preferred. Early in 1989 the Court of Appeals upheld the FCC's decision to eliminate the Fairness Doctrine. The U.S. Supreme Court decided not to hear the case. So, without legislation, the Fairness Doctrine died.

Nevertheless, there has been some legislative activity to codify and thus to resuscitate the Fairness Doctrine. Following President Reagan's veto of the "Fairness in Broadcasting Act" in 1987,[9] the Congress attempted to codify the doctrine several times in 1989, but failed. Today, congressional attention seems to have drifted from the Fairness Doctrine, and legislative activity is like the sound of thunder from a distant storm.

The Fairness Doctrine is the most recognizable effort by the government to exercise broad and general influence on television content. It argued that broadcast station licensees are using a scarce public resource and therefore are obligated to serve public interests. Instead of violating constitutional protections of free speech as opponents claim, defenders of the doctrine asserted that not providing balanced coverage of controversial issues—presenting only the views of station operators—violates the public right of free speech.

The arguments that defeated the Fairness Doctrine had three parts. First, there is no longer an environment of broadcast scarcity. New technologies have opened the floodgates of programming options, providing a rich assortment of ideas and ideologies in the public marketplace. Second, by adhering to provisions of the doctrine there actually was a chilling of speech since many broadcasters chose to avoid a controversial topic rather than risk the consequences of not providing adequate counterbalancing. They would prefer to say nothing than to say the wrong combination of things.

Finally, there is the constitutional protection of free speech. As noted previously, the FCC has always said that a failure to provide open debate with representation of all viewpoints violates the public's right to free speech. Broadcasters argue that the requirement to carry any sort of content limits their constitutional right of free speech. What really killed the Fairness Doctrine was the explosion of channels laying waste the issue of broadcasting as a scarce resource. But what worries broadcasters is the fact that bills on fairness keep popping up in congressional hoppers.

Deregulation of America's industries during the 1980s was a dream come true for some, a nightmare for others. For everyone it was a grand experiment. Would government loosening the reins improve or worsen the lives of citizens— private or corporate? The answer has come in for the savings and loan industry and one is taking shape for the airline industry and the insurance industry. No such clarity exists for broadcasting. Dismantling the broadcasting regulatory structure took longer, and the Fairness Doctrine was not discarded until late in the decade. We should have a clearer answer by the late-1990s. For now, broadcasters are free of Fairness Doctrine restraints although bills to revive it continually surface in Congress.

Equal Time Provision

The Equal Time Provision forces broadcasting to walk a straight line during campaigns for public office. The Communications Act of 1934, Section 315, reads:

> (a) If any licensee shall permit any person who is a legally qualified candidate for any public office to use a broadcasting station, he shall afford equal opportunities to all other such candidates for that office in the use of such broadcasting station. . . .
>
> (b) The charges made for the use of any broadcasting station for any of the purposes set forth in this section shall not exceed the charges made for comparable use of such station for other purposes.

The provision exempts stations from equal time requirements for newscasts, news interviews and news documentaries as long as the broadcaster continues "to operate in the public interest and to afford reasonable opportunity for the discussion of conflicting views on issues of public importance." Exemptions also include political conventions and debates among candidates. Finally, in 1984, the FCC lifted the rules for talk shows, no doubt recognizing that Oprah, Geraldo and Phil were ungovernable by definition.

During campaigns, the law demands equal treatment for all but does not require broadcasters to offer free time to any. Whenever one candidate is charged to air a message during a given time period, other candidates also must be allowed to purchase an equivalent time slot for the same cost.

The Equal Time Provision then imposes an *agenda* on broadcasters rather than compelling *content* considerations. It requires them to make provisions for candidate discussions, but it says nothing about what should take place in the context of those discussions. In fact, this law prohibits broadcasters from censoring political messages. Candidates and their campaigns are responsible for the content of their messages and any indiscreet or libelous content is their responsibility alone.

Perhaps the only exception to the hands-off policy for political messages has to do with the use of profanity and offensive language. In 1984 the FCC ruled that stations can set aside the noncensorship measures in order to remove language not customarily used in the station's programming.

In these matters the government has allowed broadcasters to exercise some content control. That's quite different from compelling them to provide particular material or to shape content according to government prescriptions. Consequently, the Equal Time Provision sets boundaries for stations and candidates but does not affect the intellectual content, if any, of speeches and ads.

OTHER CONTENT CONTROL ISSUES

There are two areas in which the government has become more assertive in regulating the actual content of television programming. For the past twenty years or so there has been considerable attention to the special needs of children.

The other issue is the use of offensive language, finally settled as constitutionally protected for print media, but equitable for broadcasting.

Children's Programming

Academic research conducted since the mid-1960s has demonstrated the special vulnerability of children to television's influence.[10] These findings have inspired not only broadcast regulators, but a host of peripheral agencies and organizations to pressure the industry. Concerns for children's television clearly have been in a category separate from all other programming genres. Even though networks balk at attempts to control children's programming, they must tread carefully, not appearing to disregard concerns of specialists and of parents who can fuel the fires of broadcast regulation.

Regulation of children's programming has been an on-again off-again activity. After several years of studying the content and influence of children's programming, in 1974 the FCC issued a "Children's Television Report and Policy Statement," which outlined several guidelines for network consideration in the preparation and presentation of children's shows. It concerned limitations on certain advertising practices that the commission said had particularly adverse effects on young audiences.[11] It also issued a general call for the networks to consider several studies that outlined improvements in the quality and educational components of children's programming. These were only guidelines, however, and did not have the force of law.

Children's television has been a topic of national debate for thirty years. Organizations such as Action for Children's Television have supported studies, encouraged public dialogue and hounded Congress with evidence supporting the power of the medium over youngsters. In 1979 the surgeon general encouraged the National Institutes of Health to conduct a review of current research on the influence of television in general but with an eye focused on children. NIH gathered leading behavioral scientists and other scholars, and three years later, in 1982, issued its well-documented report.[12] Essentially the study recognized a convergence of research findings confirming television's impact on child viewers. In a nutshell, it concluded that heavy television viewing can produce adverse effects on children, making them more aggressive and less attentive in school.

One year later, after reconsidering the evidence in the giddy atmosphere of deregulation, the FCC terminated its ongoing investigation into children's television and issued a Report and Order rejecting the idea of mandatory programming controls. The commission emphasized its abiding concern for diversified and quality children's programming but said such matters were not for them to decide and were for programmers alone to determine.

The Report and Order recognized the special programming needs of children and suggested that broadcasters might wish to "consider a variety of factors in determining what programming they should present, e.g., service area demographics, existing children's programming in the market, network affiliation or independent status, market size, prior commitments to locally produced programs, the availability of television, etc." (National Association of Broadcasters, 1988). In the true spirit of deregulation, the FCC shifted the responsibility from itself to the industry.

Action for Children's Television sought a review of the Report and Order soon after its release. In 1985 the Court upheld all provisions of the FCC's action, noting two conditions. First, it recognized the expansion of programming options through cable and noncommercial outlets. While it noted the growing number of available programs, it also said broadcasters must be mindful that not all children have access to this assortment.

Apparently the Court recognized an erosion in the scarce resources argument under current industry conditions. It said there were more channels and a greater opportunity for viewers to find agreeable programming. It also maintained that not everyone had such choices—not yet. The wording suggests the Court recognized an industry in transition from one of scarce to more plentiful resources.

Congress, often under heavy public pressure, has given lip service to children's television. There is a good deal of emotion in the issue and its high profile ensures a reasonable level of constituent attention. Protecting children, along with the defense of apple pie and motherhood, has political draw and thus a natural congressional following.

In most recent congressional activities on the subject through the late 1980s and into the early 1990s, various bills have been submitted in both houses that would have compelled television stations to provide one hour per day of informational and educational programming for children. Along with such program content provisions have been a handful of bills concerning the frequency and content of advertisements aimed at children.

For instance, H.R. 3996 would have required "the FCC to reinstate restrictions on advertising during children's television, (and) to enforce the obligation of broadcasters to meet the educational and informational needs of the child audience . . ." (H.R. 3966, Summary of Legislation). The legislation was not embraced by the industry, but leading broadcast advocacy organizations, such as the National Association of Broadcasters (NAB), did not oppose it. The bill was passed by the full House in June 1988, and in the Senate by voice vote in October 1988. President Reagan pocket-vetoed it in November of that year.

After a decade of wrangling, the Congress finally passed the Children's Television Act of 1990. Without President Bush's signature, it became law on October 18, 1990. The bill has two main provisions. First, it reinstated commercial time guidelines for children's shows on both broadcast and cable stations. On weekends they were limited to 10.5 commercial minutes and on weekdays to 12 minutes. The bill includes a provision for a reexamination of these limits after January 1, 1993, through public notice and comment arranged by the FCC.

Second, the bill imposes a responsibility on broadcasters to serve the "educational and informational needs of children through the licensee's overall programming . . ." (Public Law 101-437, October 18, 1990). This legislation dropped the specific provisions for a daily hour of educational programming and instead evaluates the station's overall service to children. This includes not only the programs aired, but other community educational activities and assistance for educational programming to other stations in the marketplace.

This legislation seems to have calmed the storm over children's television. Marketplacers effectively toned down more restrictive legislation, and champions of government intervention saw some action, even though it was less vigorous than they may have hoped and it has a built-in time limit for reconsideration of commercial time restrictions. To us, this seems like a reasonable compromise.

Will the battle over children's television resume later in the 1990s? A few developments lead us to believe the big bouts are over. First, new programming channels and sources will expand children's options, thereby limiting protectionist arguments of scarce resources. Second, the war may lose its toughest soldiers. For instance, Peggy Charren of Action for Children's Television, the leading advocacy organization for government intervention, announced in January 1992 that the national arm will lock its doors by the end of the year. After years of bloody battle, these warriors enjoyed victory in the 1990 legislation and decided it was time to retire.

Compared to the 1980s the United States is changing today in ways that may make "shock" arguments against television less alarming. Baby-boom parents have grown up with television and most can offer their own development as evidence of the medium's inability to transform normal people into adult monsters. People may like to have television help educate their kids, but they will not buy the strong claims once made about its insidious effects.

In the face of a maturing, program-enriched industry, a population comfortable with its own viewing experiences is not likely to take to the streets over television programming for children. Unless the major broadcast and cable companies do something stupid that rekindles public anger, we may have seen the last of government action over children's television.

Controls on Language

Most of the other content controls are fairly specific. For instance, limitations on permissible language usage focus on a handful of objectionable words—illustrated in the renowned "Seven Dirty Words" skit by comedian George Carlin. In this case WBAI, an innovative, noncommercial New York radio station, played a short skit in which Carlin discusses—and repeats—seven words "they will not let you say on the air." He said them and the station got a mild tongue-lashing from the FCC, which decided the language was not obscene but was "patently offensive," particularly for audiences listening when the program aired around midday.

Owners of the radio station appealed and the case ultimately went before the Supreme Court (*FCC* v. *Pacifica Foundation*, 98 S. Ct. 3026 [1078]). The

Court also ruled that the words were not obscene (since they did not meet the "prurient appeal" portion of the definition), but said they were indecent. Although indecent words can be used in the public square, they are not constitutionally protected on the public air. In writing for the Court, Justice John Paul Stevens said, "Patently offensive, indecent material presented over the airwaves confronts the citizen not only in public, but also in the privacy of the home, where the individual's right to be let alone plainly outweighs the First Amendment rights of the intruder."

In addition to recognizing the lack of constitutional protection for such language, the Court referenced nuisance law, saying such language is "merely a right thing in the wrong place—like a pig in the parlor instead of the barnyard." The Court said, "We simply hold that when the Commission finds that a pig has entered the parlor, the exercise of its regulatory power does not depend on proof that the pig is obscene" (*FCC* v. *Pacifica Foundation* [438 U.S. 726]).

Since *Pacifica*, the FCC has fined several radio stations for their use of indecent language, but the trend appears to be a loosening of restrictions.[13] It is not uncommon to hear actors in primetime programs using mild profanity, especially in later hours. "Saturday Night Live" even used the word "fuck" a half-dozen times in one of its programs in 1989. In fact, in a segment discussing the more relaxed content of television programs, the NBC Evening News replayed a verbatim tape of that "SNL" skit—during the dinner hour! (NBC claimed that the work used was slightly different in sound and, of course, meaning. An informal panel convened to view the videotape—over and over again—could not hear anything but the F-word.)

Early in the Bush administration, the FCC attempted to ban "indecent" radio and television broadcasts at any time of day. Its argument was that even late-hour broadcasts, though less likely to have young audiences, were accessible to children. The administration said the issue "was a matter of concern to virtually every American household," and so in an interpretation of 1988 legislation sponsored by Senator Jesse Helms, the FCC sought to prohibit such language at all hours. The issue was resolved in early March 1992 when the U.S. Supreme Court refused to allow the FCC to enact the prohibitions citing such blanket rules as a free speech violation (Marcus, 1992).

There are few other direct content controls on broadcasters although occasionally the FCC taps its foot and wags a finger. One such instance nearly twenty years ago concerned the airing of songs with lyrics condoning or glorifying drug usage. The FCC said it would not tolerate the playing of drug-oriented music. Its rules were upheld by a federal appellate court (*Yale Broadcasting* v. *FCC*, 478 F. 2d 594 [1973]) but they became almost impossible to administer. Rock lyrics rarely are clear enough for fifty-year-old bureaucrats to understand so that drug advocacy in a song may not even be recognizable to adult listeners. In addition, the use of double entendres and coded language may provide sufficient insulation of meaning to undermine successful prosecution of stations playing such songs. The issue is rarely discussed anymore.[14]

CONCLUSIONS

There are two categories of governmental content control. The first, which once included the Fairness Doctrine and still includes the Equal Time Provision, is more of an agenda-setting mechanism. Such controls do not necessarily affect what is said as much as they provide for balance in what is discussed and gets air time to discuss it.

The basis for the agenda-setting controls has deep roots in the belief that broadcasters are using a scarce and public resource. Because of this, they must return something of value to the public from which they are borrowing something of value. This idea is central to the Communications Act of 1934.

Broadcasters who traditionally have recoiled at government controls cite as defense the First Amendment and the Communications Act. The First Amendment guarantees free speech and a free press; the Communications Act says the government may not censor broadcast material. The question is, do FCC rules requiring broadcasters to self-regulate content constitute censorship?

The history of response to such questions is deep and wide. The courts and the FCC have expressed the view that freedom of speech includes not just the broadcaster's freedom to air speech, but also the public's freedom to hear speech. Moreover, the courts and the commission have maintained that the public has a more compelling right than the broadcaster. They have argued that if left to present only a single viewpoint, the broadcaster would violate the public's right to receive other perspectives on an issue. This would limit lively debate and curtail the public discussion of issues deemed so important in a democratic society.

It has been argued that an operational definition of censorship includes an active governmental review of content material which then stands to be altered. To date, there are no instances of such government activity and only limited examples of government concern for specific content matter (e.g., language proscriptions). As Robinson and Gellhorn point out, "The (Communications) Act does not essay to regulate the business of the licensee. The Commission is given no supervisory control of the programs, of business management or of policy" (Robinson and Gellhorn, 1974).

This position is supported by conservative Harvard law professor Douglas Ginsburg, who discusses these "content neutral" aspects of government regulation:

> They (do) not involve any branch of the government in determining that a particular program, point of view, statement, or idea either must be or may not be broadcast by a licensee. Many of the regulations, for example, are directed toward increasing "diversity" in programming. . . . Each of these rules may affect what is ultimately seen or heard by the broadcast audience in ways that are difficult to predict, but none of them involves the government either in making programming decisions or in penalizing those decisions as made by broadcasters. Their impact upon the electronic press is not significantly different, therefore, from the impact of the antitrust laws, or the labor laws, or the tax laws, applied without discrimination, to all of the media of communi-

cation, electronic and printed. And none of these regimes can seriously be said to run afoul of the first amendment of the Constitution. (Ginsburg, 1979)

Semantic debates over censorship notwithstanding, the dominant justification for government involvement in broadcasting has been the issue of public interest. For the first eighty years of broadcasting, and the first forty years of television, the government has had to balance broadcaster and public rights in an equitable use of a limited resource. Inevitably such an arrangement offends the interests of some.

Early in broadcasting history the government adopted an approach that accommodated the greatest number of opinions and ideas possible within the physical limitations of a scarce resource. It could do nothing else in this pluralistic culture. Competing interests and rights were balanced through the issuance of general directions that expressed a philosophy rather than a slate of writ for every broadcasting activity. With the benefit of hindsight we might offer refinements to avoid some of the rancor over government decisions, but it would be difficult to improve materially the general approach to regulation. There are few alternative plans that would grant reasonable broadcaster freedoms while protecting public rights to a rich marketplace of ideas.

But much has changed in recent years to warrant a reconsideration of the relationship between the government and broadcasters. The most compelling reason strikes at the heart of broadcast regulation: the spectrum as a scarce resource.

From the beginning of popular television during the 1940s through the mid-1970s, there were few changes in the availability of channels or the spectrum utilization for commercial broadcasting. New stations logged on the air giving viewers a gradual increase in the assortment of programs. Even so, with such moderate increases, it would be difficult to argue there was a fundamental change in the scarce resource conditions of the market.

Everything changed in 1975 with the launch of SATCOM1. Cable stations, which before this time served primarily as a conduit for distant signals, were given a new and exciting option. Home Box Office rented a transponder on the satellite that it used to beam movie signals to cable companies. Cable owners then resold the movies to homes throughout their systems. As a result of satellite technology, three related benefits have accrued to the cable industry:

- Cable companies were provided with a product that set them apart from broadcast stations and gave them something valuable to sell to customers.
- This new revenue source increased the capital available to the industry, enabling cable operators to invest money in the development and procurement of yet additional programming options.
- The expanded repertoire of programs increased cable's popularity, thus expanding its audience and income base.

Cable expansion erupted after 1975 as hundreds of companies opened shop, and millions of households tied into community systems. Growth continued throughout the 1980s and into the 1990s. At the time of this writing 60.6 percent of American homes subscribe to cable, and more than 92,000 homes come on line each month.[15] Many experts believe a "wired nation" is within reach by 1996, and is a certainty by the end of the decade.[16]

As cable television matures, two characteristics are evident:

- Cable offers an almost unlimited number of station choices. During the mid-1970s cable systems had a capacity of 20 stations. This expanded to 50 during the 1980s, and new super cable systems have 107 channels available. Sets bought today are "cable ready" for 150 slots. Although the newer, larger systems may not be using all the available channels, it is the capacity for additional programming that matters.

- Cable boasts a direct relationship between the number of channels and the number and selection of programs. To land new customers cable operators first include the most popular program services at the basic cost, then add options that may not appeal to large audience segments but that can amass an audience large enough to pay operating costs. Consequently, programming material that may never find sufficient audience to support a costly broadcast operation can become profitable on more efficient cable. Therein lies the economic incentive for cable stations to include program services that otherwise would not be available to viewers.

Cable, of course, is only the leading example of an emerging genre of technologies that are expanding the viewing repertoire for U.S. audiences. Singleton describes many such systems that have entered the market since the mid-1970s: low-power television, multipoint distribution service, direct broadcast satellites and satellite master antenna television (Singleton, 1986). In addition to programs available over the air, through cable and from satellites, there is an endless assortment of material available on videocassettes and disks. Through rentals, purchases and loans, viewers have a remarkable program selection. Such a variety was unimaginable just several years ago.

The critical result of growth in cable and other technologies is the massive infusion of programming options. What happens to the scarcity argument when the macho clicker can graze across scores of channels while readers are limited to one or two newspapers per town? What about the fear that the blessed few in control of stations, if left to their own devices, might impose on the population their views and ideologies to the exclusion of all others?

As long as the scarce resources argument legitimately can be defended it makes sense for government to play a strong role in broadcast regulation. But the fact is we are entering an era of abundant resources, with large numbers of broadcast participants contributing to the sweet cacophony of voices so valued in this society. Under such conditions, there is less need for government intervention. The reregulation of cable, if successful, will reduce consumer costs while permitting broadcast stations to charge for programs carried by cable—a huge victory for free TV.

With the explosion of channels, one must argue for a reduction in government attention to richness and variety in entertainment and information. The balance government correctly has sought among the few available stations increasingly can be handled by natural market forces developing from the many new entrants to audiovisual communications.

At this point several questions remain. First, are we far enough along in the development of new channels to warrant a reduction in governmental oversight as it existed in the past? The 1990s is a watershed period in which to open the issue to public debate. Such discussion may not lead to immediate changes, but it will prepare lawmakers for a different kind of oversight as expanded program options reach near saturation toward the decade's end.

Second, should the government ever entirely abandon regulation of broadcasting? One kind of government regulation always will be necessary to ensure the technical integrity of broadcasting. Original FCC controls of frequency allocations and power will be required in a period of new technologies, perhaps even more so.

But for government control of television agenda and content, it is an open debate. In the best of all worlds, with hundreds of available stations and an equitable distribution of those stations among all segments of the society, there would be little reason to defend the continuation of government attention to the medium. As the gap between the ideal and the reality grows, however, so too does the strength of argument for government intervention. Even 200 stations—all in the hands of conservative corporate barons—would not achieve the desired balance of viewpoints, to say nothing of variety in entertainment. If every show is aimed at the barely adult crowd, who will serve the interests of folks over the ancient age of thirty?

While large numbers of stations improve the chances for the airing of many voices, and perhaps many genres, they do not guarantee it. The basic philosophy of government controls is this: the broadcast spectrum should provide a stage for the diverse views of the many players in this pluralistic society. That is why, for example, Congress has passed bills reregulating cable. Is it fair for cable systems to carry over-the-air entertainment without reimbursing the networks and stations producing this material?

A note about the influence of government on the creative community in television. Apart from the inevitable compromise on financial-syndication (fin-syn) rules, the effect of government regulation on the creative community is twofold:

First, the decency provisions of federal law and FCC rulings still set the boundaries on language and sex. The Supreme Court action restricting around-the-clock indecency did not open the door to anything goes; it just confined the airing of blue material to limited hours when children are unlikely to be viewers. Producers still are not as free to use "R" and "X" material on television as they are in film. Thus, federal regulation still sets the margins for networks and gives writers something to press against.

Second, the tradition of fairness in the news, with or without a Fairness Doctrine, still prevails. This factual integrity carries over into documentaries and docudrama. Although Oliver Stone has cut a deal with ABC, he will not be as free to distort history as he was in his film *JFK*. A network requires either balance in a given show or later programs that offer contrasting opinions. Even in pure drama, networks ask suppliers to avoid one-sided presentations on issues like abortion. No one in Washington says broadcasters must abide by "truth in drama" the way they must abide by "truth in advertising," but the expectation of responsible oversight on content takes its tone from that original ethic, broadcasting in the "public interest, necessity and convenience."

NOTES

1. For more information on Hoover's early efforts to regulate radio, see Daniel E. Garvey, "Secretary Hoover and the Quest for Broadcast Regulation," *Journalism History* 3 (1976), pp. 66–70.

2. We would not consider readers to be cynical if they raised eyebrows over the coincidental hiring by NBC of FCC chairman David Sarnoff—just four months after the color signal decision.

3. A similar debate is ongoing today over the adoption of standards for High Definition Television (HDTV), which provides a crystalline image but is incompatible with current receivers. Today, of course, Nielsen reports there are 93 million sets in operation rather than the relative handful in place during the mid-1940s.

4. The Communications Act of 1934, Section 326, expressly forbids interference with "the right of free speech by means of radio communication."

5. Proceedings on this bill (H.R. 315) are before the Subcommittee on Telecommunications and Finance of the Committee on Energy and Commerce in the House of Representatives. This bill is "to clarify the Congressional intent concerning, and to codify, certain requirements of the Communications Act of 1934 that ensure that broadcasters afford reasonable opportunity for the discussion of conflicting views on issues of public importance." (Official Subcommittee description)

6. George A. Richards, owner of several large stations, misused his facilities to promote hard right-wing political activities. Richards' news distortions, editorial policies and racist, threatening programming compelled the FCC to consider license revocation. Toward the end of the commission's considerations, Roberts suddenly died. His widow was granted license renewal in exchange for an agreement to curtail the offensive practices.

7. Readers interested in the legal and rational arguments supporting the Fairness Doctrine are encouraged to examine *In the Matter of Editorializing by Broadcast Licensees*, 13 FCC 1246, June 1, 1949.

8. Detailed information about recent Fairness Doctrine history is provided in the National Association of Broadcasters, "Annual Report on Broadcast Regulation" (Washington, D.C., 1988).

9. The Senate passed S. 742 by a 59-31 vote. The House adopted H.R. 1934 by 302-102, then S. 742 by unanimous consent as a procedural matter.

10. See, for instance, E.L. Palmer, *Television and America's Children: A Crisis of Neglect* (New York: Oxford University Press, 1988).

11. For a discussion on advertising to children, see D. Kunkel, "From a Raised Eyebrow to a Turned Back: The FCC and Children's Product-Related Programming," *Journal of Communication* 38(4) (1988), pp. 90–108.

12. D. Pearl, L. Bouthilet and J. Lazar, eds., *Television and Behavior: Ten Years of Scientific Progress and Implications for the Eighties*, 2 Vols. (Rockville, Md.: National Institute of Mental Health, 1982).

13. *Pacifica* said that indecent language during time periods when children could reasonably expect to be absent or in bed was not necessarily proscribed.

14. The Parents Music Resource Center has attacked indecent lyrics in records. See chapter 6 for information on the activities of this group.

15. Telephone conversation with David Grenkevich, Research Project Assistant for the National Cable Television Association (January 1992). Adoption figure calculated from Nielsen statistics, November 1991.

16. Telephone conversation with Wayne O'Dell, President, Cable Television Association of Maryland, Delaware and the District of Columbia (March 1991).

6

"Public" Interest Groups and the Interested Public

During the 1980s and 1990s pressure groups have confronted broadcasters with a litany of complaints, suggestions and demands. Regarded as a "reverse influence" on the industry, they provide the purest feedback from the public at large since most represent chunks of the population. When the American Association for Retired Persons (AARP) alleges that Hollywood writers are not aware of sex after sixty, or when the PTA complains about Saturday morning cartoons, or when Catholic leaders deplore video violence, you can be sure that these groups speak for an authentic segment of the nation, not just a few irritated viewers.

That's why Hollywood's term "pressure group" with its implication of narrow, elitist protesters, is inaccurate. The fairer name is "interest group" since "pressure group" is pejorative, "single interest group" is too narrow for those with multiple interests, and "public interest group" too broad for constituencies that may be large but do not speak for the entire public.

How powerful are interest groups? Taken one by one, they have seldom been able to stop a show in its tracks (NBC's antebellum "Beulah Land" was an exception) nor hound a program off the air (although Morton Downey, Jr., came close). But taken cumulatively, the collective voice of American social organizations has been surprisingly effective, particularly when their values dovetail with those of the TV industry. Year after year, writer-producers and programmers have had their "consciousness raised" by groups small and large, rich and poor, pacific and so angry that they are "mad as hell and won't take it anymore."

Who are interest group people? What makes them think that their voices will be heard along the corridors of Sixth Avenue skyscrapers, much less on the backlots of Fox, Paramount or Universal? Which ones have brought about changes in given shows? Finally, have their demands for changes in program content been representative of the public they claim to serve? Do writer-producers ever hear them, much less heed them?

Some of the protesters are friendly adversaries who have been in touch with networks since the days of radio. Forty of the most prominent were welcomed in the front door when NBC reached out to national organizations through its seminars in the seventies. CBS and ABC opened a few doors through their community relations departments, whose staffs stroked the feathers of the religious establishment and bought $100 seats at fund-raisers for some of the safer charities.

During the eighties, however, uninvited guests began to beat on the doors of the networks, demanding executive time and making expensive claims. Often as not, these were alienated groups who had discovered an effective way to make points with their members by standing outside network offices and banging their drums loudly. Their abrasive tactics changed the tone of "external communications" on the part of the networks, which had always treated petitioners with noblesse oblige, handing out largesse here and a rebuke there as the occasion demanded.

That attitude changed when NBC management was first asked in 1979 by its standards department to sit down with the leaders of national interest groups for lengthy, give-and-take discussions. At first the executives in law and public relations were appalled. "Are you seriously proposing that our top officers surround themselves for three days with people who want to attack them?" one of them asked the ombudsmen-censors. Despite these fears, management went along with the seminars, which turned out to be a courageous step forward in public responsibility and a helpful exchange on both sides.

The initial hesitation on the part of managers, however, arose from a prudential attitude widely held in an industry that resists anyone outside of shareholders and clients presuming to tell them how to run their business. To NBC's credit, it not only sat down with the "intruders" but listened to scholars like Robert Bellah of Berkeley and James Kuhn of Columbia University make the case for a two-way relationship.[1]

Bellah, a social scientist and philosopher, told NBC's managers that interest groups were no new thing. He invoked the words of the French aristocrat Alexis de Tocqueville, who traveled across America in the 1830s. According to de Tocqueville, the only thing that kept America from the anarchy of individualism, with its demands for liberty and equality, was the emergence of "associations." The French observer was continually amazed at the American enthusiasm for "joining up":

> Americans of all ages, all stations in life, and all types of disposition are forever forming associations. There are not only commercial and industrial associations in which all take part, but others of a thousand different types — religious, moral, serious, futile, very general and very limited, immensely large and very minute. Americans combine to give fetes, found seminaries, build churches, distribute books. . . . Hospitals, prisons and schools take shape in that way. Finally, if they want to proclaim a truth or propagate some feeling by the encouragement of a great example, they form an association. . . .

As soon as several Americans have conceived a sentiment or an idea that they want to produce before the world, they seek each other out, and when found, unite. Thenceforth they are no longer isolated individuals, but a power conspicuous from the distance whose actions serve as an example; when it speaks, men listen.

The first time that I heard in America that one hundred thousand men had publicly promised never to drink alcoholic liquor, I thought it more of a joke than a serious matter and for the moment did not see why these very abstemious citizens could not content themselves with drinking water by their own firesides.

In the end I came to understand that these hundred thousand Americans, frightened by the progress of drunkenness around them, wanted to support sobriety by their patronage. They were acting in just the same way as some great territorial magnate who dresses very plainly to encourage a contempt of luxury among simple citizens. One may fancy that if they had lived in France each of these hundred thousand would have made individual representations to the government asking it to supervise all the public houses throughout the realm.[2]

How ironic that many business leaders today are blind to the French nobleman's understanding of interest groups but privy to his prejudice. Like de Tocqueville, they wonder why people who are bothered by something like drinking or bad television don't just stay "by their own firesides" instead of forming national associations that put pressure on those who make their profits selling liquor or entertainment. (The Hollywood version of this is, "if they don't like it, let 'em hit the off button.")

The answer to this individualistic mentality is simple: Just as 100,000 Frenchmen possess only limited power as individuals but huge clout collectively, so individual Americans, confronted with faceless power blocs, realize that only by banding together can they make their voices heard. In other words, citizens have the right to exercise their community-mindedness just as individuals have the right to do "their own thing."

When 8 million individuals join the PTA, they create a communal power base. Or, again as de Tocqueville said, "when it speaks, men listen." Even today, Americans who pass a season in France or Mexico are struck by the fact that so few voluntary associations exist to make the government stand up and listen to the immediate claims of individuals who band together, to say nothing of the charitable vacuum that exists when there are no United Ways, Civitans, retired persons' associations and minority fronts.

Adding an economic voice to that of Dr. Bellah, Professor James Kuhn of Columbia's Graduate School of Business chides corporate America for resenting interest groups, which are "as American as apple pie." Indeed, corporate America built its business system on "foundations of individuals to associate themselves for the sake of economic gain . . . (but executives) have not been easily persuaded that nonbusiness groups should enjoy such a right . . . they have not liked to have people outside business defining public policy toward business, by the public for the sake of the public."

Professors Bellah and Kuhn, together with the prophetic de Tocqueville, would doubtless agree that not all associations are responsible, much less representative of the public at large. Some are "futile and very limited" and some, as we shall see, are paranoid and possibly dangerous. But, like apple pie, they are very American and very significant for the public interest.

The first portion of this chapter will examine the tactics of the leading groups that seek to affect television program content, and the difficulty of gaining access to network executives, giving special attention to changes brought about by negotiations, demands, boycotts and regulatory actions. It will take note of the changes that networks refused to make, sometimes despite intense pressure. In the second portion, a somewhat brash and suspicious question will be asked the leaders of these organizations: Do public interest groups really represent the public's interests in television?

"PUBLIC" INTEREST GROUPS

To begin with, what kinds of interest groups are successful in realizing their aims at the networks and how do they do it? Of the thousands of community organizations and voluntary associations in America—variously called public interest, special interest or, pejoratively, "pressure groups"—only a handful can hope to get a top-level hearing at the networks.

The first step in advocacy, therefore, is simply getting a foot inside the door. That task is complicated by the oddly irrational way in which networks handle external communications. Despite the thousands of work hours consumed in responding to pressure tactics, no network has ever analyzed its relationships with interest groups. None has evaluated interest group powers, strategies and influences that impinge upon program content, nor has any followed the managerial advice of Professor Kuhn, namely the strategy of treating groups as legitimate constituencies that have to be served in order to save money and time.

The one exception occurred during the leadership of Ralph Daniels, the vice president for broadcast standards for NBC during the late 1970s and 1980s. According to the testimony of many group leaders, Daniels' office was ever open for dialogue and negotiation of conflict.[3] Reporting to him was Vice President Bettye Hoffmann, who liaisoned with more group leaders than anyone in the industry. To our knowledge, she was the only full-time ombudsman[4] in the industry. A score of national organizations counted on her for access as needed. When the General Electric Co. bought RCA/NBC, it wasted no time in "delayering" Hoffmann's office, the reason being that outreach to interest groups was not a "profit center" and therefore expendable. When Ralph Daniels, like Grant Tinker, saw the G.E. handwriting on the wall and left NBC, President Bob Wright gave the standards department to a man whose idea of good programming was the Home Shopping Network.

Today, when group leaders have a problem, what office do they turn to? They can no longer count on a concerned standards department with sufficient staff at the networks, and the community services departments are not experienced in the handling of outraged groups. Elder statesman Frank Stanton, who ran CBS for twenty-five years, making it the "Tiffany Network," told us in an interview that the new owners of CBS, ABC, NBC and Fox are "back-pedalers." The networks wait until a crisis develops and then engage in furious managerial back-pedaling. Stanton added that downgrading standards sent a grim message to staff, namely that the tradition of responsible broadcasting—viewing the airwaves as a public trust—had ended.

Not wishing to be identified, a network executive told the authors, "You have to understand that the old system whereby the networks could afford liaison with fifty groups has ended. Our president couldn't care less what pressure groups think. His attitude is, we program as we please and when the feathers hit the fan, hunker down 'til the crisis passes. And if somebody wants to sue or lobby in Washington, that's what we pay our lawyers for."

Today, the initial access to networks is capricious and unpredictable, having less to do with a group's size or budget than with the network's perception (often distorted) of how much damage a group can do. When David Burke at CBS suspended Andy Rooney of "60 Minutes" following the humorist's comments, which were considered racist and homophobic by black and gay groups, Burke seriously misread both the public mood and the power of the protesting groups. The reinstatement of Rooney humiliated CBS management and exposed it to well-deserved ridicule. Rooney, better qualified to chuckle with his viewers over the minutiae of junk mail (trivial third class paper), lost socks (why do washers eat only one?), and designer underwear (the new porn) than to comment on the genetics of blacks or gays, found himself the happy recipient of support from the likes of the *Wall Street Journal* and First Amendment groupies.

Had CBS not emasculated its standards department two years previously, it would have had on hand experienced executives who had successfully negotiated with the self-same protesters only a year earlier. In that case, the homosexual group had tried but failed in its campaign against Kellogg's "Nut 'n Honey" commercials.[5] Indeed, standards executives at all three networks had learned how to resist threats while pouring oil on troubled waters. They could have told Mr. Burke a lot about the ability of one group or another to mobilize the press for the causes they serve.

Crucial to the success of any group's access is ideology, or to be more precise, the relationship between the ideology of a cause and the corporate culture of networks. If the networks are the victimizers, and the various minorities and causes are the victims, then it is clear that not all victims are equal. The chance any group has for network access depends significantly on the sympathy that the network management and Hollywood talent have for the aims of that group. It also involves management's perception of how the press and critics might react if the network should harden its heart to the squeals of affliction.

The social consciousness of the New York–Hollywood "flyover" crowd (so called because they fly over everything between the coasts and acquire a sense that all Americans are like those in Los Angeles and New York) is typically liberal, religiously indifferent, temperamentally prounderdog and economically individualistic. This is good news for groups representing blacks, gays and women. The corporate culture takes very seriously anti-Semitic remarks but is deaf to the defamation of Arabs. It treats liberal Christian groups (National Council of Churches) with disguised contempt and it regards fundamentalists (e.g., Jerry Falwell and company) as the enemy. It is a sign of moral courage to say "condom" on the air but the word "God" is taboo except in the sitcom practice of "oh, my God."

Looked at from the outside, however, the ability of interest leaders to get the attention of network brass must seem Byzantine. For instance, on any politician's list of the five most formidable lobbies in Washington, D.C., you will find both the American Association of Retired Persons (AARP) and the National Rifle Association (NRA). In a report to one of the networks on the relative strengths of advocate groups, one of the authors wrote:

> If someone asked you to name the largest corporation in the Washington metropolitan area, you would probably think of a company in the *Fortune* 100. You would be wrong. The largest company in D.C., with over $12 billion in annual cash flow and a "cadre" of thirty million people, is the American Association of Retired Persons. The AARP serves one out of every four voters, and publishes a magazine, *Modern Maturity*, that has passed both *Reader's Digest* and *TV Guide* in circulation. It fields a full-time staff of 1,800 which recruits members at the rate of 14,000 a day. Should they get ticked off with the networks, a hurricane could hit Sixth Avenue![6]

Notwithstanding this incredible political and grassroots clout, the networks pay little attention to the AARP and to the on-air image of the senior citizen. Indeed, primetime continues its seduction of the eighteen to thirty-eight age bracket. Why so little interest in the aged?

The obvious reason lies in the misplaced contempt that advertisers have for this group's purchasing power.[7] Unlike young adults, say ad execs, older folks don't change brands and are therefore immune to the top priority of any agency cutting into the market share of one's competitor. Less obvious is the nonadversarial posture of the AARP, a passivity that suits the networks well. Although AARP staff has been studying the effects of entertainment and advertising on older people, the organization has taken no hard stands with the networks. (It has bigger fish to fry, such as national health legislation.)

Interestingly, the flattening out of the baby boom and the incremental growth of the older generation may reverse that cavalier attitude. The era in which advertisers can make more money with youth-oriented programs and ads with frenetic movements and hard-rock scoring may be coming to an end. A leading analyst of economic trends among older citizens, Dr. Alan Sloan told us that researchers still hew to the dogmatic line that young adults buy more of the high-ticket items for which sponsors pay a premium. Sloan, who did research at CBS before going independent, said that this false perception resists any factual rebuttal. Ask the buyers in their late twenties how many people in their sixties are in the market for disposable diapers. (Ironically, hospitals and nursing homes use millions of adult diapers for incontinent patients.)

The good news for senior citizens is that such conventional wisdom may change, given the new purchasing power of the fifty-and-over generation, the economic reversals suffered by yuppies of the eighties and the progressive graying of the original baby boomers in the nineties. The bad news is that most of those who program for the networks are themselves twenty- or thirtysomething and have not yet awakened to the power of the golden-agers. For the moment the AARP can be safely ignored. One thing, however, is certain: If the AARP's executive director decided to do a bit of network-bashing, he would get red-carpet treatment. As it is, no squeaky wheel, no oil.

In direct contrast, the National Rifle Association squeaks and squawks with the best and may be the most feared political force on Capitol Hill. That reputation does not faze the networks. They thumb their noses at the riflemen and dare them to retaliate. Why so? After all, the NRA staff of 390 in Washington spends a hefty $55 million annually contributed by 3 million loyalists, and they know how to hurt their enemies on the Hill. From what is known of network timidity in executive suites, one would think that ABC, NBC, CBS and Fox would fall all over themselves trying to court the NRA. In fact, the networks had the chutzpah in 1990 to turn down paid ads by the NRA, forcing them to buy nonnetwork time and triggering, if that's the right word, a national print campaign. Why the stonewalling attitude?

For the record, networks refuse to comment. But insiders confess that people in the entertainment industry simply don't cotton to the riflemen or their objectives. The truth is that the radical-chic values of the creative community conflict with the blue-collar, right-wing values of the NRA.

Most of the people who work in entertainment are pro–gun control and look with disdain upon guys in pick-ups with gun racks who may have a preference for camping out instead of watching television like normal people. (Even the corporate types who see television as a business only and who are conservative economically are more apt to join the Sierra Club or the American Society for the Prevention of Cruelty to Animals than to associate with people who kill Bambi's mother for fun.)

It's a mystery why entertainers, among the most freewheeling of all entrepreneurs, differ so much from other businesspeople in their devotion to liberal politics and ideology, but the reality is that right-wing interest groups get short shrift at networks and always have. Tom Wolfe invented the term "radical chic" and Pat Buchanan attributes it to the liberal guilt of secular Jews. George Will refers to the feminist dogma of "victimization" where middle-class white males are responsible for every known ill and all others are entitled to recompense. Whatever the reason, the Hollywood mentality rests firmly on the tenets of social and political liberalism.[8]

If networks can safely ignore behemoths like the AARP and the NRA, whom do they fear? Surprisingly, it has little to do with size. For example, a coalition called the Interfaith Center for Corporate Responsibility gets VIP attention. As gentle as the Jesus it serves, the ICCR is paper-thin (only two executives) and operates out of a broom closet in Manhattan's "God Box" — so-called because of the box-like building on Riverside Drive filled with denominational bureaucrats. Nevertheless, they sit down regularly with the high command at all networks.[9] Wise as serpents and innocent as doves, they presume to audit the networks on their public responsibility. Over the years the Interfaith team has indicted broadcasters for racism and sexism, and in the nineties has challenged networks anew on the hiring of women and minorities both on camera and behind it.

How does an obvious lightweight get away with tweaking the noses of the big guys? Two reasons: their ideology is "right," which is to say "left," and their perceived ability to stir up trouble is monumental. Today, networks totally agree with the racial and feminist objectives of standard-brand denominational leaders (e.g., Presbyterian, Methodist) and their allies (e.g., Common Cause, People for the American Way). The Interfaith audit of the networks indicates that they are far ahead of local stations and Hollywood producers in hiring female executives and blacks.[10]

The other reason is that the networks respect the financial clout of the ICCR, which gives it access to corporate annual meetings. The Protestant and Catholic affiliates of the ICCR command about $10 billion in church pension funds. Nobody takes that literally, but these denominations and religious orders do permit the ICCR to represent them at shareholder meetings, to act as their proxies on certain social issues and to use that financial slingshot to menace the corporate goliaths. Over the years, the ICCR has attended annual meetings of network shareholders and threatened actions that are extremely time-consuming and publicly embarrassing to CEOs and their boards of directors.

Some ten years ago, the word on high came down to network staffs: "Work out something with these people — now. We never want another meeting in which the chairman is embarrassed over a proxy resolution." Thus an arrangement was made whereby the church people could sit down with top network managers and review the social behavior of the networks once a year. From the Christian perspective, it must have been almost as inspiring as running the moneychangers out of the Temple.

Considering the range and complexity of demands made upon networks in a given season, one can understand why they keep the door open to so few and closed to so many. The variety of interest groups that met with NBC in 1989 and 1990 were typical of those that sat down with the other networks, with advertisers and sometimes with Hollywood producers.

- The Gay and Lesbian Alliance Against Defamation complained about the Kraft Foods "Nut 'n Honey" commercial that featured a western cattle trail scene in which the hands asked old "Cookie" what was on for breakfast. Cookie's reply, "nuttin, honey," was taken as an insult to their manhood by the cowboys, who advanced on the old coot menacingly. To gay leaders, this was "gay bashing," part and parcel of a national hysteria that had led to recent beatings of homosexuals in bars and on street corners. Having failed to get Kraft to pull the spot, they demanded that the network do so or suffer the revenge of the gay community. (Note: Although received with civility, the leaders did not persuade the vice president of broadcast standards at NBC to meet their demands. NBC argued that the dialogue was deliberately equivocal and that the overall impression would not offend the "average reasonable viewer." There were similar outcomes at the other networks.)

- Toyota Car Dealers of America. Having learned that they were on the "hit list" of the Rev. Donald Wildmon for the alleged sin of being a "heavy" sponsor of sex and violence on NBC, visiting executives complained that some of their dealers (in fact a very few) had been called by local clergy who wanted to know why Toyota was pushing "porn."

  "That explanation should come from NBC," snapped a Toyota VP, who added that his company was not in the business of alienating customers, and if the network could not "clean up its act," Toyota would have to take its business elsewhere. NBC politely explained the facts of life about Mr. Wildmon's biased and unscientific monitoring of television and agreed to send the vice president a letter outlining NBC's rigorous standards of morality. Toyota forwarded a copy of NBC's letter to its beleaguered dealers with happy results.

- Black Clergy United, with NAACP support, protested what it saw as racist elements in the sitcom "Amen." They claimed that the lead character was unlike any black Protestant deacon, the women were treated as servants, the plots were guilty of trivializing the faith and the inner-city work of evangelical black churches in the war on poverty and drugs was never depicted. Take it off the air, they warned, or suffer severe consequences. (The producer had previously agreed with NBC's recommendation to hire as a consultant a highly regarded black pastor and historian. After the consultant signed on, the clergy group quietly withdrew. Interestingly, many black Christians are ardent fans of the program because of its authentic, exciting gospel music.)

- The U.S. Catholic Conference and various Protestant leaders objected to the growing use of priests and ministers in commercials. From the monastic "brother" pitching his copying machine to the various in-church endorsements of soaps and soups by ministers fictional and real, the denominational spokespersons said such tastelessness had gone far enough. They asked for a ban on the use of sacred music, especially the Hallelujah Chorus, and sacred facilities in television advertising. (The network responses were not sympathetic.)

- Accuracy in Media (AIM), a conservative group that monitors television for liberal inaccuracies, stays on the network case. For example, it objected to a docudrama called "Shootdown." Director Reed Irvine managed to get a meeting with Bob Wright, the president of NBC, who listened to their documentation of the distortions in the made-for-TV movie. "Shootdown" argued that the Reagan administration had sent the Korean airliner into Russian airspace to spy on sensitive installations, deliberately risking the lives of 298 civilians. AIM was not mollified by NBC's assertion that their show merely exercised poetic license. The group retaliated with ads in *Broadcasting* magazine, accusing the network of falsification for the purpose of ratings.

Many groups, stonewalled by the networks, turned to other tactics. For example:

• Several hyphenated-American organizations, spearheaded by the National Italian American Foundation, complained about the sleaze in the 1988–1989 television season. When their calls to networks were not returned—due in large part to the cutback in liaison staffs—they organized a coalition of ethnic groups that complained to various congressmen. In the opinion of the director of the foundation, Fred Rotandaro, these complaints have played a part in the unsympathetic hearings that networks have received on a number of matters crucial to their interests, such as the FCC's handling of the financial interest and syndication rules. If true, this would exemplify a penny-wise-and-pound-foolish policy on the part of network management wherein the mishandling of relationships with interest groups could end up costing millions more than the savings realized from cutting the staff formerly responsible for the ombudsman role.

• A coalition of mainstream religious communities, dissatisfied with the response at all three networks, met with the congressional chairs of the major communications committees to register their dismay at the "bottom-line" policies at the networks. They also condemned the new attitude of the corporations that had bought the networks, charging that these nonbroadcasters were busily substituting "market" principles for public interest principles. They asked Congress to hold the Federal Communications Commission to a rigid oversight of networks and to reinstitute both the Fairness Doctrine and the Children's Television Act, which mandated improvements in Saturday morning shows.

These litanies of protest sound much the same, whatever the group: Thus, there are continual representations from Asian-American leaders who still wince at Dr. No stereotypes; from Polish Americans who object to dramas on the Holocaust that omit the sufferings of Poles; by Grey Panthers who decry the demeaning portrayals of the old; by educators like the PTA who object to violence; by Jewish leaders who were dismayed at the "Jew/No Jew" skits on "Saturday Night Live"; by Arab Americans who wonder why Arabs are the only villains left on the air; and by watchdogs of conservative morality who turn red at penis jokes and condom references.

Altogether the pressures put on broadcasters day by day are greater than those aimed at any other industry or service in America. Franchises and federal regulation aside, the price of barreling into most homes seven hours a day is the scrutiny of every civic force capable of raising its voice in protest against television's perceived power to influence attitudes and set the national agenda.

What exists, then, in the galaxy of voluntary organizations and public interest groups is a cottage industry of pressure and protest, much of it legitimate, some of it efficacious and a lot of it frivolous, muckraking and self-serving. In fairness to the networks, one reason they treat interest groups so unevenly is that executives are overwhelmed at the sheer numbers and complexity of it all. A scorecard helps:

- Of the roughly 250,000 "voluntary organizations" in America, about 25,000 have staffs.

- Roughly 500 take an interest in media, usually monitoring only their own images or concerns.

- Some seventy are heavy hitters, usually in the area of antidefamation.

- Of these, only about forty have the power, clout and determination to hurt the networks.[11]

It also clarifies matters when groups are properly categorized. We mentioned earlier that networks rarely study what journalist William Emerson has called their "natural enemies," despite the fact that millions of advertising dollars can be lost and thousands of work hours wasted whenever a network gets into a publicized fight with a civic organization. The industry doesn't even know what to call them. Broadcasters refer to them variously as pressure groups, special interest groups, single interest groups, voluntary organizations, lobbies, public interest groups, social activists and "do-gooding, com-symp bleeps."

Some helpful distinctions:

- A *single* interest group has one overriding aim and sticks to it relentlessly (e.g., the National Rifle Association).

- A *special* interest group adopts an issue or constituency that may be quite heterogeneous but is nonetheless sharply focused (e.g., all hyphenated-Americans, most minorities, the National Organization for Women).

- A *public* interest group usually concentrates on broader social and civic issues like the environment, voting rights, justice in the courts (e.g., Common Cause, People for the American Way).

- A *voluntary organization* enlists people from a broad spectrum for welfare and service activities (churches, Red Cross, Salvation Army, Rotary, American Cancer Society).

- The fairest, most neutral term covering any organization with impact on the networks is simply "interest group," or IG for short. (NBC first called them Public Interest Groups but the acronym (PIGS) was not thought politic.)

Motivation provides another handle on IGs. What drives some IGs into television while others ignore its effects on their members? Professor James Kuhn eschews Bill Emerson's notion of the networks' "natural enemies," and thinks of them as the networks' competitors, and thus a legitimate business constituency that a network needs to manage. Speaking at an ABC-TV seminar, Kuhn told the people who make programming decisions that interest groups are special competitors who are trying to "unsell" the audiences cherished by industry and advertisers. The IG leaders who succeed are entrepreneurs, not commercially (although some do very well) but ideologically and socially. Like business entrepreneurs, the educational, religious, ethnic or racial entrepreneurs have a service that their "customers" are willing to buy. In most cases that service for members is "protection" from insult, distortion and misrepresentation. Their "customers" are those willing to pay enough in dues and fund drives to keep them in business.

Thus, if you are a card-carrying member of the NAACP or the Italian-American Foundation, and ABC runs an "Amos and Andy" clone or a typical Mafia piece, you are happy to pay your leadership to investigate the episode and protest in your behalf. If sufficiently aroused, you may join a boycott and a letter-writing campaign. Such pressure, according to Professor Kuhn, might as well be competition from other networks because the result is a possible loss of audience or advertising. At the very least, it represents an increase in the cost of doing business because of the work hours required to meet with or resist the IGs.

Just how costly in hard dollars are IGs? So far, no network has suffered the tens of millions of dollars that Nestlé lost in its infant formula battle with a tiny outfit called INFACT and the Protestant-Catholic coalition, the Interfaith Center for Corporate Responsibility. That may have been the all-time high for corporate stupidity and humiliation.[12]

Network losses, however, are not easily shrugged off. Insiders told the authors that in the 1988–1989 season NBC suffered net losses from advertising "buy-backs" of well over $15 million, and that the other two majors lost as much or more. When a sponsor defects, usually at the last minute after a screening service has reported something on a show that might trigger unwanted publicity, the ad money is refunded. Meanwhile, other sponsors circle the cancellations like vultures and "buy back" the commercial slots for much less than the going price. Often these sponsors, like those lined up for the Geraldo Rivera show on satanism, are marginal or less prestigious companies. That being the case, the network suffers not only financially but loss of image as well. The "aura" of their time, as salespeople call it, diminishes and over a season pulls down the price of spots.

Obviously, the first line of response to IG pressure is the protection of the ad dollar. That dollar was at the root of hysteria over Michigan housewife Terry Rakolta when, in 1989, she wrote top corporate CEOs about her unhappiness at the vulgarities in Fox's "Married with Children." Her letter pushed a hot button in the minds of corporate advertisers who worried lest her attitudes represent millions of housewives who buy their products. Ten of the Fortune 500 companies pulled out of this show or threatened action. Meanwhile, their agencies sat down with the top management of at least one network to urge more stringent self-regulation.

For example, following the Geraldo Rivera show on satanism, a group of agency buyers met with NBC head Bob Wright and read him the riot act on sleaze, threatening to move their advertising to other media. It was shortly after this meeting that NBC beefed up its standards department, which had been cut in half.

When networks suffer media and public backlash as they did during that "sleaze season" of 1988–1989, they employ as their outer line of defense (the inner one being corporate communications, standards and legal services in New York City) their lobbyists in Washington, D.C. Should senators and congressmen put regulatory bills in the hopper or call for increased oversight by the FCC, the industry sounds the bugle for battalions of lawyers. This sensitivity to Capitol Hill does not go unnoticed by interest groups. The larger national organizations maintain offices within walking distance of the Congress. Whenever the broadcasters lobby for a decrease in their public interest responsibilities, one or more groups or coalitions can be counted upon to counterlobby.

Whether putting pressure directly on networks, or indirectly through Congress, the White House or advertisers, the interest groups employ several strategies, which, taken together, constitute their power and therefore their ability to effect changes in program content. Among these strategies are the following:

- "Insider" tactics can work within the establishment, by means of dialogue with the network and more or less civil negotiations. Generally, large national organizations with broad interests use insider tactics based on their assumed clout (i.e., the iron fist in the velvet glove.) In effect, advocates convince networks that it is cheaper to negotiate with them than for the advocates to go public. This civility has been frayed by the cutbacks in liaison staffs at the networks along with a tougher corporate hide.

- "Outsider" tactics can work beyond established channels and are generally employed by those who feel they cannot get a hearing any other way. The civil rights movement is the prototype for outsider strategies that lean heavily on confrontation, demonstrations, boycotts, publicity, litigation and shareholder pressure to embarrass the networks.

- "Grassroots" tactics work indirectly through memberships and regional pressure. Historically, the churches — with local congregations all over the map — have urged their individual members to write letters of protest on particular issues. For example, the environmental groups, which were instrumental in getting the networks and tobacco companies to take cigarette ads off the air, began their drives locally by pressuring affiliates.

- "Coalition" tactics bring together the power staff and budget of two or more organizations having some ad hoc concern. Churches, racial and minority groups and educational and environmental groups have found coalitions useful. The benefit: a group with multiple interests can farm out a bit of advocacy here and there without slowing down its main operations.

How successful have interest groups been in changing program content? No one can say with complete assurance because multiple influences are hard to trace. Some tactics succeed quietly in "raising the consciousness" of both network executives and Hollywood producers while some of the louder watchdogs get good press but no results.[13]

The best we can do is visit a few groups and illustrate their concerns, their tactics and some of their limited gains. This review is based on fifty interviews we conducted with leaders of national organizations with claims on network programming of primetime entertainment. To illustrate the breadth of their concerns, we will highlight a variety of the pressures they directed at the major networks. ·

One of the most interesting groups is the American-Arab Anti-Discrimination Committee (ADC). During the sixties and seventies, and on into the mid-eighties, nobody at ABC, CBS and NBC — including their news departments — was aware of Arab Americans. As one after another stereotype fell before the pressure groups, only two villains seemed safe for the bad guy role — communists and Arabs. The very word, terrorist, was a synonym for Arab, and to say that the video and film industry was pro-Israel was to understate their allegiances. For years, the three major Arab groups used outsider tactics to no avail. Then, in 1984, NBC became the first network to recognize their aspirations by inviting U.S. Senator James Abourezk, founder of the ADC, to an interest group seminar. He sat cheek and jowl with the late Rabbi Marc Tanenbaum, renowned international scholar from the American Jewish Committee. They got along famously. But network ears were scorched when the senator described show after show on all three networks that portrayed Arabs as dirty, ignorant, murderous, camel-riding fanatics, or as fat, oil-rich, predatory billionaires.

Today's Arab leaders like Faris Bouhafa, the erudite director at the ADC, pointed out in our interview that Arabs are the last "niggers" on television and that the antidiscrimination tactics take the same path as that trod by the NAACP during those days when blacks were either absent or stereotyped on the air.

Bouhafa referred to black tactics toward "Hill Street Blues" when it first hit the air. In the commendable effort to be realistic, the cop show depicted most of the arrested "perps" as blacks. As mentioned previously, this may have been statistically true in the inner city, but it gave many white viewers the false impression that since most of the criminals arrested were black, then most blacks were criminals. This is not only untrue but perverse since most of the victims of inner-city crime are black. In this case, fair play and justice won out over literal truth; the criminals on "Hill Street" were deliberately varied racially and ethnically.

Today, the ADC and its sister groups are slowly raising the consciousness of both networks and Hollywood producers. The Gulf War probably helped dispel the notion that all Arabs are alike; it certainly gave winsome, articulate Arab Americans a chance to shine on McNeil/Lehrer. Their next aim: an Arab-American hero in sitcom television. To accomplish this end the ADC has begun to use the "insider tactics" of negotiation and persuasion. Should the networks pull back from their previous standards of trying to balance the necessities of good story-telling with sensitivity to interest group images, the ADC, among others, will quickly adopt more adversarial strategies.

The National Association for the Advancement of Colored People (NAACP) stands apart from any other interest group intent on influencing television. The NAACP's president, Benjamin Hooks, was a commissioner of the FCC. Earlier, he played a prominent role in the institution of the original Fairness Doctrine. In an interview with the authors, Dr. Hooks said the following:

> One of the most troubling developments in broadcasting . . . has been the traffic in licenses. It used to be that anyone wanting to buy a television station had to meet certain standards. No more. Today if you have the money, you buy a public franchise the way you would a fast food franchise . . . and sell it the next day, if you wish. Thus you no longer have broadcasters running stations, only business people looking for a quick profit.
>
> I am disappointed in GE. They have such high standards for products and yet are willing to let NBC go into the sleaze game . . . and pull back from public responsibility.
>
> News has become in some ways a disgrace . . . infotainment! Any gimmick to attract an audience!
>
> Broadcasting is a proud and honorable medium. I would like to see it return to its sense of excellence and integrity as our eyes upon the world.

With this kind of leadership, it is not surprising that the NAACP worked hard behind the scenes of the Bush administration to put teeth back into the FCC.[14]

On the other hand, the NAACP is not as ardent as it used to be in monitoring the airwaves on behalf of black images and interests. Asked why, Dr. Hooks replied that many battles have been won, many stereotypes broken and most producers sensitized to racial integrity. These battles won, others had to be fought.

This is a guiding principle in antidefamation behavior: The more successful (and powerful) an interest group becomes the less it has to be concerned with its image and the more it becomes involved in broader civic responsibility. Although edifying for society, the broadening of objectives has its downside. As a group becomes more institutional and bureaucratic, it loses much of its original zeal. Charismatic leaders die out and the group identity, forged by the agony of victimization, begins to fade.

The reverse principle is that the smaller and more recent the interest group, the more militant and effective it is in getting public, advertiser and network attention. These two axioms — bigness blurs and smallness focuses — underlie interest group influences.

Several smaller ethnic and racial groups appear to be gaining strength in national politics: The Japanese American Citizen's League, the Mexican American Legal Defense and Educational Fund, the National Italian American Foundation and the Organization of Chinese Americans.

By contrast, the U.S. Catholic Conference (USCC) illustrates the paradox of antidefamation efforts: the bigger you are the less you get. The USCC could hardly be bigger. It serves the hierarchy (National Conference of Catholic Bishops) as a voice to the nation beyond the walls of the church. It has a full-time staff of 400, a budget of $31 million and a distinct presence in Washington, D.C. Even though Catholic bureaucracy is more decentralized than outsiders think, it still represents 50 million people just as legitimately as, say, NOW represents its 160,000 members.

A staff executive at the USCC, speaking anonymously, told us about a letter that Cardinal Joseph Bernardin, then president of the conference, had written to the heads of CBS and NBC shortly after both companies had been taken over by new management. The CEO of CBS, Larry Tisch, had just cut the standards staff by half and had announced that programmers and producers in Hollywood were perfectly capable of editing their own shows for sex, violence, language, stereotyping and antisocial behavior. Bob Wright from GE had gone on record during his first month in office at NBC saying that if cable did not need standards editors, he couldn't see why networks needed them either.

Bernardin, convinced that both companies were retreating from self-regulation, urged CBS and NBC to reconsider such actions as part of the long tradition of broadcasting self-regulation. According to the USCC executive, one network wrote back with soft soap and the other network did not even bother to reply.

One can be sure that a letter from the National Organization for Women would have been given top priority. Why would the powerful Catholic Church receive such cavalier treatment? The simplest answer is heterogeneity. Perhaps the only thing American Catholics have in common is the liturgy and the Pope, and sometimes not even the authority of His Holiness prevails across the Atlantic. The rest of the time, 50 million Catholics disagree on politics, sports, race, business, ethics and education. The networks (and Washington politicians) know that no bishop can speak for that many different interests. The USCC can drown its members in an ocean of ink with its periodicals, but it cannot gain anything like unanimity on issues dear to its heart like abortion and contraception.

At the moment, the USCC, together with its colleagues from the National Council of Churches, the Southern Baptist Convention and Jewish Theological Seminary, is locked in a battle with ABC and NBC over the traditional Sunday shows. The oldest sustaining shows on television — "Look Up and Live" and "Lamp unto my Feet" — were canceled by CBS some years ago, along with the CBS tradition of producing quality religious programming on an ecumenical basis. (NBC and ABC had one sustaining show apiece.) With CBS out, the field was open to the Falwells, Bakkers and Robertsons. When the new managements took over at ABC and NBC (Pharaohs who knew not Joseph), they soon negotiated a pull-back package in which each of the faith groups would receive a quarter of a million dollars or so to produce one hour each year. Today, the USCC and its Protestant-Jewish partners are in danger of being frozen out entirely.

Their response was to get high-level meetings at both networks where their requests for larger budgets were denied. They also started a cable network called VISN. As a result, the faith groups went to Washington, met with congressional heads of communications committees, and began a new strategy of confrontation.

Evidently, the networks feel they can take these huge organizations lightly because they know that the staff does not have the power to unleash the hounds of outrage and protest. After all, most Catholics, Protestants and Jews couldn't care less about "mainstream religious programs." Moreover, the networks have been accustomed to dealing with these religious groups in a civil manner, across friendly tables of dialogue without anger or the mention of a boycott.

Ironically, the previously mentioned Interfaith Center for Corporate Responsibility, which is a tiny protégé of the Catholics and Protestants who fund it, carries a bigger stick with the networks than either the U.S. Catholic Conference or the National Council of Churches because its aims, activities and potential for trouble are narrowly conceived. Prediction: The USCC and the National Council, tired of being nice guys who finish last, will soon turn from "insider" to "outsider" tactics toward the networks.

The National Congress of Parents and Teachers (PTA) has for twenty years been an activist in network television. Its continuous pressure on networks has paid off in several ways, notably in the improvement of Saturday morning kid-vid and in the monitoring of violence. The PTA's studies of television effects on children have had wide currency, contributing to the boundary-setting that made the 8 P.M. timeslot a haven for family sitcoms. In its 1989–1990 legislative directives, for example, the PTA supported "federal legislation which would require each commercial television broadcaster to air at least one hour per day of appropriate television programming for children during their prime viewing hours . . . (and) legislation that would exempt broadcast stations from antitrust laws for the purpose of developing industry guidelines which will reduce the exposure of children to programs depicting violence."[15] Generally speaking, the networks take the PTA seriously and try to avoid its condemnations.

Ann Lynch, the 1990 national president, told the authors that a new mood has surfaced among parents with small children.

A whole generation of parents [is] turning ugly over the content of TV . . . the risk is great that they will have us abandon our traditional distaste for censorship. Elementary school parents are whooping mad over the recent defeats of the bans on commercials on Saturday morning. It is their pressure which has caused our government relations staff to support the bills aimed at violence, and now, sex as well.

What is [the networks'] public responsibility? [Isn't it] more than delivering millions to the advertisers? What about the content of what television is delivering? It is only half-true to say that (network) service is legitimated by the numbers who watch . . . the people who are being denied a real choice are the very young and the very old . . . our parents are younger and more conservative than they used to be and on television sex and violence, they have reached the boiling point. When that happens, watch out.

The militancy of the PTA is matched by Planned Parenthood Federation of America, which took out full-page newspaper and magazine ads in 1988 saying "They did it 20,000 times on television last year" but nobody used a condom. This was "outsider" tactics with a vengeance and the president of Planned Parenthood, Faye Wattleton, knocked 'em dead on "Donahue" and "Oprah," using all manner of distorted statistics to make her point. The networks, however, did not give in to these questionable tactics and the tempest subsided. Surely it is a sign of the times that Ms. Wattleton resigned Planned Parenthood in 1992 to host her own talk show. (Trojan and its competitors reaped a golden harvest of free publicity, however; much more than they could ever have afforded on national television with their very limited budgets, all of which would have been exhausted after a few weeks of primetime rates.) On the other hand, the spread of AIDS and bombshells like the infection of basketball hero Magic Johnson have led to a new policy at Fox that permits condom ads if presented as disease prevention. NBC and CBS are likely to follow suit.

At the other pole of educational advocacy is the American Library Association. To our amazement, the librarians are First Amendment absolutists who would place no limitations or restrictions on network primetime. The ALA's Dr. Thomas Galvin said that librarians would not even favor a ban on the attendance of children at X-rated films, much less to the relatively bland fare on television. They so fear the chilling effect of any standards review of producers' shows that they have set up a foundation to support network freedom and to battle the likes of CLeaR-TV and other censorial groups.

Closer to the PTA norm is the National Educational Association. The NEA has formed a coalition with both PTA and the American Medical Association to re-regulate network television. With a full-time staff of 600 and a $75 million budget, the educators are pushing hard for regulation of children's programming. In a 1989 interview with Dr. Don Cameron, the NEA director said that television is a major "legitimating" influence, setting attitudes and values for children. He stated that "the three major broadcasters should be the most publicly responsible of all corporations in America. Instead, they are among the least, pandering for ratings only and giving back nothing to the public." He asked for legislation and a tiger-toothed FCC.

As sports anchors put it, there is "absolutely no question" that the most interesting players in the television content game are the mostly small, incredibly loud and surprisingly effective guardians of television morality, ethics and taste who are known as "watchdogs." Roughly fifteen nip at the heels of network brass. The following deserve a passing mention:

- Action for Children's Television (ACT), founded and headed by Peggy Charren, over twenty years ago, is an example of what a handful of housewives can do when they get mad. A tiny staff of four working on a mere $160,000 per year has hurt the networks more than the writers' strikes. Fighting against the Reagan philosophy of letting the market decide what is best for America's children, Mrs. Charren and her 140 chapters have kept alive legislation to uplift Saturday morning, eliminate toy-show tie-ins, add quality and taste and demand some public-responsibility commitment from the networks. Her ability to embarrass industry executives has made her truly effective. Newspapers have learned to call her for colorful quotations whenever the industry commits new sins of child-hawking irresponsibility. Much to network relief and constituency astonishment, Mrs. Charren closed ACT's doors in 1992, saying that the Children's Television Act of 1990 (mandating local station educational considerations) has made a national voice unnecessary. (There is some talk about local ACTs continuing.) Without her voice, the public interest in broadcasting will suffer. Chester Cheetah, the Frito-Lay mascot, is now free to flog Cheetos on Fox's Saturday morning line-up!

- Americans for Responsible Television (ART), a creation of Terry Rakolta, opened a Washington office in 1990. Mrs. Rakolta, wife of a wealthy Michigan contractor, became an instant celebrity when her letters to heads of corporations resulted in advertising cancellations on the Fox sitcom, "Married with Children." She is trying to establish herself as the moral counterpart of Peggy Charren, avoiding the extremes of Rev. Wildmon and fellow adversaries. She objects to sex and violence from the standpoint of a parent with small children. If ART has indeed tapped into a parental rage that is real, it may become a formidable watchdog. So far, networks note that the Fox show has increased slightly in ratings since the attacks. On the other hand, the 1990 stance of Fox seems to be less permissive and more conventional as they cut into the broader expectations of primetime audiences. Not much has been heard from Rakolta in 1991 and so far in 1992, but she has reportedly been building a community-based constituency.

- CLeaR-TV and the National Federation for Decency. The Rev. Donald Wildmon is a Methodist moralist who began as a sports journalist, pastored a small church and became nationally known when his watchdog organization made common cause with the Moral Majority. Wildmon is the classic example of the "outsider" tactician who serves his members by pulling the lion's tail. His "monitoring" of television stands as a case study of social science distortions. University content analysts have denounced his procedures as scandalous. During one of his "evaluations" in which he was grading the networks for sex, violence and profanity, he tripled the negative score of NBC because a comedian on "Saturday Night Live" used the F-word during the sign-off. His periodical is the *National Enquirer* of network reviews, pulling words and actions out of context, making the exceptional sound like the norm. The articles imply that primetime is a collage of fornication, bloodletting and obscenity.

His success, however, in entrepreneurial terms, has been phenomenal. From a garage office with a mimeograph machine, he has graduated to one of the most sophisticated and expensive plants in all of the voluntary sector. His base, the National Federation for Decency, has a narrow fundamentalist support. In an effort to widen his constituency, he created CLeaR-TV, which adds the National Association of Evangelicals to his cause and enlists a few Methodist and Catholic clergy besides. An informal phone poll of the middle-of-the-road clergy on his list revealed that half had either never heard of him or were not aware of what they were supporting.[16] Even with these allies, he has not been able to change network programming. (The Moral Majority, shortly after affiliating with the NFD, cut its ties when the two reverend gentlemen, Falwell and Wildmon, could not see eye to eye.) The networks ignore him programmatically, but his yellow journalism affects them indirectly when certain advertisers are periodically spooked. What keeps him in business are network experiments that "push the envelope" of taste and values, and the tendency of advertisers to take the attitude of "better safe than sorry."[17] Were primetime to go G-rated, he would go bankrupt overnight. Nevertheless, his nuisance threat to advertisers, particularly those with high-ticket items like automobiles, is considerable.

- Parents Music Resource Center (PMRC). Founded by the wives of congressmen and high officials (Tipper Gore, Susan Baker, Sally Nevius and Pam Howar), the PMRC has done to the record industry what ACT has done in broadcasting. It took this tiny group (five paid staff members and a few local affiliates) only two years to bring the largest record companies to their knees, forcing them to print lyrics on album covers or display a parental advisory. A national poll found 80 percent of the public favoring their objective of giving parents advance notice of lyrics that were possibly pornographic, drug-oriented, unduly violent or verbally vulgar. The Recording Industry Association of America and the four leading independent companies have signed a disclosure agreement with the PMRC despite cries of censorship from heavy-metal rock stars and others of elevated civic concern. The year 1990 marked renewed interest in the excesses of a small number of rap groups that used vulgar language, talked bloody and endorsed drugs. Predictably, the ACLU has said that once society limits hardcore sexual references, the public will no longer be able to buy records like "I Saw Mommy Kissing Santa Claus."

- Accuracy in Media (AIM). Chairman Reed Irvine runs a team of neoconservative journalists who are devoted to mobilizing the public on accuracy in news and entertainment. With the exception of the Interfaith Center, AIM has been the most formidable intruder at shareholder meetings of large corporations. Unlike the Christian activists who lean to the left, Irvine's views are close to those of most shareholders. He is anticommunist, pro–free enterprise, Republican, religious and a stickler for accuracy as he understands it. AIM's ads in *Broadcasting* magazine are short, clear, hard-hitting and bellicose, a textbook of advocacy journalism. The networks, owned by businessmen who are genuinely conservative but dependent on Hollywood producers who are genuinely liberal, give Irvine hearings but seldom change course for him. Network staffs are convinced that Irvine needs a shrink. He plays hardball against media moguls who are surprisingly thin-skinned. How will he fare with Clinton Democrats?

Summary of Part One and Evaluation of Impacts

To repeat two axioms on the ability of public interest groups to gain access to networks and effect changes in program content:

- One, the narrower the focus the greater the power. Thus, the smaller but sharply focused Interfaith Center for Corporate Responsibility has more clout on Sixth Avenue than its larger, diffuse parents, the National Council of Churches and the U.S. Catholic Conference. In short bigness blurs your impact; narrowness concentrates your impact.

- Two, the closer the ideology of a group is to the corporate culture of the entertainment industry the easier it is for it to present its claims and elicit changes in scripts. Since the Hollywood/network culture is liberal, pseudointellectual, secular and prosocial, the groups that represent blacks, gays, intellectuals and feminists will get a warmer hearing than groups that represent religion, big business, the aged, neoconservative or hyphenated Americans like Italians and Poles.

One way to measure the success or failure of interest groups is to look at the elements of programming that they complain about most and ask how the networks have reacted to their various claims.

Those issues and areas are:

- antidefamation (group image and treatment)
- gratuitous violence
- offensive language
- exploitative sex
- religious offense.

Led by Jews and blacks, the history of the antidefamation movement has been one continuous stream of successes in raising the consciousness of writers, producers and network executives. Looking at reruns of ten years ago, much less twenty, one is struck by the fact that blatantly demeaning portrayals no longer appear. Overt racism, sexism, homophobia and ethnic insensitivity have virtually disappeared. (Pay cable, with its unrestrained sex, violence and language, is another matter.)

Many groups can take satisfaction in their positive role models on air. A few have received inverted compliments. Take blacks. Having filled series with strong black characters, particularly in sitcoms and police dramas, writers are now emboldened to use blacks as villains. Or take women on television. At the moment, many shows feature mature characterizations of women. Critics who doubt this, as NBC's Susan Baerwald said, must not see much television. The distance from Lucy to the women lawyers on "L.A. Law" is infinite. Or homosexuals. From "Love, Sidney" to "An Early Frost" to a spate of movies-of-the-week about AIDS, that segment of society is getting more sensitive treatment.

In other areas we see a mix of successes and failures. Italian Americans still resent the Mafia characterizations, but the number of positive Italian role models has increased in ten years. Native Americans are no longer "injuns biting the dust" but dignified people with a special feel for the environment; for example, John Taylor on "Paradise." Protestant clergy often were once depicted as pious wimps or fanatics, but one occasionally sees a strong and authentic minister. Blue-collar people seem to be riding high with shows from "Who's the Boss?" to "Roseanne." Asian Americans say that stereotyping persists, and as reported, Arab Americans have yet to receive one positive portrayal on a television series, including most of the film reruns featuring Omar Sharif. Nevertheless, Hollywood—and the networks they supply—deserve a huge "well done" for the diminution of stereotypical and insulting depictions. In our opinion, the lion's share of the progress is attributable to interest group pressures.

Violence is harder to figure. In the first place, what is the difference between violence and action, between action and adventure? How can stories about cops and robbers be told without car chases and how can a western be shot without fistfights in bars and how can war stories be told without a shot fired in anger?

Standards editors make decisions like football umpires, who officiate a violent game but manage to draw acceptable distinctions between normal force and unnecessary roughness. Editors label as "gratuitous violence" anything that does not drive the story, fit the characters and meet the comfort zone of viewers for free television. This is called "contextual" judgment. A case can be made for basic improvements in network treatments of violence without being drawn into the morass of how harmful are the alleged "20,000 acts of violence" each season.

The PTA and the AMA would not agree that a great deal of progress has been made. They oppose violence whether or not it is integral to the story or used as a protection of the innocent or redeemed by the condemnation of violence. ACT and the PTA can take pride in some network reprogramming of children's shows, now models of prosocial, team behavior instead of the previously violent cartoon and monster shows. Meanwhile Teenage Mutant Ninja Turtles continue their mutant ways, and many small children prefer them (and the old Disney and Hanna-Barberra cartoons) to the programs designed by teams of prosocial scientists.

Objectionable language suffers from the same problems in editing as do violence and sex. Writers seek realism. Realistically, street talk is often rude, coarse or profane. A bit later, we discuss Supreme Court rulings on "dirty words" and "fighting words." The latter are mostly defaming and are not normally permitted on primetime — words like "nigger," "fag," and "spic," — but the former have slowly crept into network scripts, much to the regret of older viewers, apparently without offending younger people whose classroom and job talk is earthier than that of their parents.[18]

A subjective monitoring of primetime language reveals that damns and hells rain down promiscuously, an occasional SOB is complemented with bastard, and the name of Jesus is often slurred as "Jeez." Until recently, NBC held the line on the casual use of God, but ABC and CBS allow anyone mildly surprised to say "Oh m'gawd" to the cheap-shot delight of the laugh track.

Given the competition of cable and social usage, few verbal taboos will last the decade on over-the-air television. Advocates of "family values" want less sex and the "cultural elite" want less violence, but only your English teacher wants to keep a civil tongue in your head. Someone like Disney may come up with a G-rated channel for those who want scrubbed language only. Humorist Russell Baker of the *New York Times* wrote in his December 7, 1991, column that Americans in the past "could say 'dirty talk' without feeling disgracefully unenlightened, repressed or inhibited." Today, any verbal boundaries are considered un-American in New York and Hollywood.

Linguistically, "Hill Street Blues" was inventive, substituting all manner of hear-alike words such as "dogbreath" and "snotbag" for bad guys and scouring the dictionary of slang for Yiddish and Spanish synonyms for what they were forbidden to say in English. Grant Tinker used to say that forcing talent to write around dirty words evoked juicy euphemisms.

To our knowledge, few interest groups hound the networks on language, leaving that to the taste of the viewer and the wrath of CLeaR-TV. Standards editors will admit anonymously that they let slide rough language on the quality shows and come down hard on the rudeness in the cotton candy of third-rate material.

Exploitative sex comes and goes, alternating with gratuitous violence for media and interest group attention. Networks used to say that there is no "sex" on free television, meaning that nobody "did it" once, much less the 20,000 times claimed by Planned Parenthood. True, primetime has yet to display hard-core intercourse. But the "befores" and "afters" are no longer the quick fade-ins and fade-outs of five years ago. Considerable activity takes place under the sheets and despite the AIDS scare, long sucking kisses are current.

In defense, producers tell their critics that the best stories since Adam and Eve, to say nothing of David and Bathsheba, are sexy. The network approved term is "romance." But what is the dividing line between romance and exploitative sex? The authors believe that, like gratuitous violence, those calls are best left to experienced editors in standards who consider the context and quality of stories when they ask for cuts or permit a hot scene to play.

Pressures from the religious right have had no permanent effect on primetime sex, although the Moral Majority scared sponsors enough in 1981 to cause a brief limitation on the "jigglies" the next season. The late 1980s and early 1990s saw another attempt at regulation by advertisers. What really triggers network programmers to change, one season to the next?[19] It would be difficult to distinguish between pressures generated by the groups, those generated by the press (always obliging with the lip-smacking delight of hypocritically condemning the immoralities of their competitors while blind to their own eroticism), the cries of advertisers and the sense of the entertainment president that the present cost of exceeding boundaries is too high. So far in the 1990s, at any rate, it seems that unsafe sex endures, pressures or no pressures.

Religious offense might sound like an afterthought where group critics are concerned. Of the 250,000 letters of complaint that NBC receives annually, those protesting one form of religious prejudice outnumbered those on sex, violence, language and stereotyping.[20] (Form letters and special campaigns are not counted among the 250,000 average, but are treated as single communications and are rarely read individually. Thus one letter, carefully written by a single member, is just as effective as two thousand letters from every member of a given church.) Many of these have to do with sex, violence or language but are delivered from a religious perspective. Most, however, complain about some insensitivity toward their faith.

For example, networks used to depict Mormons as polygamists, drawing no distinction between sectarian Mormons and those in the mainline denomination who live lives, by modern American standards, as pure as the driven snow. Today networks are careful not to defame Mormonism, a tribute to the patient and tolerant witness of people like Beverly Campbell, the church's Washington official.

The loudest religious noise is made, to no one's surprise, by Rev. Donald Wildmon. He accuses the networks of being anti-Christian. Reading between his lines, the faithful can infer that what Mr. Wildmon means is that the Jews who run television are not sympathetic to the Christian cause. The Wildmon accusations of programming prejudice against Christians are not only ludicrous but blind to the real problem.

Professor Martin Marty, writing in *TV Guide*,[21] put the case cogently when he said that religion is not sinned against on the air so much as it is ignored. There seems to be a conspiracy of silence that ignores this aspect of American life in which Gallup reports each year that 95 percent of us believe in God, 80 percent accept the deity of Christ, 60 percent say that the Bible is the word of God and a solid 40 percent of the nation attends church at least once a month. And yet, you could watch sitcoms, dramas and movies-of-the-week for a solid month and never get this impression.[22]

Evangelicals (regarded as the mainstream of Christian denominationalism today as contrasted with the more sectarian and fanatical fundamentalists) are badly used by television. From Elmer Gantry (fictional) to Jim and Tammy Bakker (all too real), evangelicals have suffered from the excesses of the few that have demeaned the honor of the many — all 45 million of them.

The churches and synagogues will survive, but it would be nice to see an occasional writer-producer with the knowledge and insight to present the clergy in human and authentic terms—warts, halos and all. For insight into lay religion this side of Norman Lear, we must leave it to heaven.

In summary, the interest groups have surely changed the features if not the face of primetime television. The tube is kinder, more accurate, less harmful to vulnerable people. Perhaps the greatest achievement of most public organizations is their very presence. There they are in the background, ready to defend their honor, open to dialogue and hopeful of quality. The most responsible of them will continue to raise the consciousness of the creative and managerial community in the entertainment industry. Even those whose methods are nasty and aims problematical have their place in the marketplace of clashing values.

How closely those values represent the public at large as against the elite values of group leaders is another question. What happens when these conflicts over sex, violence, language, stereotyping and religion spread into the halls and courts of government, and how the public's expectations factor into the equation will be the next consideration.

ON WORKING OUT AN ACCOMMODATION BETWEEN BROADCASTERS AND GROUPS FOR THE PUBLIC'S SAKE: DO PUBLIC INTEREST GROUPS REPRESENT THE PUBLIC?

This question is akin to asking if government really represents the people. Much depends upon which people you mean and what their interests really are. In a republic, individual congressmen serve some of the people most of the time and all of the people none of the time. The president must assume the responsibility of serving "all of the people" on those occasions when the larger welfare transcends factional interests. The Supreme Court, reading the Constitution above political pressures, serves the "best interests" of the people, whether majority or minority interests.

In broadcasting, the interest groups parallel the activities of congresspeople, each representing a legitimate constituency whose aims are often incompatible with those of other constituencies. The question is, who in American broadcasting assumes a "presidential" role of speaking for "all the people" and who assumes a "judicial" role of speaking for the "best interests" of the people?

Both interest group leaders and network brass would answer that, yes, they serve that larger well-being of society, however hard it is to define. As seen from our corner, neither successfully meets that broader standard. The networks argue that their news programs serve the mass appetite for information and that their entertainment shows, validated by the millions who watch them, serve the recreational needs of the public. This is a specious argument in light of "infotainment" and nightly news shows that are produced *as* entertainment. The interest groups argue that they serve collectively the interests of so many minorities that the total effect adds up to serving the wider public. We have our doubts.

To put things in context, look at the relationship between the "interested public" thought of as ratings and the "public interest" thought of as the mandate of broadcasters to act as trustees of the public air. Clearly, the networks concentrate on the efficacy of supplying the entertainment and information needs of the larger public while the interest groups rally around the concept of the mandate to serve the public at large.

Take interest groups first. In the case of the AARP, the PTA and the church groups, to name some of the more prominent ones, leaders serve those who "elect" them with their dues and support. Taken whole, such organizations probably come as close to preserving an ecological balance of interests as is possible in a plural culture. Thus, Arab fronts balance Jewish fronts; the National Rifle Association balances People for the American Way; the liberal religionists of the National Council of Churches balance the conservative religionists of the evangelicals; the National Organization for Women and its allies balance the antiabortion consortium; and the ACLU with its "freedom" faction balances all the "order" groups from the Association of Attorneys General to the U.S. Chamber of Commerce. The overall pressure generated by the cumulative power of interest groups serves to underline the network's double responsibility toward minorities and the well-being of society itself. The tension of opposites may create a balance between entrenched forces fighting for minorities and fractional points of view, but it may not serve the mass of viewers who are more interested in their favorite shows than in the prosocial activities of the interest groups. This clearly is the case in the program diet on network television. An illustration shows why.

At one of the NBC seminars (in which forty group leaders spent three days with forty network managers and producers), Harvard professor of law Arthur Miller staged one of his role-playing dramas. Miller often presides over such simulated debates on public television with celebrity role-players who react to his baiting questions on various controversial issues.

At the NBC conference, Professor Miller was playing the devil's advocate with a panel composed equally of group leaders and television producers. His simulated "case" had a famous TV "auteur" making a pitch to a fictional network for a new show he wanted to produce. The show he had in mind was, to say the least, pushing the boundaries of sex, violence, stereotyping and language. Introducing each character, Miller had the audience (and panel) in stitches over the tasteless, exploitative and offensive portrayals. Like "Saturday Night Live," his show was an "equal opportunity offender."

Turning to the panelists, Miller asked each for a comment on the acceptability of his characters and their perspectives. Those representing the "hyphenated-Americans" pointed out how harmful such a show would be to Italians or Poles or blacks and therefore to the public interest at large. Church and educational leaders deplored the intensification of sex and violence. Network officials swore they would never accept such caricatures. Feminists deeply resented the "bimbo" image. The audience nodded piously.

At this point, Miller turned to a former producer of "Hill Street Blues," a man who claimed to be completely sympathetic to minorities while at the same time an outspoken critic of network censorship. "Having heard these complaints, Mr. Producer, would you make any changes in your show?"

"Yes, I might even call my writers in and demand a different concept. There's no way we can outrage that many segments of the public. And, I imagine, the standards people would be spitting and scratching every inch of the way. Sure, I'd reconsider."

Pausing dramatically and shooting his silver-linked cuffs, the elegant Miller inserted his needle: "But suppose your new series went on the air with all those portrayals so offensive to public interest leaders and nevertheless garnered a 40 rating. What would you do then?"

"In that case, I tell every leader in this seminar to go to hell." (Applause from network attendees; groans from group attendees.) "A 40 rating and a 65 share means that the public has spoken. They belong to me. It means that your so-called representatives of the public are out of touch with their own members. Like the title of this meeting, the interested public truly foreshadows the public interest."

Sound thinking? Not entirely, but persuasive because of its half-truth. The exchange illustrates partly valid arguments: (1) that the Balkanized world of interest groups speaks more for fractions of the public than for the public en masse, and indeed, may sometimes be out of touch with majority audiences; (2) that there is a real relationship between numbers and what people want for entertainment, between the public interest and the interested public. The fact is undeniable that serving the public interest *includes* an interested public. That's part of what the original Communications Act intended. Now, some sixty-five years later, both the American people and the American government agree that a commercial system devoted to entertaining the public is part of what it means for broadcasters to "serve the public interest, necessity and convenience." Not many watchdogs understand this truth.

However, there are also fallacies at work in the producer's stance. He was suggesting that grabbing such high entertainment ratings exhausted the public interest responsibilities of networks. This ignores the moral argument (see below) that questions the right of majority audiences to see material that injures minorities, much less the right of the masses to material that is inherently contrary to community standards (i.e., snuff movies that film actual murders).

The larger fallacy has to do with numbers and public welfare. In the minds of most entertainers, an audience of 40 million viewers is a bold demonstration of the public interest. Big numbers prove that the public is served. But is there such a simple identity? What about the 200 million who are not watching a sleazy show but who are outraged and defamed and just annoyed that such antisocial values are being legitimized to the other 40 million? If 40 million viewers were willing to watch Godzilla eat Morton Downey, Jr., on the Geraldo Rivera show, would that harm the public interest? If not, why not step up the ante and endorse cocaine on the Noriega Show? It likely would draw a crowd.

No, Mr. Producer, persuasive as huge ratings are, they don't fulfill the mandate of the "interest, necessity and convenience" of the public. Conveniently overlooking that mandate, network managers like to say that viewers vote with their remote controls in this, the purest of democracies. Why listen to "so-called" public interest groups when the market polls the public?

The argument has a convincing, antiintellectual appeal. After all, leaders of interest groups are prone to give the masses what is good for them rather than what the masses find good. Or as the longshoreman and writer Eric Hoffer put it, "Intellectuals are always asking the people to get down on their knees and love what they hate and hate what they love."[23] Networks could never be accused of such highmindedness.

The plain truth, as we see it, is that interest groups speak for legitimate fractions of the public, the networks speak for their pocketbooks and nobody speaks for Everyman in the viewer's chair. Add up the fractions represented by groups and the larger public is well served, but no interest group speaks for "all the people," or the viewers en masse. In fact, it is doubtful if either groups or networks completely understand what the general public regards as its stake in the content of free television.

Cynics may scoff but our vote for the persons most delicately tuned to the viewing public's "desires" and "desirables" are writer-producers—entertainers who know instinctively what the public will entertain.

NOTES

1. One of several seminars designed for networks by Charles Brackbill and Richard Gilbert, The American Values Institute. Professor Kuhn told his audiences of industry executives, producers, programmers and standards staff that "the right of any group of people to challenge any other group on grounds of any value or interest is an unassailable right in the mainstream American democratic tradition." In James Kuhn, "The Emergence of Corporate Constituencies," unpublished manuscript, 1989.

2. Alexis de Tocqueville, *Democracy in America* (New York: Anchor Books, 1969), p. 513.

3. Richard Gilbert, "Public Interest Groups," NBC Corporate Communications, New York, 1989, p. 68.

4. All networks have community relations executives whose aim is public relations, gathering awards, doing promotional work for prestigious programs. Only Hoffmann's role was that of ombudsman, liaison for standards, responding to complaints and reaching out preemptively to responsible groups leaders.

5. See the Gay and Lesbian Alliance Against Defamation case discussed later in this chapter.

6. Gilbert, "Public Interest Groups," p. 8.

7. Dr. Alan Sloan, a leading market consultant on the buying habits of senior citizens, has exploded this myth by noting that people over fifty not only buy most of the "big-ticket" items like large cars but underwrite many of the purchases of the so-called yuppie generation.

8. See Tom Wolfe, "Radical Chic," *New York*, June 1965 (entire issue); see also Ben Stein, *The View from Sunset Boulevard* (New York: Basic Books, 1979).

9. Based on phone interviews with ICCR staff.

10. "Television and Minority Hiring," Interfaith Center for Corporate Responsibility, New York City.

11. Gilbert, "Public Interest Groups," p. 91.

12. Those who have seen the 1990 documentary *Roger and Me* might add General Motors to the list of dinosaurs that can't handle change.

13. For a snappy look at case studies of pressure group tactics, see Kathryn Montgomery's *Target: Prime-time* (New York: Oxford University Press, 1989). It suffers, however, from the selection of incidents that date back to the good old days of network standards responsibility. The new network owners have a different attitude toward interest groups and therefore a different set of responses.

14. See chapter 4 for additional discussions of changes in broadcast regulation.

15. The National PTA "What's Happening in Washington," pamphlet. See also April 1988 issue of the *PTA Today* on "Children in the Electronic Age."

16. NBC Research, 1988.

17. Ten years ago, the president of P&G flew in his private plane to Tupelo, Miss., in an effort to appease Rev. Wildmon and made a speech condemning network sex.

18. An unpublished focus group–based study by Charles Brackbill and Richard Gilbert for NBC Research, "Language Problems and Young Adults," (1989), was conducted with focus groups. The members took a permissive attitude toward most of Carlin's words and advocated an uncensored television vocabulary with the exception of "fighting words" and racial/ethnic slurs.

19. See chapter 3, "The Network Programmers."

20. Based on NBC standards analyses, unpublished.

21. *TV Guide*, December 1980.

22. "Amen" is an exception of sorts, portraying a black pastor who is neither wimp nor pious hypocrite, but the setting is more George Jefferson than ecclesiastical. Father Dowling is more detective than priest.

23. Eric Hoffer, *The Ordeal of Change: Essays* (New York: Harper & Row, 1963), p. 56.

7

Advertiser Influence on Television Content

Several years ago the National Audubon Society produced a one-hour television special about the destruction of ancient forests in the Pacific Northwest. The program, underwritten by the Stroh's Brewing Company and eight other advertisers, was scheduled to air first on the Turner Broadcasting system and several months later on the Public Broadcasting Service.

"Rage over Trees" is a biting film on conservation. It contrasts clear, wide-angle footage of century-old virgin woodlands against scorched-earth hillsides denuded by timber industry chainsaws. It presents interviews with conservationists, forest service officials and lumber company representatives. Actor Paul Newman narrates the award-winning film, concluding with his comments on the film's desperate message:

> You don't have to be an expert to perceive that once a forest of 400-year-old trees is cut down, that forest is lost forever. . . . President Thomas Jefferson spoke of his concern for posterity — for the thousandth generation of Americans to come. He was thinking about us. Are we thinking about our children and grandchildren? . . . This nation needs lumber, but there are millions of acres of timber in the United States besides ancient forests. . . . These forests belong to the American people, and you have to let Congress know what you want done with them.[1]

The logging industry, which learned of the program through station promos, complained to Stroh's threatening a national boycott unless the company withdrew sponsorship. Stroh's, in turn, pressured the Audubon Society to tone down the message that so angered the loggers. Audubon refused and Stroh's pulled out several weeks before the scheduled airing. Just days and in some cases hours before air time, eight other sponsors — Exxon Corporation, Citicorp, New York Life Insurance Company, Ford Motor Company, Sears, Roebuck & Co., ITT

Corporation, *Omni* Magazine and Michelin Tire and Rubber Company—also canceled sponsorship, leaving the program without a single backer. Despite these advertiser pressures, Turner Broadcasting refused to drop the program and ran it at a quarter-million-dollar loss.

This example of advertiser influence on television program content—and broadcaster courage—is particularly conspicuous, but it is by no means unique. The power of the purse is nothing new. It is difficult to believe the networks, or any broadcaster dependent on commercial underwriting, could completely discount the power of advertisers who are their sole source of revenues, and yet there are scores of cases where they did resist, particularly on news and informational shows.[2]

Public television has a variety of funding sources: the government through the Corporation for Public Broadcasting; viewers and listeners; foundations; and corporations that contribute as underwriters, not in exchange for a specific allocation of air time. Operational funding is defused among many sources with diverse interests, diminishing the power of any single contributor. Public broadcasters, consequently, enjoy greater autonomy in programming decisions.

This came about as a result of former president Richard Nixon, who was no fan of what he saw as liberal public affairs programming on the Public Broadcasting Service (PBS). As a means of sapping the strength of PBS, he diverted federal money from the network directly to individual stations.[3] Although Nixon's strategy successfully decreased public affairs programming, the funding cuts forced PBS to cultivate its own funding sources as it reduced its reliance on government subsidies. In the long run, this has granted PBS greater freedom from political and governmental influence. Richard Nixon unwittingly strengthened the PBS funding base and, as his luck would have it, expanded the role, loyalty and size of its audience.

By contrast, the networks have only commercial advertisers to pay their bills. Despite the hundreds of companies that buy time, networks must listen to the same sad story from each. That's because, when it comes to demands from broadcasters, the hundreds think as one.

For instance, advertisers who select television want the same thing: large, heterogeneous audiences in a fairly passive state, not aroused to anger or charged to seek revenge from the bearer of unpleasant messages. We call this the "sleepy viewer" concept.[4] Programming that would upset this audience dormancy would be equally as undesirable for one advertiser as for another. Since the goals are the same for all—to sell products—they all want the same phlegmatic audience. This became clear in the Audubon case when advertisers as diverse as ITT, Exxon and *Omni* Magazine found reason to withdraw sponsorship. The domino that toppled one company upset the others as well, whether caused by the fear of a charged-up audience or the threat of consumer boycotts.

Further, companies that advertise on television are similar in other respects. All are large. Mom-and-Pop operations do not buy network television. At $150,000 for a thirty-second spot in prime-time, only big companies can afford the medium. They all need to show profits, to pacify shareholders, to meet government obligations and to play internal corporate politics. Such forces acting on corporations create cookie-cutter structures that mold their messages into lookalike shapes. Hundreds of corporations may advertise, but their ads are of the same genre and do not reflect hundreds of individual personalities. Wasn't it humorist Dave Barry who said that British royalty has intermarried so often, working out of a minute gene pool, that their fingerprints are all the same? So with giant companies.

Advertisers are subjected to other homogenizing forces. Purchases of television advertising time are funneled through a handful of large advertising agencies and production houses. These too are cookie-cutter operations. Ad agencies use similar formulas for their clients, departing little from standard treatments current in this trendy industry. When humor is in, it is in for the group. When fifteen-second spots become the rage, everyone gets into the fifteen-second pool. When the latest demographic is the under forty crowd of impulse buyers, that audience is de rigeur for all.

Most national advertisers also employ program screening services to preview shows for questionable content.[5] The screeners look for material that reflects badly on individual products, such as automobile crashes in programs sponsored by General Motors, or peanut butter poisonings in programs sponsored by Jif. But screening services also look for content that might be more generally objectionable. For instance, they scan for offensive language or sexual material that might provoke viewers or interest groups. They look for strong and controversial themes that might set off some segment of the audience. Disagreeable topics are anathema to the "sleepy viewer." At such a sighting the screeners light a red flare for all would-be sponsors of the program. Depending on the strength of the material, only the weak-hearted may defect. Or there may be a stampede for the door as there was in the Audubon case.

So, despite the appearance of diverse advertiser backing, the networks do not enjoy a "diffusion of sponsorship" that would allow them greater latitude in content development.[6] There are many advertisers, but they present themselves as a fairly undifferentiated block. Consequently, the networks do not venture far from group norms. Offenses for one, it turns out, are offenses for all.

The dependency of networks on their advertisers defines a two-step business relationship different from the more linear arrangement found in public broadcasting and pay-for-cable TV. In public television, with its heavy viewer funding, and in pay-for-cable television, with revenues coming directly from viewers, the audience is clearly the "customer." The people who watch pay for large portions of the programs. There are fewer middlemen or peripheral patrons to please or to fear. A show makes the grade almost entirely on its success with the viewers and underwriters who are one and the same.

The networks, though, are not in the business of selling programs to viewers—not directly. Viewers pay for programs but only remotely through added costs to advertised products; we all pay whether we watch or not. Since networks sell audiences, not programs, their "customers" are the advertisers who pay for the audiences. The bigger the audience, the more advertisers pay—you buy 'em by the pound—and lately, by age and income. In practice, the networks strive to develop programs with great audience appeal, and while the motivation for many professionals at the networks is to please the viewers, their ultimate aim is to sell this or that audience to advertisers. Fox, having the lowest ratings, aims for youth. CBS, the surprise winner in 1992, goes for the largest audiences, banking on the fact that the 18 to 38 viewer is proportionately represented in that mass. Programs, therefore, are not the ends of network operations as they are for public and pay-for-cable-TV, but a means by which networks yield a salable product. Details of this arrangement are no small matter, for they get to the heart of advertiser influence on content.

Any business is beholden to its customers. When customers are pleased they continue their business. Networks, now fixed more on the bottom line than they have been for the past thirty years, wish nothing more in this era of increased competition than to please their customers. Millions of dollars may be lost when advertisers withdraw from a program or refuse to be associated with a particular program or program genre. Networks, therefore, see it in their best economic interest to listen to these concerns and do what is necessary to carry accommodating programs.

Although we have staked out the position that networks sell audiences, the formula often involves more than just the sale of advertising targets. The Audubon program, which won critical awards, drew in sizable audiences for Turner Broadcasting, and so, in theory, it provided a salable product. Advertisers, however, prodded by the loggers, looked beyond the audience and fixed on program content. Despite Turner's success at delivering viewers, the vehicle itself became more compelling. Advertisers attempted to soften the Audubon message.

Even though the nine advertisers did not succeed in getting the Audubon Society or Turner to alter the content, don't conclude that content is beyond the reach of advertisers. We will cite a number of examples later in which advertisers *have* changed content. Moreover, even though the broadcaster did not comply in this case, how often will it be willing or able to shoulder the financial burden of programs that advertisers view as troublesome—even though such shows may attract substantial audiences? Commercial stations earn money only from advertisers. If Turner earned money directly from viewers, it would be a safe bet the broadcaster would continue airing such material. However, since its customers are advertisers, it must consider more than viewer wishes. Unlike Turner, who has a lucrative business as well as his superstation, NBC, CBS and Fox get only a trickle of money from cable. Only ABC through its interest in sports channel ESPN profits from this revenue stream. In any event, networks must keep their broadcast customers satisified.

This chapter will examine how the relationship between networks and advertisers affects the content of television programs. Technological changes during the past fifteen years have imposed additional competitive pressures on the broadcasting industry and have complicated the network-advertiser relationship. We will consider the effects of these recent program changes on content. First, let's take a look at the historical alliance between advertisers and broadcasters.

HISTORY

To understand commercial television, first understand commercial radio. The origins of broadcaster and advertiser relationships began long before anyone thought of "watching" a program. The arrangement now so familiar to American audiences was established during the 1920s.

The earliest radio stations literally were back-room operations. The most widely accepted account of the first station involves the amateur radio activities of one Frank Conrad, a Westinghouse employee living in East Pittsburgh, Pennsylvania.[7] Conrad talked a lot on his amateur radio set to other hobbyists in the area, and occasionally for the fun of it, he would air records by jamming a microphone into the horn of his Edison phonograph.

Before long Conrad established a following for his broadcasts as amateur radio enthusiasts spread the word of his novel use of the wireless. Soon he received requests for certain tunes, and to accommodate the growing interest he set aside designated times for music. Ever the innovative programmer, Conrad added general commentary and recruited family members to perform live for the growing body of listeners.

Conrad's "concerts" received press attention that further expanded his audience. A local department store advertised in a newspaper the sale of receivers with which anyone, not just amateur radio hobbyists, could tune in the concerts. A Westinghouse executive saw the ad and contacted the one-man band about expanding his operation beyond the garage. Conrad accepted the proposal and, after receiving authorization from the Commerce Department, set up radio station KDKA.

KDKA and other pioneer stations soon expanded the concert concept in which live talent and phonograph recordings were woven into feature-length programs. New, creative formats were tried as additional stations logged on the air, staffed by people on loan from large companies. Radio in those days was not a money-making enterprise; programming often served as a pretext for the sale of receivers rather than as the purpose for broadcasting.

The notion of selling air time was tried but quickly dismissed in the belief that listeners in the privacy of their homes would resent the assault of commercial messages. It was argued that people tuned in to be entertained and informed, not to be pitched. With such quick abandonment of advertisements, early commercial radio ironically came to resemble the current public broadcasting concept in which advertisers stay in the background, serving only as quiet program sponsors. A number of other funding solutions were proposed, including government backing and foundation support, but only the restrained commercial underwriting approach took hold. Over time, the increasing financial requirements of radio stations and the more liberal national mood toward commercial promotion allowed greater boldness in advertising. By the end of the decade few restrictions on commercial announcements remained. Advertisers continued to produce and sponsor programs, only now they could blow their own horns. This model served the industry for the next twenty years. Broadcasters supplied the equipment and the forum; advertisers supplied the programs and the commercial hype.

And so it was in this environment that television entered the American mass media market. Television was subsumed under the same set of broadcast regulations governing radio (see chapter 4). It also contended for the same audience, and to underwrite its operations it needed the same commercial sponsors. The nation's transition to television was easy but it meant hard times for radio. Immediately after the television freeze lifted in the early 1950s,[8] advertisers and viewers moved swiftly and naturally to television. Radio survived—even thrived—after a bumpy transition into new configurations, while television grew like Topsy, endowed by the rich commercial coffers.

Inheriting the radio model meant broadcasters provided the forum and advertisers provided the programming. Here was the ultimate form of advertiser content control. Although the networks worked hand-in-hand with the sponsors in program development, the sponsor—with control of the purse—dominated. Of the three networks, CBS adhered most faithfully to this single-sponsor format.

It must have worked; CBS-TV led the industry in ratings throughout the decade. NBC-TV, whose roots go back to the earliest radio days, first sought a greater distribution of sponsors for its programs. To gain better programming control, NBC-TV produced its own shows and sold air time to advertisers whose combined contributions supported production costs and yielded the networks a healthy profit. Although such an arrangement shielded programming from advertisers' control, it did not remove program content from their influence.

Two forces in the late 1950s acted to shift the broadcaster-advertiser relationship almost entirely in the direction of the NBC model. First, costs escalated. The success of television with American audiences greatly enriched the value of air time. After a decade of audience growth the networks were able to charge advertisers substantial sums. Costs also increased because of growing celebrity salaries, more sophisticated filming techniques and better quality of writing and production. These towering costs prevented most advertisers from going it alone as sponsors. Although advertisers might have formed consortiums through which they jointly could have produced and underwritten programs, the networks could more efficiently orchestrate production and sell the advertisers small blocks of time on selected shows. This freed advertisers from the burden of program production, allowed them to distribute their messages across channels and times and enabled them to reach a better audience blend. Such a strategy is more efficient than single-program sponsorship in reaching patrons for general consumer products typically advertised on network television.

Scandal was the other force putting networks in the driver's seat. Throughout the latter part of the 1950s, television quiz shows hooked huge audiences for their sponsors. The concept was not new—quiz shows were introduced to radio audiences years earlier—but the glamor of television and the size of the winnings piqued audience attention.

Most quiz shows were produced by advertisers who had creative control. Sponsors and their agencies selected the formats, the contestants and, as it turned out, the winners. The networks played a peripheral role, allowing advertisers to manage all the details. But arms' length was not distance enough to protect the networks from the fallout resulting from charges that the contests were fixed. Congressional investigations revealed that participants were fed answers to win or were paid under the table to lose. A national potboiler became grand theater as revelations of the scandal were augmented by findings of perjury and other sins by leaders prominent in the industry.

According to federal regulations, broadcast licensees, not advertisers, are responsible for televised material. So, member stations (licensees) were placed in jeopardy as a result of network laissez-faire attitudes toward programming. Throughout all this the networks claimed they were innocent by way of their ignorance, but vowed, nonetheless, to exercise firm control over their programming in the future. In such a visible industry, forewarned broadcasters could not risk other scandals that would bring public and regulator condemnation, and moreover, that would threaten valued network–member station relationships. Remember, the networks have always made more money from their owned stations in the major markets than they made from network operations.

So all three networks assumed operational control of their programs, settling almost exclusively for the magazine approach to broadcasting. Networks acted as publishers with editorial control, independent producers acted as writers who submitted material and advertisers paid the bill. Parenthetically, each of the big three beefed up its standards departments, and censors became the network shields against fraud and corruption. Broadcasters made programs and advertisers bought time. In this arrangement, advertisers no longer wrote the scripts, but they hardly yielded editorial influence. They had given up the pen but not the sword of financial power.

ADVERTISER PERSPECTIVES

Our examination later will demonstrate how easy it is to view advertisers as villains who manipulate network programming to suit their own selfish, economic motives. Their concentration of financial power positions them as a significant force within the industry. The Audubon story offers a poignant example of big business—the biggest of businesses—poised against the creative treatment of an important national topic.

Indeed, there are many examples of advertisers brandishing their powers to pummel television programming into self-serving images. We will explore later in this chapter how advertisers use their clout to affect the content of programs not only directly as in the Audubon case, but also in more subtle and perhaps more manipulative ways. Such discussions left unbalanced, however, distort the true relationship between advertisers and broadcasters. One can understand the mutual dependency better by examining first the advertisers' concerns.

The American broadcasting industry would not be the healthy, diverse, enormously popular system it is today without the participation of companies that have written the checks for the past forty years. Viewers may pay the tab in the long run through higher consumer prices (to offset advertising costs),[9] but advertising has proved a successful and painless funding source for this expensive enterprise.

The alternatives to advertiser-sponsored television are not without substantial drawbacks. Consider these. Government-run television invites government censorship, political influence and inevitable limitations on the creative and aggressive exploration of new program forms. All this and, through taxes, the public still pays the bills. Examples of government-run television worldwide make the case against this funding approach in which the people pay for programming that may serve political needs of the state rather than entertainment and information needs of the viewer.

Pay-for-view programming, now becoming a popular option in the maturing television industry, would, if it were the only available funding approach, have changed the character of American broadcasting in two ways. First, it would have retarded the rapid acceptance and adoption of the medium, limiting the number of stations and receivers.[10] Free services are adopted more rapidly than those that charge a fee. Second, such an approach would have undercut a population-wide participation in the medium. The pay-as-you-watch approach would have limited the participation of people less able to afford the service. This would have disenfranchised large segments of society, and not only reinforced economic disparities, but imposed informational barriers as well. People in lower socioeconomic groups, who today are the heaviest users of commercial television, would have been deprived of access. (If pay-per-view services continue to outbid free television for special events, that disenfranchisement will become a sad reality.) Political, cultural and economic prices of such isolation would have been high indeed.

As it turns out, government anxieties with broadcasting in the early 1920s left it uninterested in exploring more active participation. A government-run system thus was never a serious possibility. Because of technological limitations, pay-for-listening options were not feasible. And so the urgent need for funding sources during these early years opened the activity to a commercial support system mutually beneficial to the industry and to business—and ultimately to viewers.

Although advertisers came through when they were much needed, they were hardly knights in shining armor. They were in it for profit and they benefited from the arrangement as much as the industry and viewers did. Nonetheless, it is important to recognize the value of the commercial broadcasting system. If you find it lacking, just consider the alternatives.

What do advertisers get for their money? Why are companies willing to spend millions of dollars annually to broadcast ephemeral messages to viewers who may or may not be listening, who may be zipping around the dial or who may be in the kitchen opening another beer? Why are advertisers so concerned about the environment in which their messages appear? Answers to these questions provide the key to advertiser concerns about program content.

Companies advertise for two interdependent reasons: to sell their products and to sell their images. While on the surface these reasons are simple enough, consider television advertising not as an isolated undertaking but as part of a more involved marketing activity encompassing all the events that bring a product from the factory to the consumer. Moreover, individual messages must be viewed in the context of companion messages — on television and in other media — in order to understand the goals of an advertising campaign.

Television is an ideal medium for the direct promotion of consumer goods. Advertising messages spotlight products in glowing terms and show the virtues, never the vices. Everything is upbeat, supportive, positive and buoyant. Never is heard a discouraging word. Promoters are happy, actors are happy and everyone hopes the viewers are happy, too.

Many advertising textbooks examine the use of television to promote products directly. We leave the subject to them and focus on image advertising as a factor of advertiser influence on television. Here advertisers set out to enhance public perceptions of a company with an expectation that the image of the company will transfer to the image of the product. Favorable company images thus yield favorable product images, and if everything works by the book, this translates into favorable product sales. In other words, company image advertising is a roundabout way of product advertising.

The J.M. Smucker Company offers an excellent example. It has become a standard advertising procedure for Smucker's to promote its company image alongside its promotion of jams and jellies. The company name echoes over warm strawberry patches at sunset, American Gothic scenes and grandma's country breakfast table. Its slogan, "With a name like Smucker's it has to be good," doesn't proclaim the wonders of its jams but the goodness of its own image. Like the company, love the jam. J.M. Smucker, for all its down-home goodness, is actually a major international foods distributor with tens of millions of dollars in annual sales.

McDonald's Restaurants offer another example of company image advertising. While McDonald's engages in product promotion, its television strategy involves substantial company image building. Consider one Clio winning commercial[11] in which McDonald's is shown to be significant in the lives of two youngsters who, in the course of a sixty-second spot, grow from toddlers to graduating high school seniors. The misty lens, swelling music and cozy images project an emotion not easily forgotten. Hamburgers and other products are noted only in passing. Everyone knows McDonald's sells fast food and naturally will make the connection. The purpose of such spots is to sustain the warm, familial, wholesome image of McDonald's. Love McDonald's, love their burgers. McDonald's is an international, multibillion-dollar outfit adding new franchises at the rate of nearly one per week.

Most image advertising accomplishes the dual goals of company image enhancement and product promotion by focusing on company credibility. It does so by manipulating audience perceptions of three credibility components: charisma, expertise and trustworthiness.

Charisma building seeks to position a company as a growing, dynamic, exciting, forward-looking enterprise with its sights set on the future. In the hype and excitement of the television environment, companies enjoy a natural setting in which to show themselves as charismatic and vital. Expertise, the second image component, applies most directly to companies involved in the production of high-tech products. Automobile companies, for instance, are especially likely to use television to advance public perceptions of technical competence and skillful workmanship. These companies exhibit their expertise as proof of their ability to manufacture technically excellent cars. "Ford One" commercials, for instance, show workers using the latest technology to construct and test Ford cars. Ford emphasizes the technical excellence of its assembly operations and the innovativeness of its engineering and design facilities. Expertise is promoted by electronics manufacturers, airlines and home appliance companies, among others.

While television well serves the advertiser's need to enhance perceived company charisma and expertise, it is unparalleled among media in fortifying perceptions of company trustworthiness. This concept involves a complex of images related to the honesty, believability and dependability of a company. It addresses the question: do you, the potential customer, trust this company first to be good and honest, and second, to provide a product that will satisfy your needs? Companies perceived to be trustworthy enjoy public affection and confidence that translates into positive product images.

The Smucker's and McDonald's advertisements strike at the core of the trustworthiness issue. They evoke images that beg for audience trust—warmth and goodness, patriotism, the innocence of youth. Companies today yearn for audience trust as never before. Sad tales of defective and dangerous products, savings and loan disasters, toxic spills, air crashes, executive indictments, foreign takeovers and a host of other woeful stories have contributed to a gloomy public view that American enterprise is preoccupied with profits and its own self-interests. There is an emphasis these days on the enhancement of corporate images, and television has played a major role in bringing these messages to American audiences.

We cannot overplay the importance of a corporation's public image. Billions of dollars are spent annually to bolster favorable or to change unfavorable images, and while television provides only one forum for the presentation of a corporate image, it is of singular importance. The popularity and influence of television place it center stage for vast numbers of American citizens who as consumers and voters sit in judgment. Public image maintenance is more than a matter of vanity or corporate boasting. While there always are elements of personal pride at stake, these companies invest considerable resources to develop a market for their products and to cultivate a unique corporate persona for practical business reasons. These motivations drive companies to protect their public image:

1. Internal perceptions

2. Corporation expenses

3. Product sales

1. *Internal Perceptions:* Few people enjoy working for a company that is in public disrepute, least of all corporate executives. They steer the ship, and if it runs aground, it will have done so with them at the helm. Despite stiff public posturing typical of executives following major company embarrassments, we cannot believe CEOs and other corporate leaders fail to experience distress when troubles mar the company image. Typically conservative, these men and women do not like controversy, particularly when it is focused on matters over which they have some power. Corporate executives are visible not only in business circles, but also in the social community and on association and foundation boards. Company image problems transfer to personal embarrassments, and, therefore, have implications beyond the board room. Such personal matters can have a greater impact on corporate decisions than the cold logic of the marketplace.

A tarnished company image also presents challenges with stockholders. Any event with the potential to affect profit makes them nervous. Image problems may affect sales and costs simultaneously and as a result are no small matters for shareholders. No CEO enjoys facing angry shareholders, particularly over matters that easily might have been avoided. Thoughts of such confrontations motivate corporate executives to seek conservative approaches that avoid public controversy and protect the company image.

2. *Corporation Expenses:* Negative images cost money. Depending on the extent of damage to its persona, a company will need to bankroll corrective advertising campaigns and costly public relations efforts. It may have to scrap short-term promotional plans that already have cost development money and staff time. It also is likely the company will suffer a sales loss that may affect not only revenues but also reshelving and transportation costs.

Affected companies must anticipate that short-term problems may incur long-term damages through the yielding of market shares. Customers are creatures of habit who establish comfortable patterns that they are content to follow. Successful companies do not want distractions that derail customers from stopping by the same fast-food restaurant, tossing the same beer in the cart or booking tickets on the same airline. Skillful marketing goes into development of these customer behaviors; it is difficult to reestablish them once they are disrupted. Widespread flack about some real or manufactured complication can mar the image, rub off on the product and forever change desirable customer patterns.

Procter & Gamble provides a textbook example. One of the largest U.S. manufacturers of consumer goods with sales exceeding $12 billion, P&G has been using the same trademark since 1851. The symbol depicts a crescent "man-in-the-moon" surrounded by thirteen stars, each representing one of the original American colonies. Through the years, Procter & Gamble has chosen to retain the familiar icon for the sake of continuity, tradition and because it was arguably attractive.

A rumor started in the late 1970s that Procter and Gamble, as revealed somehow by its trademark, was in alliance with Satan.[12] The man-in-the-moon with thirteen stars was read by some as a Satanic symbol, proof enough of P&G's demonic alliances. Letters poured into the company's headquarters complaining about the symbol. Many described a talk-show interview with a P&G spokesperson in which the company's Satanic connection was discussed. Letter writers said they either heard the interview themselves or they heard about it from friends or in church. Boycotts against P&G products erupted around the country.

Procter & Gamble fought the spreading rumor with a bold public relations campaign, disavowing any link with the devil, explaining the origins of its assailed trademark. They exhibited a personal letter from the talk-show host proving that no P&G spokesperson had ever confessed on air that Satan was a member of P&G's board of directors. Procter & Gamble used every media device Madison Avenue could provide, and it sent letters to regional and national church leaders explaining its position and asking for help in setting the record straight.

The P&G thumb in the dike was partially successful, but even today new waves of superstition pound against the barriers. Finally, after years of assaults by fundamentalist groups, and not willing to sustain another costly battle, P&G dropped the trademark symbol from its consumer products packaging. Thus, a negative image, falsely generated, impacted the company's sales and cost millions of dollars—and the use of a valued trademark.

Network sales executives closely monitor the image problems of buyers. You can bet that none of the P&G soaps worked satanism into their scripts during that troublesome period. There is no way to tell how often a sponsor's fever results in a producer's chill, since these matters are delicately handled.

3. *Product Sales:* We already discussed the direct relationship between corporate image and product sales. Favorable images transfer favorably to products. If Smucker's has a good name it probably makes good jam, even worth a few extra cents at the cash register.

But a corporate image–product relationship has a dark side. A negative corporate image can lead to lower product sales. People who dislike the company because of something it has done or because of something with which it has been associated, or who lose trust in the company's ability to provide an acceptable product, are less likely to purchase the product. This is particularly true in a rich consumer market where companies face formidable competition. The loss of product sales is an important reason for corporations to step carefully around controversial matters.

This point is well made by General Motors' response to an episode of CBS's "Wiseguy" that included a sexually suggestive scene. Shortly after the program aired, G.M. Chairman Roger Smith received a phone call from the self-styled media critic, the Reverend Donald Wildmon, head of CLeaR-TV (which budded from the National Federation for Decency). Smith also received letters from angry viewers. In response to these complaints—and mild complaints at that—John McNulty, vice president of public relations at General Motors, said, "We took this very seriously. If we lose a car sale, that's a lot of money. We could also lose the next car sale five years from now" ("Screeners Help Advertisers Avoid Prime-Time Trouble," *New York Times*, January 20, 1989). In order to avoid such a recurrence, McNulty said the company was considering augmenting the role of its screening agency. He said, "We hope to empower them in our interest to take our commercial off a program." General Motors felt the heat and recognized its potential impact on sales. G.M.'s eagerness to authorize a screening service to pull its ads demonstrates the impact of a mild threat to its corporate image and sales.

TWO THREATS TO CORPORATE IMAGE

Negative images may arise from two sources. First, corporations may become the victims of their own negligence, malfeasance or misfortunes. A product may cause injury, a policy unfairly may disadvantage another company or bad luck may bring about a round of unfavorable publicity. For instance, Exxon had its Alaskan oil spill, an event partly Exxon's fault, partly bad luck. Automobile companies have recalls—usually as a result of their own engineering shortcomings. Johnson & Johnson faced the Tylenol nightmare, a problem any other pharmaceutical company just as easily could have faced; J&J just had the misfortune. All of these problems are dealt either by the company's own hand or by chance.

Second, as a means of coercion, a negative corporate image may be generated from outside the company. In such cases, the corporation is charged with guilt by association. Interest groups or ad hoc organizations with no substantive complaint may associate the company with something it considers distasteful. For instance, a group may link an advertiser with an objectionable television program. Although a company may have had nothing to do with the program production or content, it may be tarred with the same brush. In the Audubon example, Stroh's withdrew sponsorship because it felt the heat from loggers who were quick to link the brewer with the program message. Similarly, the remaining eight sponsors pulled out because of their anticipated identification with the message and an expected assault on their image. The relationship of the sponsor with the program was one only of association, not of substantive participation in the concept or in program development.

From the corporate viewpoint, there may be little difference in the costs between image damage by internal problems or manufactured means. The end result is the same. To avoid public thrashings from powerful interest groups, companies may yield to demands and withdraw sponsorship. The network then must find other sponsors, air the program with fewer or no sponsors or pull it entirely.

The greater danger to freedom of speech and the diversity of programming is more subtle. Anticipating negative public reaction, how many sponsors and programmers establish a lowest common denominator standard for programming? Or to put it positively, the establishment of quality controls by sponsors and networks may serve as a governor on program material known to offend segments of the public. Either way, program content is limited or shaped in advance. By remaining well below the controversy threshold, networks ensure tranquility and the preservation of the all-important advertiser corporate image.

SUMMARY

A marred company image, then, is anathema to large corporations that annually spend billions of dollars on public relations efforts, goodwill programs, lobbying activities and other undertakings designed to project a favorable impression. The last thing these companies want is unfavorable press, boycotts and grassroots efforts to challenge their good name in public forums. George Mahrig, director of media services at Campbell Soup Company, revealed that his firm had a list of programs on which it avoided advertising because of the rub-off of program material on company image. He said, "Shows are unacceptable if they're not in keeping with the company's (wholesome) image" (Walley, 1989). As we have seen, negative images are personally distasteful for corporate executives and shareholders, and they are costly because of lower product sales and the cost of remedial efforts.

Business leaders expect to be held accountable for their company's activities. They find it particularly onerous, however, to be held responsible for the sins – or perceived sins – of others. Why underwrite the content excesses of maverick producers who push the envelope or deal with taboo themes? The cost for such support might be considerably higher than the bill for a few thirty-second spots. Other program vehicles, void of controversial material, are available and at a cost that includes insurance against negative public reaction. Stroh's can just as easily sell its beer on programs less steeped in controversy than the Audubon special. Audiences can be found in other forums at no greater expense and in a less charged atmosphere. Why pay for advertising exposure that ultimately may not only reduce sales, but also bring down all the miseries of controversy?

In the next section we will consider the implications of image concerns and examine ways in which advertisers affect program content.

ADVERTISER INFLUENCES ON PROGRAM CONTENT

Although in practice the relationships between programmers and advertisers are complex, in theory they can be described simply: advertisers pay networks to provide audiences. Advertisers usually seek the largest audiences for the lowest cost. This is no different from any other transaction seeking the biggest bang for the buck.

Commercial television, however, offers two notable exceptions to this simple rule. First, not all audiences are created equal in the demographic mix of viewers that advertisers find desirable. Beer companies do not aim at child audiences. Manufacturers of expensive sports cars don't pitch to poverty-line viewers. Fast food joints care little for the Perrier crowd, and, to repeat the litany of the nineties, brand sponsors show little interest in viewers with brand loyalties (e.g., senior citizens).

Second, the price of negative feedback from protests must be factored into the normal cost-per-thousand viewers. Programs with the potential to incite public reaction may incur long-term expenses that offset the benefit of reaching a mass audience. Therefore, advertisers must expand the formula in calculating costs to include the potential for a program to elicit public disapproval. Because interest group outcry is emotional and by some standards, irrational, it is hard to predict exactly which scenes may create a stir. One program may draw fire while another with almost identical content may slip by without comment. [13]

An increase in the perceived egregiousness of a program leads to a greater potential for public outcry, higher levels of public and interest group indignation and closer association of an advertiser with the offending program. Advertisers always have been interested in television content, but with recent changes in the industry, they have given greater attention to program elements and themes. On the other hand, programmers have felt the need to keep pace with cable competition, and in the process they more frequently test conventional standards. There have been substantial cuts in standards departments at each network. This has left fewer hands experienced at steering programs toward accepted mainstream tolerances. Finally, there has grown up a cottage industry of network critics that has dogged programmers with media scrutiny and threats of consumer boycotts, both of which have dragged networks and advertisers into the unwanted public spotlight.

Increasingly, networks find themselves in tight spots as they develop audience-rich shows that advertisers desperately need for good demographic exposure, yet understandably fear for provocative potential. When networks successfully run the gamut, they earn premium revenues. When they fail on either side, they stand to lose money and possibly become involved in bitter public disputes. Networks, therefore, spur programmers into a full gallop while holding back on the reins.

Since advertisers pay the bills, they have some right to mandate what is acceptable in network shows, even if only by their decision not to buy time. In fact, nonparticipation may be their chief tool in effecting network programming. Withholding support ranks among three methods by which advertisers influence television content:

- Withholding advertising from a program
- Producing their own shows
- Buying their own network

WITHHOLDING ADVERTISING FROM A PROGRAM

When companies withdraw spots from a program or instruct their agencies to avoid a particular program or program genre, they achieve two effects. They make an immediate impact on the program or program type in question. When one advertiser defects, it casts a pall on that program that affects the perceptions of other advertisers. If a chain reaction occurs, the value of the air time plummets and with it network revenues for the program. Worse, defections force networks to scramble, often at the last minute, for other advertisers willing to fill the spot, the inducement being time at a discount. The scavengers among time buyers know this and run a thriving business for clients with limited ad budgets. Somehow the market usually finds a way.

For networks, their worst-case scenario is when a group of advertisers pulls out of a program. Mass exodus sends up a red flare to image-conscious sponsors and a green flare to the less fastidious. It says, this show is dangerous—stay away or expect bargain basement prices. If replacement advertisers cannot be found, the network must run an alternative program, or it must bear the cost itself. Either way, the network loses.

Despite the immediate punishment inflicted by advertiser withdrawal, the long-term fallout affects not only the networks but also the viewers. How often can a network submit programming that meets with such negative advertiser response? Since networks are in the business to sell air time, there will be considerable pressure to search and destroy the offensive elements that have provoked advertisers. In the long run networks are likely to establish policies that align program content with advertiser wishes.

Recent industry events are a case in point. Taking aim at Fox's "Married with Children," Michigan housewife Terry Rakolta conducted a one-woman crusade and made her fame in a heated letter-writing campaign to advertisers. Rakolta complained about the sexual content of the program and threatened to boycott its sponsors. Within days of receiving her letter several companies agreed to reevaluate their participation in the show. Tambrands, one of the advertisers, said in a letter to Rakolta that it is "continually reviewing editorial content of our advertising, and upon further review of "Married with Children," we have canceled our participation . . ." (Walley, 1989). Kimberly-Clark and Procter & Gamble also pulled out. The defections were troubling except for one thing: "Married . . ." increased its ratings and replaced its sponsor support.

"Saturday Night Live," NBC's free-wheeling late-night program, always at the leading edge of content exploration because of its more permissive adult audience and innovative staff, has been dropped by General Mills and Ralston Purina. The triggering offense was a short skit in which the actors attempted to see how many times they could say "penis" on network television. Ralston Purina said it felt such programming "crossed over the line of good taste." The defection cost NBC more than $1 million ("Protests get Saturday Night Live ads pulled," *New York Post*, 1989).

A relatively new genre of programming known as "tabloid TV," or "trash TV" has met with audience ratings successes but failed advertiser content tests. Twenty-four national advertisers, who collectively spend more than $2 billion annually, have decided to boycott sponsorship of "A Current Affair," "Inside Edition" and "Hard Copy." The industry calls this the "Hit List." According to one buyer for several major advertisers,

> The tabloid magazines on the air are so geared to getting an audience through sensationalism that it's almost a waste of time to try to screen every show to find an episode that won't be offensive to one of my clients. I buy syndication mostly as a supplement to network buys, so my attitude is: Why bother? I just don't need the grief. ("24 Advertisers Boycott 'Affairs,' 'Edition,' 'Copy,' " *Variety*, 1990)

In this case advertisers have repudiated an entire program genre for its unacceptable content. With such unified advertiser assault these programs can rarely succeed without a major content overhaul or economic salvation by other advertisers willing to take on the inevitable interest group harassment.

Ironically, the viewers of these shows do not hold sponsors responsible for the alleged excesses. The authors, working as consultant to Twentieth Century Fox, surveyed a national sample of viewers of "A Current Affair" and reported that no one was so offended as to call a sponsor. None changed brands, even if angry. So much for commercial umbrage. Thanks to the "Hit List," the tabloids get less prestigious sponsors.

Other sponsors have pulled out of programs that did not recover their losses. Chrysler and Sears withdrew sponsorship from "Nightingales," a program that offended nurses in unprofessional positions. The "Log Line," bragged about nurses in tight uniforms and the air conditioning failed! The Mennen Company abandoned "Heartbeat" after hearing complaints about an episode discussing prostitutes having abortions. "Crimes of Passion II," an ABC sequel, could find no sponsors and was killed even before it was penciled into the programming log. "It happened because there is a sensitivity on the part of advertisers to programs of this nature. That's clear, that's obvious and that's growing," explained Ted Harbert, senior vice president of programming for ABC ("A Shock to 'Shock' TV," *Washington Post*, 1989). He might have added that made-for-TV movies and specials, being one-shot affairs, are more vulnerable than series that develop loyal audiences. Indeed, once a viewer commits to a show and buys into its characters, s/he will tolerate small offenses before switching.

NBC experienced difficulty over a made-for-TV movie, *Roe v. Wade*, not because of tastelessness but because of the program's theme. The Reverend Donald Wildmon sent letters to some five hundred advertisers expressing his displeasure with the subject and brought national attention to the program. NBC pleaded with advertisers to stay with the show, and as an inducement for participation lowered the price of air time. Even with the discounts many advertisers avoided the program altogether, and NBC lost close to $1 million ("The Missionary's Position," *Manhattan, Inc.*, July 1989).

Still, in defiance of the natural law of programming, "Saturday Night Live" continued to enjoy public and commercial support. Jon Mandel, vice president of national broadcast for Grey Advertising, Inc., said, "I have clients who are staying in and clients who pulled out. . . . It happens to be good, quality television, but it's a subject matter that hits a fuse, and it will probably upset both sides" ("Screeners Help Advertisers," *New York Times*, 1989).

Even "good, quality programming" dealing responsibly with controversial subject matter gets hit hard when interest group pressures threaten jittery advertisers. Steve Leff, vice chairman of the Backer Spielvogel Bates advertising agency, said, "There's a saying in this business: 'When in doubt, get out' " ("Screeners Help Advertisers," *New York Times*, 1989). This is underscored by General Motors Corporation's Buick Division Assistant Ad Manager Sue Yahr, who described her company's policy: "If it's borderline, we pull out" (Walley, 1989). So much for giving the benefit of the doubt to creative efforts and innovative programming. On the other hand, why should advertisers pay to jeopardize their products? Such calls at the margin drive programming ever closer to a dead center—as defined by vocal interest groups.

Many advertisers have established recent policies that deal uniformly with programming material. If network programs fail to measure up, there now are alternatives in cable and other innovative programming technologies to which advertisers can turn. Rigid guidelines may take the guesswork out of programming decisions, but they also ensure a consistency, predictability and blandness that will work against imaginative uses of the medium. Audiences may have "safety" in viewing but not the creativeness and experimentation audiences have sometimes known during the past forty years.

What worries the creative community is the prospect for television content in the face of an industry-wide adoption and strict interpretation of policies such as these Kodak "Guidelines for Television Program Acceptance":

> Kodak's corporate reputation is a most important company asset. It has been established by consistently providing quality products to our customers and consumers all over the world. With such a reputation, we desire to place our advertising messages in quality media. We take this position because the environment is critical to the perception of the advertising in which it runs. Therefore, with respect to broadcast programs available to be prescreened, Kodak/Sterling agencies are instructed to prescreen all prime-time programs. . . . The agency will alert Kodak when any of the conditions detailed below are contained in the program carrying Kodak messages. If upon review by Kodak and/or Sterling advertising services personnel, the program is deemed unacceptable to carry the Kodak/Sterling message, the agency will be so notified and the network will be asked to remove the commercial from the program.

> 1. The principal theme of the program relies on sexual, violent, or profane behavior and/or language without public censure and retribution.
> 2. Minors are used as pivotal characters to advance a storyline of sex, violence, perversity, or greed.
> 3. Members of the clergy (ministers, priests, rabbis, nuns, etc.) are portrayed in a manner that clearly denigrates or satirizes their position.

4. Controversial social issues, e.g., prostitution, incest, wife-beating, alcoholism, drug abuse, etc., are treated in a gratuitous, glamorized, or simplistic manner without regard for the general public morality.
5. Individual scenes portray excessive or gratuitous sex, violence, and/or profanity used for shock value and not necessary to the basic storyline.
6. Individual scenes are in some way antithetical to a Kodak or Sterling brand, e.g., film used (implied or actual) to record scenes of questionable taste . . .[14]

Interest groups, and, in many cases, unallied viewers upset over programming content, have struck a raw nerve with advertisers. They have threatened company images and triggered chain reactions that ultimately affect programming for all. As we have seen, advertisers respond seriously to these threats. They often do so out of proportion to the size of the challenge. In the Rakolta case, a few letters from an articulate viewer in Michigan were sufficient to stimulate advertising defections from Fortune 500 companies.

During the past few years, the squeaky wheels have gotten the grease. Networks have heard the complaints, directly and through advertisers, and they have begun to impose restraints on programmers consistent with advertiser demands. Compared to the notorious, envelope-pushing, outlaw seasons of the late 1980s when networks blessed the risky and daring audience grabbers, shows now, at least temporarily, are being pushed back toward the safe center. Some are steering clear of content that involves depictions of sex and violence and the use of strong language. Themes are becoming less provocative, and controversy of all sorts is becoming scarcer. A phrase making its way around television circles is "advertiser-friendly shows." Cynics with a sense of history might be pardoned for observing that such pull-backs always have been temporary, part of the network tactics of two steps forward (e.g., 1988) and one step back (e.g., 1989) and then three steps forward (e.g., 1990, 1991). And bear in mind that independent producers, who are once removed from Madison Avenue, are busily pushing the boundaries to hook the baby-boomers.

Reality-based shows, specializing in sexy, gore-laden recreations, have toned down, at least temporarily. Paul Siegel, president of LBS Entertainment Inc., sees advertiser complaints bringing about a softening. Siegel says programmers will reduce graphic reenactments that have offended some viewers. Additionally, he predicts a change from themes of physical violence and action to those like fraud and scams. For these programs, Siegel said he had no trouble getting advertiser support (" 'Reality' TV Shows Continue to Spread Despite Critics and Nervous Advertisers," *Wall Street Journal*, May 1989). Well, we shall see.

Opponents of advertiser control are concerned not only that advertisers will impose their views on program content, but that the networks, in anticipation of the pressure, will wield a sharper axe themselves. Such long-term effects of advertiser control are more insidious because they presuppose an opposition that may or may not ensue. By anticipating contentions, the networks are likely to become even more restrictive than their concerned advertisers. Producer Michael Jacobs fears that trimming program edges "leads to boring and boring means we're back to the great wasteland." This concern may not be ill-founded given recent examples of network controls. Meanwhile, a chill from New York often produces a deep freeze in Hollywood where producers, despite cries of censorship, sometimes knuckle under to the buyers' demands.

There is evidence of network concerns — call it censorship or quality control — not as a general standards matter but to head off advertiser protests. An article in the *New York Times* discussed the network position on the matter:

> In trying to drain television programs of any hint of propaganda, the censors are trying to forestall press criticism as well as protests from pressure groups who frequently complain about biased programming. These groups have a strong weapon: a threatened boycott of products that advertise on a controversial program. Sometimes advertisers, anticipating controversy, take it upon themselves to cancel commercials. . . . The network censors freely admit that loss of advertising revenue is one of their concerns when they require a balance of presentation of any controversial social issue ("They Watch What We Watch," *New York Times Magazine*, May 1989).

Advertisers have responded to the challenges and pressures they perceive as threatening to their corporate image. With increased sophistication of interest groups, and a viewer corps sensitized to the issue of program content, advertisers are seeking the safety of programs whose content and themes provide a shelter from criticism. The costs to a company in terms of sales and image rehabilitation have become too great. At least the potential for higher costs is seen as great, and in today's conservative corporate milieu, no more than a perception of such a threat is enough to send advertisers packing.

The networks have gotten the message. They have issued orders to producers and remaining fragments of their standards staff to tone down the content that has so angered the bill payers. In part this reaction may be because of the network's notorious late-eighties season excesses. As they sought to trample the cable competition and cling to their supremacy in the television market, they abandoned their usual standards and encouraged producers to employ less restrained cable approaches to programming. This ill-advised, desperate attempt failed not only to slow the movement of viewers to cable and alternative program vehicles, but it also created a climate in which interest group critics grew. As a result, in the 1990s networks are dealing from a weaker position. Cable has continued to siphon network audiences, interest groups grew stronger, viewers are more critical, advertisers are more nervous and programming elements that once may have slipped by unnoticed now trip the content alarms. Parodoxically, the result of all this — advertising and network pressure together with declining ratings — has been the blanding of most shows and the sensationalizing of some shows.

How long or how far this will go is anybody's guess. The industry is in a great state of flux as advertisers, viewers, networks and cable companies come to terms with the vast expansion of programming options. Confusion is everywhere. The deck is shuffled and nobody knows if aces are high or low. Will nudity win or lose? Will shock scenes draw youth but spook sponsors? New stations enter the programming mix, and audiences are reapportioned among the programmers according to an unknown formula. As we will describe in chapter 9, new cable stations are carving out audience niches to draw viewers with special interests and needs, leaving the networks to decide for themselves how they will retain an audience base adequate to attract large advertising dollars. These natural market pressures have caught the networks by surprise. Their response to advertisers so far has been compliant and accommodating. They appear to be at the end of a pendulum that is bouncing off both walls.

Some interest group watchdogs see advertisers as new underwriters of quality. Direct petitions to the networks have had little effect on programming decisions until the threats were joined with the power of interest groups to attract press attention and deliver real damage to corporate images. This two-step process, therefore, has proven demonstrably successful from the interest group perspective. Pulling advertisements and the threat to pull advertisements have brought about a considerable level of advertiser control of television content.

ADVERTISERS PRODUCE THEIR OWN SHOWS

An old idea in the industry is coming around for the second time: advertiser-produced programs. As we discussed at the beginning of this chapter, during the earliest days of radio, advertisers supplied programs and networks supplied the air time. Television then inherited this comfortable single-sponsorship approach, which served it reasonably well through much of its "Golden Years." In the late 1950s, scandals, production costs and the increasing value of air time altered this relationship as advertisers bought spot messages and networks assumed the primary role in program development.[15]

Conditions that brought about the end of advertiser programming have changed. The quiz-show scandals that attracted national attention and inflicted public shame on the industry have long faded from public memory. There have been no recent suggestions of impropriety in network productions or in syndicated programs that serve as the primary source of quiz shows. Networks have been vigilant in maintaining rigid standards for such productions. Syndicators, mindful of the heavy costs paid in the 1950s, have certified the integrity of their programs. Advertisers have stayed out of this programming for the past thirty years and so carry no such unwanted baggage into the 1990s.

The once prohibitive production costs and the increased value of air time have not improved for advertiser-producers so much as have related regulatory and economic conditions. Federal regulations that limit networks from selling programs for syndication benefit producers who may earn a substantial profit on the "back end."

Theoretically it works this way: A producer sells a program to the networks that pay the producer enough to cover production costs. This provides the networks with programming and the producers with a forum for their shows. While a sale to the networks is a plum for any producer, the reality of license fees is painfully different: studios are lucky if network contributions come anywhere near production costs; usually they cover 80 to 90 percent, sometimes less. Today, only producers of older hits such as "Cheers" can renegotiate license fees that truly cover expenses. Producers make real money only by syndicating their material to broadcast and cable stations, and that takes several seasons.[16]

Since the heaviest production costs already have been paid by networks during the original airing, syndication sales offer producers a low-cost, high-profit opportunity. Mega-hits like "M*A*S*H," "Andy Griffith," and the omnipresent "I Love Lucy" run over and over again, snowballing producer and syndicate earnings with every airing. Today, with so many more independent stations and cable channels gobbling up programming material, there is a much larger market for network shows, and thus even more money on the table. Suppliers gamble on hits that will make it to the syndication market. But as Grant Tinker remarked about the TV "non-business," producers can "deficit" a show for $200,000 per week and end up taking a bath if the show is canceled after a season or two.

Producers were not always in a position to capitalize on program syndication. Prior to 1971, the networks participated substantively in the development of programs. They produced them, aired them, then syndicated them, thus exercising complete cradle-to-grave control of the airtight vertical system. Although networks rightly claim that independents subcontracted 90 percent of primetime, they can't deny that suppliers were forced to accept deals advantageous to the Big Three broadcasters. They do that only to a limited degree today. Such creative and business control was seen to have the ills of a monopoly: product uniformity and an insurmountable barrier to market entry by other producers even though the networks never produced the bulk of their own shows.

The Federal Communication Commission issued its "financial interest and network syndication rules" (fin-syn rules) in 1971, which changed the formula in favor of producers. Essentially, the FCC said the networks could not own part or all of the programs aired (except three hours per week—expanded to five hours in 1988), nor could they become involved in the syndication of programs. In effect, networks bought the right to run the show twice, after which all rights reverted to the supplier. At the same time the FCC issued the "prime time access rule" that, for the largest fifty markets, prohibited stations from carrying network programming in the first hour of the former primetime block,[17] which extended from 7 P.M. to 11 P.M. The intention was to induce development of local programming; the effect was to create a ready market for syndicated material. The 7 to 8 P.M. time slot made billions for syndicators, especially the game show producers.

After so many futile attempts to rid themselves of the heavy fin-syn yoke, the networks found just a little relief from an FCC ruling in the spring of 1991. Although they expected—or at least hoped for—a lot more, the ruling allowed networks to produce "in-house" up to 40 percent of primetime programs, to participate in foreign syndication, and to ally with studio partners in domestic syndication. These were lightweight concessions, compared to the two-ton anvil that remained: the networks still were not allowed to engage unimpeded in first-run syndication activities, and thus were deprived of the considerable revenue available in syndication (FCC 91-336).[18]

But the last line is not yet written on network regulations. FCC Chairman Alfred C. Sikes became a strong advocate of further industry deregulation and proposed a sweeping plan to erase many of the current restrictions. New services, delivery mechanisms and programming options, he said, are changing the industry more rapidly than anyone would have imagined just a few years ago. Sikes argued that new conditions merit a change of the rules to allow market forces to operate without government impediments (Farhil, 1992).

Since advertisers discontinued most of their program production during the 1950s, the ground rules have changed. At least for now, program producers, not networks, stand to benefit financially from syndication. Advertisers who produce their own shows would be in a position to market their material after its initial airing. Reruns of a typical, long-airing sitcom can earn more than $100 million (Grover, 1990). Advertiser-producers also can take advantage of an expanding foreign market for U.S. programming. In addition to the usual customers, radical changes in the former Soviet Union, Eastern Europe, Africa and Latin America may open markets not dreamed of just a few years ago. In 1990 the European market, just beginning to free up because of the abolition of state-run monopolies, is expected to spend more than $1 billion on American-made shows (Grover, 1990).

From the advertiser's viewpoint, then, program production may not be the costly venture it once was; it now may represent a substantial source of revenue. Moreover, with widespread corporate diversification, thoughts of engaging in profitable sidelines are not so alien.

In addition to financial inducements, advertisers are becoming increasingly more interested in program production because it gives them creative control over content. If they commission the scripts, they can avoid the assaults of interest groups. Furthermore, they might be able to build subtle but effective advertising messages into the program. David Braun, director of media and promotion services at General Foods, which produces movies in the General Foods Golden Showcase, says, "Producing our own shows gives us a better chance to showcase our brands and also have control over the program" (Fanning, 1989).

Most recently, Chrysler, AT&T, Campbell Soup and Procter & Gamble (which always produced soap operas) have gotten into the production business. These companies coincidentally have pulled back from conventional spot advertising — some because of direct interest group pressures, some because of internal policies to avoid controversial content and themes.

Advertiser-developed programs deal quietly with centrist themes. A Campbell Soup production dealt with the quiescent story of Jessica McClure, the toddler who fell into a Texas well. General Foods Golden Showcase programs develop themes that could offend no one. If these early installments foretell the future of advertiser programming, viewers cannot expect much in the way of innovative themes or provocative treatments.

The pressure is on these advertisers to make conservative judgments. They cannot afford to venture over the line drawn by interest groups because as sole sponsors, the show is clearly their production and theirs alone. They have no wiggle room to escape the clutches of critics who may be offended. It would be foolish for an advertiser to spend the energy on production then to be condemned as the sole author of an objectionable work. An increase in the popularity of advertiser productions probably means an increase in the banality of television content, the Hallmark Playhouse and Mobil Oil's Masterpiece Theater notwithstanding.

Resistance to sole sponsorship, suggested earlier, is twofold: First, the best demographics can be attained only by spraying one's spots across several programs appealing to a variety of audiences. Second, only a handful of companies can afford to sponsor the same show week after week.

CREATION OF ADVERTISER NETWORKS

If you don't like the hand you're being dealt, with enough money, you can buy the casino — or open your own down the street. Buying a network — the definitive answer to advertiser image woes — is a serious undertaking but not as unrealistic as it initially might seem. While content problems with networks may provide one reason for some advertisers to consider hanging out their own shingles, there are other motivations to do so.

First, because of financial incentives, cable has been spawning new networks for the past dozen years. Nielsen now measures twenty-one cable networks with its People Meter system ("Nielsen Media News," 1990). New programmers typically appeal to a specialized market segment. Cable News Network, The Discovery Channel, The Nashville Network and The Total Sports Network target audience niches. Turner Broadcasting, HBO, Cinemax and Fox demonstrate the potential for success with more generalized programming. Much of the erosion in Big Three audiences is not because of a decline in network programming as some critics would suggest (and as some in the industry believe), but because there is an expanded assortment of alternative stations from which to choose. With the correct blend of programs or segmentation of audience subgroups, new broadcasters can find room in the industry. There is no reason an advertiser consortium could not compete successfully with the networks and with others in the business.

While cable has made feasible the addition of new programmers, changes in corporate structures have made the activity a logical economic consideration. Large corporations increasingly are becoming amalgamations of many companies. Corporations have become wheels within a wheel, manufacturing wide assortments of products and performing services that have little in common. In such an environment it is not unreasonable for corporations to consider involvement in the formation of yet another enterprise — a new network, one controlled according to the rules laid out by image-sensitive backers.

Although there are no blueprints on the table, just a few years back a consortium of advertisers discussed the development of just such a network. Burt Manning, chairman and chief executive of J. Walter Thompson, "told a convention of the Association of National Advertisers that frustrated agency clients are mulling the creation of a new television network backed by the nation's one hundred largest companies."[19] The idea is still alive.

The bombshell resignation of Fox's CEO, Barry Diller, in February 1992, has set off a spate of buying rumors. Diller, who pioneered the Movie-of-the-Week genre while at ABC-TV, says he wants to own the shop, not work for Rupert Murdock. Time-Warner and Disney, to say nothing of foreigner entrepreneurs, are listening.

Whether or not the concept of advertiser-owners materializes, on the surface it appears that it would give advertisers the greatest control possible over content. If these advertisers have been burned by controversial network programming or simply want to avoid guilt by association, they can as owners prescribe a formula that locks out offensive programming. They can promote their own products in the context of the shows, and they can determine what other companies, if any, may be permitted to buy advertising time.[20] They could have that cradle-to-grave control now denied the Big Four.

This is an interesting concept, but assuming such a venture is based on a desire to escape from network failings, rather than on a demonstrated audience need for spotless programming, we believe it will fail for these reasons. If an ad-network were to come about, it would be operating in the same environment as ABC, NBC, CBS and their growing competitor, Fox. It would be subject to the same audience rating pressures, to the same need to sell advertising time (even to its owners) and ironically to the same interest group scrutiny that has motivated formation of such a network in the first place.

How would the owners react if safe themes and quiet treatments, void of objectionable material, failed to attract audiences of sufficient size to support the new enterprise? Would "G" be the kiss of death as it is in motion pictures? Would they reevaluate their programming philosophy? If they should decide to open the door a bit wider to some of the proscribed material, wouldn't they be subject to serious challenge, not just as sponsors of a program, but now as owners of the network?

If so, they would suffer double blows. First, they would have to subsidize production costs themselves. Lower audience ratings mean lower advertiser participation and someone must pay the bills. Second, owner companies would not receive the audience exposure they need to maintain the market positions of their nonnetwork operations. Advertising successfully promotes products if it reaches potential buyers. When no one watches, no one can be motivated to buy. The slipping network would drain the member companies, and the low audience participation would deprive them of necessary exposure.

Could these companies hedge their bets by buying time on the Big Three? Maybe so, but that would admit a problem in paradise and cost money needed for the advertiser network. Nor is that the worst of it. Back on the networks, the advertisers would be where they were before their breakaway venture – under the gun from the same irritating interest groups who once linked them with controversial content.

We've built a worst-case scenario. What are the chances of such a start-up network succeeding? After all, with one hundred of the biggest television advertisers sponsoring the enterprise, it would have the capital necessary to get it off the ground in a big way. Big money, big talent, big promotion — all would be possible with the backing of such enormous resources.

We have to remind ourselves that we are talking about a network, not simply a few random programs distributed in a monthly lineup. All the shows might be squeaky clean, and they might receive the seal of good housekeeping from every interest group in the country. They might attract hard-core viewers in search of sanitized programming, and with their novelties they might draw the curiosity seekers. But could they attract sufficiently large audiences?

The problem lies in the nature of the programming. Despite some bad press and complaints from several quarters, something in the network formula appeals to American viewers. Network power has eroded, but the Big Three Plus One still are giants. Their programming formulas consistently draw immense audiences. We do not see the great outcry against network programming where it matters — in mass audience defections. We see audience movement among the variety of new stations but not large-scale desertion from the networks. We would be surprised if an alternative network carving out its niche with disinfected programming would have the substantial audience draw and holding power of the four.

This brings us back to the exposure and promotional needs of member companies. Small cable networks are successful because they can attract selected audiences of sufficient size to sustain them. Many make nice profits. The one hundred biggest advertisers, however, require the biggest audiences. They cannot meet their need for consumer exposure on tiny cable-sized audience fragments. Even if an advertiser network survived with a reasonable audience base, it probably would not deliver the large number of viewers necessary to form an adequate viewer base for its advertising. So the new networks might draw a profitable audience, but the participating advertisers would not find the massive exposure they require for their other enterprises. Under current network conditions, advertisers receive millions of exposures daily. Makers of popular commercial products require such visibility. They need lots of viewers, lots of messages, lots of repetition to drive home the message. Would the proposed network support this formula? Could the companies get by without supplemental advertising on the Big Three or on other high-volume programming vehicles?

We see little possibility of success for an advertiser-sponsored network designed to provide a safe harbor for large corporations seeking relief from network content problems. These advertisers would be forced to break out of their gilded cage in order to achieve the exposure necessary for the sale of their goods and services. The lesson in all of this is clear: the advertisers and the networks are still in this together despite the pots and pans that fly every now and then in their lively marriage. The industry is not ready for a radically different arrangement, much less a divorce. In time—particularly if Congress should update the Communications Act as perennially threatened—it might, but for the next decade, there will be a mutual dependency between major advertisers and the major networks.

THE IMPACT OF INTEREST GROUPS

For a full description of interest groups, their emergence and relative powers, see chapter 6. For their advertiser impact, we offer a few summary comments.

For the moment the networks are still the biggest and most visible kids on the block. Advertisers are still locked in a struggle. Corporations want the large network audiences, but they fear some viewer-pleasing programs will render costly image damage. Recent success in bringing advertisers and networks to heel has emboldened interest groups. Without the pressure of these groups it is unlikely the advertisers would care much about content beyond the audiences it attracts or bother to exert much control over it. When we discuss advertiser control over content, then, we must recognize that the impetus for control does not come from within the company as much as from outside groups that have learned how mice somehow frighten elephants.

In this context, then, a discussion of advertisers' content intervention must include comment on the vocal interest groups that stimulate advertiser concerns.[21] There are several groups that monitor television programs and apply pressure to sponsors of "offending" shows. Many have fundamentalist affiliations and apply a rigid set of rules in program assessments. The groups come and go, but one has been around for a few years and has received a lot of press attention: CLeaR-TV. We will examine this organization as a case study of high-pressure interest groups.

The Reverend Donald Wildmon, founder and head of CLeaR-TV, has developed a television monitoring system that reports the number of "offensive" incidents per show and identifies advertisers and networks most associated with "offensive programs." His media hype promotes this content review process as though it were legitimate research. Wildmon, however, is not a researcher but a public relations practitioner. Honing his PR skills over his research skills has been more successful in obtaining national attention and feeding the coffers of his $5 million-a-year operation ("The Missionary's Position," *Manhattan, Inc.*, 1989).

Wildmon uses a variety of techniques to dissuade advertisers from supporting programs he deems offensive. He has access to a large fundamentalist network of churches that serve as the foundation for national boycotts—or threats of boycotts. He also has learned how to get press attention for his crusades against advertisers. Even though much of the ink tells Wildmon's story tongue-in-cheek, the man is successful in kicking up the dust advertisers most fear will soil their images. For Wildmon's purposes, any press is good press. As a testament to his success, some of his recent efforts have required no more than a letter on CLeaR-TV stationery to frighten advertisers into submission.[22]

Advertiser responses to such tactics contrast reality against perception. Do Wildmon and similar critics speak for themselves and, perhaps, a small contingent of followers, or do their concerns reflect the outlook of many American viewers? Is Donald Wildmon a Wizard of Oz—an illusion created by a small man with a big voice—or is there real substance in his threats?

The answer depends on your viewpoint. Wildmon's constituency base is minuscule. His ability to organize an effective, economically bruising boycott against a nationally ranked corporation is negligible. From this perspective the answer is no. Early successes with advertisers, however, have generated a widespread perception of a threat with some substance. In such perceptions one finds a perverse reality. Wildmon's powers are as ephemeral as a corporate image. The contest is thus illusion versus mirage. Will the projection of a threat be sufficient to convince an advertiser of inevitable stains on its image? Evidence suggests the answer is yes.

In such an ephemeral world of impressions and images, it takes no more than the perception of substance to yield results. As we have seen throughout this chapter, corporations hearing the loud voice have envisioned a giant behind the screen and so have applied pressure to networks. Advertising executive Aaron Cohen with Ayers Agency in New York told us he believes Wildmon's skills at drawing press interest have enabled him to project a larger-than-life image. "He has received press attention out of proportion to his importance, and this has given him a power with the networks he otherwise would not have."

As a general policy—whether toward Action for Children's Television or Accuracy in Media—standards editors were ordering daily content changes long before Wildmon or any of the watchdogs began to howl. The networks have conceded the economic reality of effects on image. For their part, advertisers have brought about content changes that could not be rendered by the government, viewers or even the interest groups acting alone. In this sense, advertisers' pressures on the networks have provided the amplification and focus of power necessary for interest group successes.

Despite any objections to CLeaR-TV's approach, polls suggest some public support for interest group strategies. In a 1989 survey among 500 adult Americans, Oxtoby-Smith, which services the advertising industry, said, "Most Americans not only support the actions of companies that remove advertisements from 'objectionable' television shows but also favor the idea of boycotting companies that continue to advertise on those shows" ("Screeners Help Advertisers," *New York Times*, 1989).

The consumer research firm reported the following specific findings:

- 68 percent of the viewers said "it was a good idea for advertisers to stop advertising in programs some viewers found 'objectionable.' "

- 72 percent said "it was a good idea for consumers not to buy products of advertisers in programs they found objectionable."

- 49 percent said "the amount of objectionable material on television these days bothers me a lot."

- viewers between the ages of 18 and 45 were less likely to be "bothered a lot."

- 25 percent of the viewers thought "the Government should make it illegal to show objectionable material on television." ("Screeners Help Advertisers," *New York Times*, 1989)

We could dismiss these results by saying the sample size was small (it has an error margin of approximately $+/-5$ percent at the 95 percent confidence level), and the wording is somewhat misleading, but at the heart of the study there is a truth worth noting: people favor someone watching over television content. This was confirmed more recently in a 1990 *Parents Magazine* poll that found 66 percent favored standards prohibiting the airing of certain material. The study listed a series of content categories that large portions of its sample agreed should be censored.[23]

Networks, once the guardian of their own material through rigorous standards departments, are now in danger of relinquishing the responsibility to others eager to do the job in the public spotlight. For the moment, interest groups prying the lever of advertiser fears have imposed some of their judgments on the networks and on viewers. This arrangement, in theory, may be acceptable to many viewers, but its long-term implications are dangerous and in opposition to the principles of a free society. The content of television is best left as a negotiable matter directly between the networks and their viewers. An axe-wielding values broker does not serve well the free marketplace of ideas. *Time* magazine writers Mary Cronin and Naustad S. Mehta say: "Advertiser boycotts, if successful, do not make TV better, only blander. They also reveal a remarkable lack of faith in the ability of viewers to lodge the ultimate protest: turning off the set" ("Putting a Brake on TV 'Sleaze,' " *Time*, March 1989).

Down the line where programs are made, writer-producers and programmers factor in the advertising sensitivities if they want to be successful. Automatically, they self-censor with the buyers in mind, even if the effort is subconscious. While it is doubtful if producers Steven Bochco or Bill D'Angelo have ever encountered a man in a gray flannel suit on the set representing P&G, they are aware that the president of the entertainment division has to keep these people happy. Programmers are instructed to tell producers to stay off the hit list of top 100 advertisers. The trouble is, they speak with a forked tongue. They ask for more sex and violence in the vain hope that this is pushing the envelope for those addicted to pay cable while reprimanding producers whenever there is sponsor resistance. As far as original concepts go, you can count on one thing: Nobody in Hollywood's courageous creative community has ever walked into a network with an idea for the Ralph Nader Story, narrated by the author of *Roger and Me*.

NOTES

1. Quoted in an editorial by Les Line, "Intimidation," *Audubon*, 91(6), November 1989.

2. Dr. Frank Stanton, for instance, told the president of the United States and the Congress that the "Making of the Pentagon" would air unedited; ABC resisted all pressures on "Red Autumn"; and NBC stood tall for "Martin Luther King."

3. This policy was articulated in a 1971 memo by Nixon's director of the Office of Telecommunications Policy, Clay Whitehead: "We stand to gain substantially from an increase in the relative power of the local stations. They are generally less liberal and more concerned with education than with controversial national affairs. Further, a decentralized system would have far less influence and be far less attractive to social activists. . . ." Quoted by Les Brown, "Files of Nixon White House Show Bid to Control Public Broadcasting," *New York Times*, February 24, 1979, pp. 1, 9.

4. The "sleepy viewer" concept of broadcasting states that product promotions are most effective among viewers not aroused to emotional highs. A mildly passive audience will be most receptive to commercial pitches.

5. "Advertiser Information Services" dominate the program review market.

6. The exception is the countervailing force represented by time-buyers who scatter their ads across the demographic spectrum, taking no account of program content.

7. For details of this account see F.L. Smith, *Perspectives on Radio and Television* (New York: Harper & Row, 1985).

8. See a review of television regulations in chapter 10.

9. Some economists argue that advertising, by stimulating consumption, reduces costs to the consumer and contributes to the efficiency of the marketplace. For instance, if Crest can promote substantial consumption of its toothpaste, it can lower production and distribution costs per unit and thereby offer its product at a lower price.

10. The smaller viewer base effectively would have reduced the number of programmers. Such a funding method would have become a serious drag on the development of the medium.

11. Clio Awards were the "Academy Awards" of television advertisements. Each year, the Clio board, comprised of advertising executives, selected the most creative and well-produced advertisements. The Clios suffered a financial collapse in the late 1980s. Several advertising executives now are attempting to form the "New Clio Awards," and are seeking financial backing.

12. P&G lawyers took action against a Florida couple for spreading the rumor throughout the fundamentalist community, but the rumor persisted.

13. The NBC miniseries "Jesus of Nazareth" was a cause celebre in the late seventies, but Pasolini's more radical version, both in theatrical release and on television, caused not a peep.

14. "Kodak/Sterling Guidelines for Television Program Acceptance," January 1989. Ironically, codes like Kodak's directly increase in proportion to the decreases in network standards control. For more on this see chapter 6 on network influences.

15. The death of former CBS comedian John Henry Faulk, who was blacklisted during the Red Channels controversy in the late 1950s, reminded the industry of another issue. Advertisers proved so timid in the face of McCarthy's threats that networks found it easier to stick to their guns when wrongly pressured. It's less traumatic to lose one thirty-second car spot on "Wiseguy" (especially when you know Ford or General Motors will reposition

that spot) than it is to lose all the advertising done by one sponsor in its own half-hour. Although CBS radio was no braver than other companies, its subsequent leadership under people like Frank Stanton was bold, even cocky.

16. Arthur Price, former head of MTM Enterprises, Inc., says everyone works toward the major figure of sixty-two episodes. Anything short of that takes a long time and overseas sales to generate substantial profits.

17. On the East Coast, for instance, this is between seven and eight P.M.

18. The rule on first-run syndication is as follows: "A network may produce entertainment programming for first-run syndication and retain a financial interest and foreign syndication rights in such programming 'solely produced' in-house. Such programming, however, shall be syndicated domestically only through an independent syndicator. As with our off-network rules, the independent syndicator must be insulated from network influence and its conduct is subject to the same affiliate favoritism safeguards. (FCC, 91-336, November 22, 1991, Sec. VI., Para. 75)

19. Comments described by E. Kalish, "A Surprisingly Good Year for the Masses," *Channels*, January 1990, p. 32.

20. Doubtless this would raise antitrust concerns.

21. For an in-depth analysis of interest group pressures directly on the networks, see chapter 10.

22. Richard Johnson, reporting for the *New York Post*, tells how Wildmon claims "to have gotten two out of three advertisers to pull their spots from 'Saturday Night Live' merely by writing a personal letter." R. Johnson, "New Targets for TV Sex Foes," *New York Post*, April 20, 1989, p. 6.

23. Vulgar four-letter words should not be permitted at any time (74%); ridiculing or making fun of religion (72%); ridiculing or making fun of traditional values, such as marriage or motherhood (64%); scenes that suggest but do not actually show homosexual activity (55%); objective discussion of Satanism (55%). In some cases, censorship is just a matter of timing. If shown only late at night: scenes that suggest but do not actually show sexual activity between adults are acceptable (55%); explicit and graphic depictions of violence (50%). What could get by the censors and be permitted on the air at any time? Mildly profane words, such as "hell" or "damn"; words not ordinarily used publicly, such as "breast" or "condom" (51%). I. Groller, "Should TV Be Censored?" *Parents Magazine*, April 1990, p. 34.

8

Technology and Television Content

People make television programs. Producers and writers, network brass, advertising executives, government officials, interest group members, each contribute to the blend of forces that determine the content of Americans' television. It's easy to show their impact. High-visibility public figures such as Norman Lear, Grant Tinker, Brandon Tartikoff, Timothy Wirth, Newton Minow and others are both forces and symbols. They not only shape the shows but they are emblematic of the professions that shape the shows. It's easy to understand that people influence television content.

It isn't so easy to recognize the influence of silicon chips, optical wires and satellite transmissions. They make programming possible, but do they influence it? Does a canvas influence the painting or does a piano effect the sonata? In a way, yes. Without the canvas there could be no painting and a sonata would be black page-bound dots without a piano. Tools allow the art. New tools allow new art. Humans sweep the brush and stroke the keys, which they could not do without the technology that shaped the brushes and fashioned the keyboards.

Technology opens the way for humans to express their creativity. In that sense the new technologies influence the content of television. Producers, writers, government and media entrepreneurs may have created the new content, but this was possible because the evolution of telecommunication tools allowed it to happen.

In this chapter we will discuss the role of technology in shaping television content throughout the eighties and into the nineties. We do this by contrasting the early days, when audiences had just a handful of programming options, with the current industry offering almost unlimited variety of program selection. This variety of news, sports, sitcoms, dramas, MTV and movies stands up even if thirty-five of forty shows are mediocre fare. The move from famine to feast occurred in just a decade and yet it's hard to remember what it was like to have such a limited program menu from which to choose.

We will look at research that assesses audience use of the new technology, then at the networks straining to hold on in the new environment. We conclude with a few suggestions for network survival in a fiercely competitive market.

BACKGROUND

The shape of the U.S. television industry is the result of an easy and natural melding of two great American passions: the love of technology and the love of television. Americans always have been enamored of technology. Our large industrial base, forged during the first half of this century, was a product of technology. We dominated space through the efforts of American scientists. Fax machines, telephone answering machines, computers, talking cars; anything born of technology is quickly adopted by U.S. consumers. The public eagerly bought into the technology of radio when it first appeared in the early 1920s, and at a glance we were heart-smitten by the sights and sounds of television.[1]

Audience adoption of the innovations discussed here has required little promotion. Viewers have sold themselves on the hardware and they are deciding for themselves how they will use it.

AUDIENCE CHANGES

In contrast to today's viewers, audiences of the past were in a state of dormancy. They could not conveniently switch stations, and even if they could, to what alternatives would they tune their tiny, drab, black-and-white sets? Fortunately, viewers were thrilled to get "moving pictures" at home. And so they sat willingly through annoying scenes and irritating commercials. They changed their channels once a day; those more daring, between programs. Although some shows were live and beautifully done, programming was pretty much the same from station to station. Networks, which provided nearly all of the shows, appealed to the same viewers, used the same formulas and came up with pretty much the same profile of programs.

The homogeneity of programming and the limited number of available channels did not frustrate early viewers. They knew only a handful of stations; why would they expect more? In 1964 only 4 percent of American households could receive nine or more stations. By 1981 this figure increased to 53 percent, and today, with over the air and cable reception, 86 percent of all American homes can tune in nine or more stations; more than half can access thirty or more.

Over-the-air stations continued coming on line during the 1960s and 1970s, but it was not until the late 1970s that programming options expanded dramatically with the introduction of videocassette recorders. Faced with an uncertain fortune at first because of movie industry opposition, video disk competition, format debates[2] and cost, the VCR became sufficiently well recognized as a consumer product in 1980. In this year A.C. Nielsen launched its first usage study (Nielsen, 1980). With recorders costing around $1,000 back then, the 1 to 2 percent of VCR owners tended to be upscale and atypical of the general population.

Consumer sales erupted during the next few years as VHS became the standard, and unit prices dropped to discount-store levels.[3] The proliferation of video rental stores also made available an unprecedented range of programming options. By November 1991, over 73 percent of all U.S. households owned VCRs ("Nielsen Media News," 1992). No longer a privilege of wealth, VCR ownership profiles now almost match demographic norms of the U.S. population, demonstrating the expansion of programming options to all viewers.

The programming repertoire further has expanded with cable, microwave relay, satellite dish and other emerging technologies.[4] For instance, SkyPix began an eighty channel satellite-to-home broadcasting system in the spring of 1992. The company has faltered in the recession, though, and has discontinued operation pending Chapter 11 reorganization (*Communication Daily*, 1992). Thomson Consumer Electronics and General Electric Company say they will launch satellites late in 1993 for DirectTV, a system that will have a 100-channel capacity (Ziegler, 1992). TCI Inc. will market 500 channels in 1994.

At this time, cable clearly is dominant. As of November 1991, more than 61 percent of homes were cable wired (Nielsen, March 5, 1992). They were served by more than 10,704 cable systems operating in some 29,040 communities throughout the United States (*Cable and Television Fact Book*, 1991). According to a General Accounting Office study (1991), the basic service offerings of the average cable station makes available some thirty-six channels to its subscribers, greatly expanding the previous number of programming options. A few dozen channels soon will seem confining as the industry scrambles to increase the number of available programs. For instance, a new cable service from Time Warner offers 150 operating channels. It includes two different Cinemax and three HBO channels, and entire channels in Greek, Hindi, Korean, Cantonese and Mandarin, along with programs in other languages. It offers the standard fare along with a channels for prayer, college-level courses, big bands and a wide assortment of other special interests. Tests indicate viewers are not overwhelmed by the vast selection; they quickly adapt to the expanded menu (Span, 1992). In just over a decade, the television industry has undergone a monumental change. Through VCRs and now cable, American viewers (and viewers in nearly all other developed countries as well) are acquiring access to an enormous selection of programs, and the end is not in sight.

Remote-control devices made it easier to sample the expanding array of programming. The infrared version, refined for commercial application in the late 1970s, has provided an integral component allowing television audiences to use the medium's many channels.[5] Through the purchase of remote control–equipped television sets, VCRs and retrofitting hardware, about three-quarter of American homes now have the capacity to change channels from across the room (Nielsen, 1992).

Split-screen and window innovations are the most recent advances in consumer television hardware. Although features differ by brand and function, they all allow viewers to position two or more programs on the screen simultaneously. The program of primary interest appears on the main screen while other selected channels are displayed on peripheral, smaller "window" screens. With a remote control, viewers instantly can replace the main program with any of the window programs.[6]

Window viewing accommodates grazing—hopscotching among channels—while reducing the need to explore each channel individually. It obliges viewers who want to monitor several programs simultaneously without abandoning a favorite program. The active and integrated use of all these technologies will allow Olympic-class grazers to monitor several programs while simultaneously zapping through others on the array of peripheral windows. This is the stuff of nightmares.

Although talk of High Definition Television (HDTV) has been around for a while, only recently has the technology become commercially available. Mexico has a HDTV broadcast facility in operation and Japan came on line with one late in 1991. The advantage of HDTV is a crystalline image, looking more like a fine print than the sand drawings of conventional television. The disadvantage is the extraordinary cost. Sets are priced above $5,000 and some well above $10,000. There also are few stations with programs to grace those wonderful screens. As with all communication technologies, prices will drop over time, program availability will increase, and consumers will jump in foursquare to support the new systems. The common use of a superior technology can only increase programming possibilities and impose yet other pressures on television content. Again, technology will affect what we watch.

This recent rush of consumer products enables audiences to access a significantly greater number of programming options and to select among them conveniently. Together these features have revolutionized the way people use television and consequently have imposed new demands on the industry. Viewers no longer settle in with a single channel for the evening. They sample among many, monitoring the progress of two or more at the same time. Increasingly, programming decisions will be driven by hardware options placed in the hands of viewers. Pandora's box is open. New devices, the likes of which we can only imagine, will continue to change viewing patterns and so programming approaches, availability and, no doubt, content. It is a safe bet we have not seen the end of "tech change."

The effects of channel proliferation on the selection of television content are like the effects of new restaurants on the selection of cuisine. Each new outlet attempts to carve for itself a unique segment from the general market and in the process expands the range of options. For restaurants the clientele are wooed by specialty menus and ethnic food choices. For television, audiences are romanced with special-appeal programs that draw in clusters of the viewing audience—sports fans, news buffs, do-it-yourselfers, youth audiences. In the process—with restaurants and television—consumers enjoy a greater range of choices. Moreover, specialty chefs and programmers alike have a chance to display their talents. In television, subject matter, topic treatments, and production styles that may not have made it to the screen when only a handful of channels existed, can now, when channels number in the dozens, find an outlet and an audience. This encourages experimentation and yields many more choices. Quality is another matter.

MEDIA EVOLUTION

The mass media evolve in stages. Most start out with a few available channels around which all audiences gather. A few early radio stations attracted all the radio audiences. There were a number of early magazines, but a few stars drew in most of the reading audience.

With the addition of new channels, audiences naturally sort themselves among the choices. Two outcomes result. First, assuming there is a natural and finite limit on audience numbers, the addition of each channel increases by one the denominator of the viewer/channel ratio. The result is a continued reduction in potential audience size for any single channel. At some point the system saturates. Channels come and go but only in a delicate balance dictated by audience economics.

The second outcome is more interesting and much more relevant to a discussion of media content. Early channels almost always appeal to large and undifferentiated audiences. The first commercial radio stations of the 1920s offered general, one-size-fits-all programming. The strongest magazines during this century, *Look* and *Life*, similarly appealed to mainstream audiences. The three television networks got off to a strong start by attracting centrist audiences with one-for-all and all-for-one programming.

Early media serve undifferentiated, heterogeneous audiences, and because these audiences contain people with a wide assortment of characteristics, they typically are large in number. But, if something doesn't like a vacuum, something else doesn't like heterogeneous audiences. Large numbers of users served an inspirational purpose during the early stages of media development, demonstrating public support and acceptance, and thereby holding out the carrot of fortune for hungry media entrepreneurs. Early outlets became victims of their own success, having to face growing numbers of competitors whose market entry they had helped to inspire.

Media outlets arriving later make their success with smaller, homogeneous audience subsets budded from the larger group. For instance, cable networks have gone after special-interest audiences: ESPN seeks sports fans, Cable News Network appeals to current affairs enthusiasts, and the Inspirational Network reaches people interested in religious programming. These audiences characteristically are parochial and uniform. They are identified by the demographic and ideological similarities of their members.

Thus, a medium starts with a few channels serving large audiences with general programming and evolves into a medium with many channels serving smaller audiences with specific programming. It cannot be known whether or not television, now emulating the patterns of previous media, will see the end of the major networks. Although a strong case may be made for such a scenario, there are exceptions enough in radio and print to argue convincingly that networks may not perish.

The outcome, however, will not be a crapshoot. It will be determined by the strategy that finally emanates from the networks themselves. Specifically, what content will the networks offer to audiences that now enjoy such an unprecedented wealth of choices?

WHAT ARE THE EFFECTS ON TELEVISION AUDIENCES?

Since three of the networks are still the 800-pound gorillas on the block—and Fox has tipped the scales at 500—much of the discussion about television content must consider the network perspective. We know that *the television medium* is providing greater choices for ever more pigeonholed audiences, but what will happen to the content of network shows in this volatile environment? Answers can be found in the way audiences are now using television. In this section we examine a variety of independent studies that report a viewing population in transition.

We should state at the outset of this discussion that audience research methodologies, like the audiences they seek to measure, are in a state of flux—they have been since the early 1980s when the new technologies began breaking big on the market. Research results have varied depending on the data gathering approach and the involvement of new sophisticated equipment used to record audience habits. Networks pay for Nielsen but dispute the findings. Diaries, phone surveys, people meters, and the varieties of heat and motion sensors yield inconsistent results that cloud the issue and make it difficult to know exactly what viewers are up to.[7] Debate over techniques provides a convenient basis on which to dispute the legitimacy of results and allows discussions to focus on the measurement methods rather than on the meaning of shifting audience behaviors. Such derailment of the debate has diverted industry attention from the implications of ongoing audience changes and impeded action at a particularly critical time. These diversions have provided some in the industry convenient grounds on which to convince themselves that nothing much is happening at all.

For instance, NBC's former vice president for research, William S. Rubens, disputes claims that viewers are making extensive use of their remote controls. He said in an interview a few years back that "the zapping concept . . . has no 'basis in reality' " (Kneale, 1988). He claims viewers overstate their use of zappers and that their behaviors are considerably more sedentary than research may reveal. That was a few years ago, but there were a lot of remotes out there and anyone who had one knew the truth—the U.S. audience was on the move.

A year later, ABC and CBS confronted advertiser defections to cable stations by attacking underlying perceptions that cable can deliver valuable segmented audiences. In CBS's "The Cable Fable" and ABC's "20 Questions Facing National TV Advertisers," the networks argue that their forums are as strong or stronger today than they ever have been. David Poltrack, CBS's senior vice president of planning and research, claims cable growth, though impressive, is "generally recognized as being more a part of its past than its future" (Kleinfield, 1989). Now, a few years into the nineties few people would dispute that cable has a bright future. Indeed, it is the networks for which the future is a bit misty.

Most of the available research on the use of the new television technologies by individual viewers comes from industry sources. We would do well to remember, however, that industry research is thick with politics. There is, after all, a lot of money at stake in statistics that report what people watch and how they watch it.

Despite disbelief by many segments of the industry, there is strong and convincing evidence of considerable movement among American television audiences. One must conclude this after viewing the mosaic of audience behaviors described in the aggregate of available studies.

Two trends are emerging. First, it is no surprise that audiences are taking advantage of the programming options available though cable and VCRs. They are spreading their viewing hours over a greater number of channels, and are doing so by grazing among the selection of programming alternatives. Second, and this is an inevitable outcome of the first observation, viewers are conceding network time to make room in their schedule for other channels. The following research summary demonstrates the validity of these claims.

The R.D. Percy & Co. revealed that audiences in the late 1980s were heavily into channel changing. On average, Percy's sample of New York City households zapped once every three minutes and forty-two seconds. Heavy zappers (17.9 percent) switched channels more than once every two minutes; moderate zappers (35.8 percent) changed one to three times every six and a half minutes, and light zappers (46.3 percent) changed once every twenty minutes. Those with remote controls, of course, changed more often than those without them; those with cable more than those without cable. Higher-income viewers tended to zap more frequently than lower-income viewers. Moreover, this research shows that during commercials, audience numbers dropped 17 percent; one-third of this number because of people zapping away to other programming (Kneale, 1988).

The Percy research, which employed a sophisticated array of new, high-tech sensors and meters, has been challenged by networks, some advertisers and the A.C. Nielsen Company, which competes in the sale of audience measurement statistics. R.D. Percy & Co. since has gone out of business. Its short life, nonetheless, yielded statistics confirmed by other research.

American Demographics magazine reported that a study by "Teenage Research Unlimited" found that two-thirds of twelve- to nineteen-year olds zap commercials and fully 89 percent fast forward through commercials when they watch shows taped on a VCR (*American Demographics*, 1988). In a study by the A.C. Nielsen Company comparing homes with and without remote controls, it was found that "on the average day, switching increased seventy three percent once a home was equipped with a remote control device." This study noted further that "one-third of all switching (remote and non-remote) occurs during the first four and the last four minutes of the half-hour" (Duff, 1986). J. Walter Thompson research reported almost identical numbers. According to one JWT study, channel changing increased 75 percent when a family acquired remote switching capability. This research also reported increased channel changing during programs, and notes that "flipping reaches its heights when the programs are short and the audience is young" (Dougherty, 1987). Less scientifically, perhaps, humor columnist Dave Barry claims that the typical zapper has the I.Q. of asphalt, and that includes every male under forty. Since wives despise the compulsive use of remotes, Barry adds, this device is the chief cause of American divorces.

In a study conducted for Act III Media, publishers of *Broadcasting*, Frank N. Magid Associates reported several observations relevant to this discussion (Magid, 1988):

- Among respondents who owned remote control devices, 80 percent said they used them sometimes or frequently.

- Nearly half claimed to zap during programs. Most said they did so because they were bored or wanted to be certain they were not missing something better on another channel.

- Some 10.5 percent of respondents claimed to change channels when commercials came on.

Magid also discovered these interesting viewing behaviors:

- Almost a quarter of the viewers who used their remote controls did so to follow more than one program at a time. More than half the younger viewers (eighteen to thirty-four) said they regularly watched two or more shows at once, while about 20 percent said they watched three or more programs at once. Based on focus-group discussions and interviews, it became clear that men grazed more than women and enjoyed it significantly more.

- In spite of the growing options, viewers tuned only to a few channels. Those with cable watched, on a regular basis, an average of eleven channels, compared with only five for those without cable.

- Despite the popular sport of television-bashing, particularly by academics and newspaper commentators, there is an underlying public affinity for the medium. The Magid study showed that many more viewers felt that television has been a positive influence in their lives than those who believed they would have been better off without it.

- Viewers consistently underestimated how much the television set is turned on in their homes. Respondents said the average is five-and-a-half hours daily, whether anyone is watching or not—well below the Nielsen number of seven-plus hours daily.

- It is still a network world. When viewers were asked which stations they stopped at while they're looking for something to watch, six in ten named one of the Big Three networks. In fact, in virtually every question asked about station preference, the networks were mentioned first.

- At the same time, cable's popularity continues to grow. The vast majority of viewers who have cable were more satisfied with what's on television than they were before they had cable. Almost half the viewers who had cable said that cable channels were better than noncable channels and more than a third of cable subscribers said cable channels are better than the broadcast networks.

- Although some viewers grazed simply because they enjoy it, grazing appears to be a measure of dissatisfaction among viewers. Boredom as well as concern that they're missing a better program elsewhere were viewers' primary motivations for grazing. Furthermore, almost half the grazers said they enjoyed television less when they were flipping through the channels rather than watching a single program.

Audience reduction during advertisements is confirmed by many available studies. In the R.D. Percy research involving New York City viewers, slightly more than 10 percent zapped commercials during prime time. This figure refutes earlier estimates of a 2 to 4 percent drop during advertisements (Kneale, 1988).

A national study conducted among 1,881 adult respondents by Simmons Market Research found that 9 percent switched channels during commercials while 34 percent switched during programming. Of course, purely random zapping would hit the programming more heavily. Additionally, findings observed in a McCann-Erickson Arbitron analyses reveal a "twelve percent dial-switching loss for the average station break versus only two percent for a typical in-program break" (Secunda, 1988).

It is difficult to argue that new technologies have not had an impact on the habits of American television viewers. This handful of studies, supported by yet other commercial research, substantiates claims that people today are dividing their time among a variety of programming alternatives and that they are doing so by sampling frequently among the options. Even if for the sake of argument one agreed there were methodological frailties in some or most studies, it would be difficult to refute the consistency of so much market research. It should become evident to all but the most resolute skeptics that audiences are changing in ways that suggest new challenges for broadcasters and particularly for the networks.

The proliferation of alternative programming options, by all reasonable measures, has resulted in an assault on network audiences. Although viewers can and do increase their total viewing time to make room for cable and VCR channels, clearly alternative viewing displaces much of the time formerly spent with the networks.

This case is made by the numbers. In 1979 the average network primetime share was 92 percent, dropping to 73 percent in the fall of 1991 ("Nielsen Media News," 1992). (Note: The 1991 figure includes Fox; thus the statistic is an aggregate of audiences for four networks, not three as reported in previous measure-ments). In the fall of 1991 it was not uncommon for the combined primetime network audiences to dip below 60 percent (Nielsen, 1992). To make the dis-placement argument more obvious, Sue Rynn, research director of the Associa-tion of Independent Television Stations, reports that independent television has been increasing its share of the primetime audience each year. Nielsen reported a 10 percent share in November 1991. Moreover, Nielsen says ad-supported cable has increased to a 24 share in early 1992, from an 11 share in 1988 (Nielsen, Special Staff Research, 1992).

Another way of looking at network defections is to examine the actual number of viewing hours spent on network channels. Of the 27.5 hours per week with television, current viewers spend only 12.5 (47 percent) with the networks. Compared to total network viewing in the 1950s, this is a 39 percent reduction; compared to the early 1970s this is an 11 percent reduction (Papazian, 1988). The trend is obvious: network viewing is declining in total hours and as a portion of overall viewing. These trends undeniably are a direct result of conditions cre-ated by channel-expanding technologies finding their way into American living rooms since the early 1980s.

NETWORK RESPONSES

Amid these dark clouds the networks correctly have found a silver lining, one that should figure prominently in their forthcoming programming and content strategies. Although their audiences are shrinking, networks clearly dominate the industry. If you want maximum public exposure you still want the networks and the call isn't even close — aggregate cable and independent station audiences pale by comparison. As David Poltrack, research vice president for CBS, stresses, networks still reach over 95 percent of all American households during a single week (Kneale, 1988). No other medium or collection of channels can make that claim. Networks also should find comfort and direction in the observation that al-most 80 percent of respondents first named one of the "Big Three" when asked about which channels they enjoyed watching. About 65 percent of respondents said their viewing sessions began by examining network programming (Magid, 1988).

These observations become particularly important in any effective strategy adopted by the networks. Such evidence suggests talk of their death is premature. Nonetheless, the networks must make decisions critical to their survival at this important time, when the vast majority of homes are equipped with cable, VCRs and remote-control devices, when viewing habits are in transition and when the roles of networks and alternative channels are not clearly defined. The first step, we propose, is the recognition among network brass that audiences really are afoot out there and that the mentality of viewers has changed drastically in the nineties.

In summary, they might reflect on this: American consumers are buying into the high-tech environment of television viewing and they are quickly adopting the new behaviors this equipment fosters. They are spreading their viewing time among an assortment of programs rather than settling in with a single program, which was once their custom. Since the new channels offer specialized content with elements not found in traditional network programming, viewers are tapping into a greater variety of programming, and as a matter of course, sampling frequently among several programs. The result: decreased exposure to the networks.

The question at network conference tables these days is, "What kinds of programs — what content — can we offer to attract and hold viewers?" The answer to this question forced upon them by high-tech innovations has been the suicidal one of trying to "outcable" cable.

NETWORK CONTENT STRATEGIES

The key to network survival is a strategy that recognizes how audiences are using the medium and accommodates the evolving viewing patterns. While everyone else is narrowcasting, networks must find new ways of broadcasting, or reaching the mass audience with mass-appeal material.

Some wonder if television viewing has become a capricious and random behavior. We say no. There is a pattern even among frenetic grazers. Their selections are not without purpose or plan. They may change stations rapidly and regularly, but most viewers do so in predictable sequences among a preconsidered, presampled, preselected program set. According to the Magid study, more than half the viewers who graze do so only among specific, predetermined channels (Magid, 1988). They graze according to rational personal interests. They sort themselves into specialized channels much as they have before; only now, with the enhanced repertoire, with more than one channel meeting their specialized needs, they settle on a collection of desirable programs, not one.

Audiences are breaking into groups identified by their mutual programming preferences. But even now, network programming remains common to most of these varied groups. Our enjoyment of food analogies leads us to liken television programming to American diets. Most of us enjoy sampling an array of ethnic and specialty foods — some of us in greater proportion than others — but we usually return on a regular basis to a meal of meat and potatoes, the traditional staple of American diets. Similarly, as the research cited earlier demonstrates, people sample among the new programming varieties, but predictably return to the meat and potatoes of network programming.

Recognizing that they never again will have exclusive hold on everybody, the networks are in the best position to remain an important touchstone for most groups. That means staying within the viewing loops of the greatest possible number of viewers. These audiences will be transient; nothing can change this. But there can be a programming strategy that merits the periodic return of loyal viewers to network stations. Networks may not have all the viewers all the time, but they can have most of the viewers for much of the time. Such a strategy, of course, is not without its challenges.

The question is how to remain within the viewing loop for such varied audience groups. The key to this strategy lies in the networks' self-perception. The answer draws from historical and fundamental network philosophies that hold as sacred the development of program content designed to satisfy needs of mainstream viewers. The networks' strength always has been their extraordinary appeal to broad-based audiences. Structurally the networks are bound to the massive majority. They seek out and develop program content that strikes a common interest among members of these broad audiences. They do so with a technical excellence difficult to match by small, narrow audience competitors who settle for audience bits and pieces, such as only country music fans, sports enthusiasts or religious audiences. In order to stay in the viewing loops of most audience groups, networks should continue to offer programming with broad-based appeal that strikes the interest of viewers across demographic and special-interest categories. At the heart of this strategy is the notion of values, tolerance limits and audience acceptance of program content.

The U.S. population is remarkably stable. Despite the assaults of savings and loan disasters, the national debt, our shifting world role in the absence of superpower rivalries and a host of social changes, the massive majority stays the course. The core of this country remains little moved, where less sturdy societies would have collapsed. The commitment of this population to a set of fundamental beliefs is not easily altered. There are deep currents of underlying values and mores that run in the mainstreams of American society. Ongoing public events may stir ripples and eddies on the surface, but the central course remains unchanged.

The election of Ronald Reagan, then George Bush, has not spelled a significant shift to the right. Democrat Bill Clinton now reigns. The majority of people today support school busing, a woman's right to choose abortion and accommodations with the former Soviet Union. During the liberal Carter years the majority supported a strong national defense policy, capital punishment and fiscal conservatism. The point is, no matter which political force dominates at any given time there always is a regression toward the mean and a commitment to those central tenets. This observation has strong empirical support in polling data that reveals people change little over time in their belief in basic religious tenets and deep underlying values.[8] Clinton knew this.

The significance for broadcasting is the recognition of stability within the U.S. population on central themes and values. Stories that embody these values will always be popular. The society changes, but it changes slowly, and it never wanders far from the center. There are fads and fashions, but these almost always are ephemeral and not to be mistaken for a radical realignment of values.

So how should networks respond? First, large, mainstream, heterogeneous audiences continue to be touchstones, and with proper cultivation will remain so. Second, the maintenance of such audiences depends largely on the networks' ability to provide programming content that lies within accepted value parameters for mainstream viewers. This second point is critical.

It would be a mistake for networks to chase after narrow audience subgroups with programming that may lack appeal to the masses. There are dozens of channels and thousands of video titles that serve well the viewers' esoteric needs. Networks are ill suited to compete in the narrow audience market. The economics are against them. Cable stations, the prime suppliers of targeted programming, can thrive on ratings of only 2 (Fuchs, quoted in Walters, 1988). Small, homogeneous audiences are their specialty, their stock and trade, their foundations. They need serve only a handful of viewers to make profits.

The networks lose money with ratings of 12. They are inherently mass-audience media in style and substance. It has been their philosophy and it is now their economic mandate. Their financial and corporate structures demand large audiences in order to satisfy advertisers, their sole source of income. Why, then, are networks still trying to win back the minority of viewers who want pay-for-view? And don't they realize that the programs that might appeal to uncut-film fans are going to drive away many more viewers than they can win back?

One must question any content strategy that would separate networks from their mass audiences. For the past thirty years, as a means of holding to accepted values and norms of mainstream American audiences, network standards divisions have evaluated programs in advance of airing. They have examined programs for violence, sexual material, profanity and other features that might have violated the sensitivities of the massive majority. Although much has been written about the problems of programming uniformity among networks,[9] and about content excesses even under these conditions,[10] the system has worked better than one might have expected given the enormity of the task. Viewers have been able to tune in a network station and be reasonably sure that programming content would remain within limits they have come to know and accept. This is the essence of the mainstream programming concept. Within the past few years, networks have departed from this way of doing business, reducing their standards divisions and curtailing the program review process.[11] Two reasons have been offered to explain such action

The first is economic. In the late eighties, each network was purchased by a corporate conglomerate whose sights were set on the bottom line. Such a view has made it difficult for new management to see a direct and positive contribution of standards work to network revenues, and so as part of a broader effort to render the enterprise meaner and leaner, review functions have been limited.

One also can argue—and though it is more difficult to demonstrate it is no less plausible—that standards reviews interfered with the corporations' impressions of profitable programming content. There always has been an adversarial relationship built in between program producers and network standards reviewers. Whenever creativity is involved there will be tension between a creator and an evaluator. These historical disputes notwithstanding, the issue has taken on another dimension with new network management.

Censors, the argument goes, were throttling content that would bring network audiences to new limits. They were interfering with a strategy that sought to "push the envelope" of network programming.[12] They were in the way. The thinking of standards personnel might have been brought into line with the thinking of current network management but for what purpose? What function would standards serve when the commitment for evaluation had been abandoned?

Paradoxically, we feel, the same strategy networks hope will save them more likely will facilitate their demise. They have been lured into believing a momentary rise in audience numbers over salacious, violent and profane content reflects an audience shift in outlook and values. With gusto in the late 1980s they adopted a plan of audience titillation over audience cultivation and ratings continued to drop. Bells and whistles drew in some crowds but evidently they could not sustain the audience for long.

Some observers suggest the days of mass-audience television have passed. We have seen the near extinction of network radio as it once was. Few radio stations can boast anymore of great, blended, heterogeneous audiences. Most have settled for a convenient slice of the pie on which they focus their creative and administrative energies. We can count the number of mass-audience magazines on one hand. *Reader's Digest* comes closest, defying all trends. *TV Guide* should be included, but we know why it enjoys mass audiences. And the new circulation leader, *Modern Maturity*, has attracted its millions from those oldsters least inclined to the sensationalist novelties of the networks. So it may be that television has fallen in line with its companion media, where mass-audience outlets begin with a bang and end with a whimper.

This may happen to broadcasting, not because it is a hand dealt by fate but by the networks themselves. There is still time while network popularity continues to dominate the industry, while loyal audiences still include network programs in their viewing loops. The network that resists temptations to adopt targeted audience strategies for momentary spikes in the ratings and embraces the mass audience approach will be in the strongest position to weather the inevitable changes. If that is true, CBS will prosper and the others will decline.

NETWORK OPTIONS

The technological developments emerging in the late 1970s and blossoming throughout the 1980s have had a profound affect on television content. First, they have affected audiences, and any influence on audience behaviors makes its impact on the bottom line and thus on the operation of industry participants.

Developments in cable and videocassette technology have expanded the number of possible program outlets. Entrepreneurs moved in quickly to exploit the use of these outlets by appealing to smaller audience groups with more focused content of interest to limited numbers of viewers. The economies of smaller cable and broadcast stations allows them to serve smaller audiences and still make profits.

Meanwhile, audiences are recognizing their expanded program options. As they acquire the means, they explore programming alternatives, generally at the expense of the networks, which once by fiat of their monopoly commanded the viewing population. Networks are seeing their audiences slowly but surely committing a portion of their viewing hours to other channels, and then returning to network stations, but not with the commitment they once displayed.

The networks now are faced with a problem: to recapture or at least to retain their broad audiences and halt further erosion in ratings points. There are two critical judgments to be made at this point. Should the networks base programming strategy on the assumption that audience defection is a predictable and natural outcome of the new technologies that provide so many competitive choices, or can audience defection be slowed, halted or reversed with appropriate content modifications? While these two positions are not mutually exclusive, they do suggest clear differences in strategy.

If the first is correct, then audience shifts are not a matter of network blunders, but a predictable outcome of a natural evolutionary process over which networks have little control. Consequently, networks must reassess not just their content, but their roles in the new mix of entertainment suppliers. They may continue to dominate the industry, but they no longer remain without realistic competition. Networks should examine their place among entertainment suppliers and generate programs commensurate with this newly defined position. As all three now seem to be doing, they also may cover their bets by investing in the very enterprises—primarily cable—that have created their problems in the first place.

If the second position is correct—if program content has been the culprit—then networks can regain lost audiences and stem audience defections with content revisions of some scale. A great burden is placed on programming when one believes altered content can regenerate network strength. Implicit in this argument is a denial of other contributing causes—such as technological advancements and changing industry conditions that sweep along the networks and all others in the television business.

By adopting the position that content problems are responsible for the rating drop—and so content revisions can fix it—the networks assume a different remedy. Old content formulas will be suspected of failing to meet the needs of current audiences. New formulas will borrow from scripts that are working for the new programmers who are pinching network rating points. After all, if small programmers are siphoning off viewers, they may be doing something right. Borrow their formula, steal their thunder.

The fallacy of this argument, of course, is that program content is hardly responsible for network audience erosion. As we have argued throughout this chapter, there is no content formula on earth that can regain for networks their former places among viewers. The time of network monopoly has passed. The trouble is not with programming but with evolution. New technology, and the resulting new options, opportunities and appeals, have forever changed the industry.

We have suggested that networks may best be suited for the touchstone role, one that assumes most viewers regularly will tune to network shows. This argues for centrist content of demonstrated appeal to the large, reasonably stable mainstream audiences. In other words, a program strategy that avoids the objectionable things that drive away family viewers: heavy use of sex, violence and profanity. Leave such content to smaller programmers who can muster modest but adequate audiences with such material.

At this point the networks must consider a broader and more sophisticated solution based on a more complex philosophy. We believe the networks will do best with mainstream content, avoiding material that repulses a significant number of viewers. They should follow shifting audience trends but avoid the temptation to target the trendy few who seek material beyond the tolerances of average viewers. Leave envelope pushing to cable and small independents who can survive on low ratings. The networks should support the mainstream audiences or continue to lose viewers beyond any hope of retaining a dominant place in the television entertainment industry.

Both Michael Eisner at Disney and Grant Tinker have made the same, essential point about programming and technology. No matter what the distribution system, the stories remain the same. Good ones will sell and bad ones will flop. And as almost every thoughtful person in Hollywood asks, "Where are the good writers, the new writers that producers can afford?"

The answer to that question is easy. Programmers, much less agents, are looking in the wrong places for the wrong people.

The novelist Louis B. Jones, writing in the *New York Times Book Review* (March 2, 1992) draws a contrast between writing that is good and writing that is sensational. He speaks of Jane Austen, "whose every sentence discovered a new tone of affectionate irony, and whose mature skepticism of all our necessary hypocrisies makes that of the Sex Pistols seem mild."

The high-tech competition of cable has simply underlined the fact that network programmers can't distinguish the originality of the Jane Austens from the luridness of the Sex Pistols. What kinds of writers sell? Those who walk in with a picture of leather-clad teenagers and the caption, "They make house calls." Or those who present the "Nightingales," summed up in the line, "nurses in tight uniforms and the air-conditioning fails. . . ." Until programmers and agents accept the fact that the edge of the envelopes they want pushed are not defined by Sex Pistols but by talent, the network's hope of retaining the mass audience seems remote.

If broadcasting's answer to cable narrowcasting is creative programming, why don't networks find and nurture that talent that alone can push the envelope of originality while capturing a pop audience? Instead of scouring the nation for "America's Funniest Home Videos" (which elicits several hundred entries per week), why not hold weekly auditions for America's Funniest Writers? Or commission some of the scores of mystery writers who turn out witty, fast-paced novels reviewed each week in the *Times*, the best of which seem to be written by middle-aged English ladies? The Fortune 500 companies talent hunt every college for future engineers and scientists. Have you ever seen NBC or Paramount on your campus looking for young writers? Don't hold your breath. Here's an industry that spends $10 billion each year on programming and offers through its Academy exactly ten modest prizes for would-be writers, 2,000 of whom send in scripts on spec. Well, that's show biz.

And so we conclude that while technology does not wear a recognizable face and cannot so easily be identified as a force that affects the content of television programming, it does play an undeniably critical role in what Americans watch. Clearly, by opening up dozens of new channels, technology has affected the assortment and blend of available shows. But, for the networks, there is an indirect effect on programming. The multitude of new outlets siphons off network audiences and forms an ever-changing programming standard. In a way, the canvas does affect the painting. Technology has made a real and tangible difference in television content.

NOTES

1. In 1948 there were 190,000 televisions in use in the United States. By 1955 there were 32,000,000. Nearly every home in America had a television set by the early 1960s. Information from F.L. Smith, *Perspectives on Radio and Television: Telecommunication in the United States* (New York: Harper & Row, 1985).

2. U.S. consumers were given the choice between two incompatible videocassette formats: VHS and Beta. VHS sets were manufactured by a number of electronics firms; Beta, because of patents, was produced only by the Sony Corporation. Although the question is not entirely settled, the VHS format appears to have dominated the market.

3. Ownership of videocassette recorders increased from 500,000 in 1979 to more than 16.5 million in 1984. Reported in Smith, *Perspectives*.

4. For instance a consortium of big industry players, including NBC, have invested in a direct satellite-to-earth technology, in which small receivers, the size of dinner plates, installed on a roof receive cable-like programming direct from orbiting satellites – cable without the bother.

5. Robert Gerson, editorial director of *Twice Magazine*, said that remote control has been around for many years, in many forms. The infrared technology, now in use exclusively, was used in Europe since the early 1970s, but was not available in the United States until the late 1970s. This was so largely because original equipment could not accommodate the larger number of stations available in the United States. (Information obtained in a telephone conversation, January 1989.)

6. Information about window technology obtained in a conversation with Robert Gerson, editorial director, *Twice Magazine*, January 1989.

7. Dispute over the Nielsen People Meter Service has created considerable controversy in the industry. Given that advertisers pay by and networks earn by the numbers of viewers, the introduction of any new measurement technology is bound to draw fire. In order to document the validity of its People Meter approach, Nielsen recently has revealed results of a major study conducted by Statistical Research, Inc. (SRI), and sponsored by the Committee on Nationwide Television Audience Measurement (CONTAM), whose members include the Big Three and the National Association of Broadcasters.

Based on a study of the seven-volume SRI report, Nielsen concluded that "This review, in our opinion, underscores the fundamental soundness of this ratings system, while pointing the way to opportunities to enhance that system." "SRI Completes Review of Nielsen People Meter Service," *Media News*, 1989, p. 1.

8. Information taken from various editions of *The Gallup Report*, 1988. *The Gallup Report* is a periodical available in most university research libraries or by subscription through the Gallup Organization in Princeton, New Jersey.

9. See, for example, G. Gerbner, L. Gross, M. Morgan, and N. Signorielli, "Charting the Mainstream: Television's Contributions to Political Orientations," *Journal of Communication* 2 (1982), pp. 100–127.

10. See, for example, D. Pearl, L. Bouthilet, and J. Lazar, eds., *Television and Behavior: Ten Years of Scientific Progress and Implications for the Eighties*, Vol. 2 (Washington, D.C.: National Institute of Mental Health, 1982).

11. We will deal with network changes in chapter 10.

12. "Pushing the envelope" is a phrase used to describe how producers test audience tolerance limits for innovative – sometimes daring – programming components.

9

Content Solutions

Two questions weave their way through our discussions of network programming content: First are TV-makers deeply influenced in what they create by external forces at networks, advertising agencies, pressure groups, government, the press, technological change and by public opinion itself? If the results of our investigations are any sign, the answer is: yes, both writer-producers and programmers are subject to the coordinates that are drawn for them by these forces, and many of their tastes and values in primetime are shaped by outside influences.

TV-makers, as Gary Goldberg suggested, are fathers, mothers, sons, daughters, brothers, sisters, aunts and uncles, and they draw upon their daily lives for inspiration. But outside of their talent, hustle and good luck—and nobody doubts the weight of these factors—they are constantly buffeted by forces that are magnified by the press, quantified by Nielsen and nationalized into public opinion.

The second question is very much unresolved. It is: Who decides what programming content is in the public's interest and what is not? If public opinion really influences TV, who should speak out for the public good? Is it viewers at large, their representatives in Congress, the courts that interpret the law and the FCC's oversight? Is it pressure groups, advertisers or the broadcasters themselves through self-regulation? No doubt, each will continue to play some role in determining the public good. But from whatever angle the question is debated in the future, one truth is as simple as the populist notion behind it. Audiences will continue to decide what they want on the basis of the choices they are offered. More than ever before, thanks to the proliferation of channels and options, the viewers of primetime television will determine what they want or do not want on the public air.

By saying that, we do not endorse uncritically the position the National Association of Broadcasters has taken for years: that the market should be the only guide to program content. Nor do we endorse the deregulation policies of the recent FCC. Ironically, the very deregulatory tactics that turned network television over to the market produced such a spate of indecent programs that the FCC flipflopped and tried to reregulate all such sexually outrageous material. Alarmed by the outcry, broadcasters assumed a moral stance. After saying that producers could be their own censors, both CBS and NBC had to turn around and rehire a battery of editors to replace those fired. How delicious!

When FCC Chairman Mark Fowler was leaving office in 1987, Tom Shales wrote in the *Washington Post:*

> For six years Fowler has howled a tirelessly repeated litany about how this holy entity called the "marketplace," not the government, should set the rules for broadcasting. Right . . . six years of anything-goes, devil-may-care, public-be-damned deregulation of the broadcast industry nurtured the environment in which so-called raunch radio was able to flourish. By announcing the FCC's intention to get tough (by cracking down on explicit language on the air) . . . (it was) shooting itself in the foot. The FCC was addressing a problem it had helped create.[1]

Shales was sounding a clear note. If the audience for a given show is the only factor the market considers, and if ratings are votes in this purest of capitalistic democracies, then who is the FCC to tell millions of "voters" who love the vulgarities of raunch radio and sleaze TV that they cannot have access to whatever they want?

Jack Valenti, president of the Motion Picture Association of America (MPAA), and consumerist Ralph Nader seldom agree on anything, but on Fowler's deregulation of broadcasting they walk identical lines. Valenti accused the FCC of changing the rules that "protect the powerless," and Nader said, "Fowler has done more damage than any of the top one hundred Reagan people. . . ." Adding a producer's voice to the chorus, David Levy of the Caucus for Producers, Writers and Directors in Hollywood wrote, "We view his years on the FCC as a disaster for the public good and as a gigantic windfall for private interests."[2]

Shales noted that NBC (under Grant Tinker) fired the "notorious smutmonger" Howard Stern even though he was their highest-rated performer. Evidently, NBC did not think at the time that the "anything goes" philosophy of a free market was entirely consistent with the public interest tradition of broadcasting. For honorable broadcasters in the tradition of Julian Goodman (former chairman of NBC), Frank Stanton (former chairman of CBS) and ABC's Goldenson and Tinker, the word "audience" covered more than just the audience for any given show. They thought of the audience as all those who listen to radio and watch television. That becomes tantamount to the public itself. Every listener, every viewer has a stake in every show on the air. And it is in that sense that the audience represents the public interest and ultimately determines program content.

The tug of war between those ancient gods, freedom and order, has animated much of this book's description of program content. It emerged in the interviews. Steven Bochco fears that any limitation on writers will chill creativity while Arthur Price is afraid that an "anything goes" philosophy will trigger reregulation by Congress. Both are right. Freedom without order breeds moral anarchy and order without freedom breeds moral tyranny.

We encountered much the same tension in the discussion of government intervention and interest group pressures on advertisers and the networks. Repeatedly the question arose: How can the freedom of expression sought by suppliers and the free access sought by many viewers be balanced against the concern parents feel for their children and the interest the public has in maintaining community standards?

We offer the following recommendation as a workable compromise between the conflicting goods of a free market that satisfies its audiences and a public interest standard that protects children and community values: Like the motion picture industry, and more recently, like the record industry, it is time for the television industry to offer the viewer a program review and ratings service. Such a service would provide advance information with which viewers could make informed decisions. It could work something like this.

ADVANCE TELEVISION PROGRAM INFORMATION

Through symbols in the daily television log, viewers could get information that would enable them to anticipate the content in shows. They would have immediate notification of strong material (violence, sex and language) and values elements (mainstream standards such as honesty, fair play, courage and caring relationships). Viewers could then make choices based on their informed judgment of program content. Networks and advertisers could benefit if the major discretionary responsibility were exercised in the home.

This approach to program selection is not without precedent. Twenty-five years ago the major film companies and theater chains faced decreases in audience, competition from television and increased pressures from Congress and public interest groups. Film producers, conscious of expanding audience interests, wanted to stretch traditional boundaries, but whenever they did, they invited a backlash of public protest and threats of censorship.

The Motion Picture Association of America's solution was to create a rating scale that said in effect to parents: "The responsibility for what children see belongs in the home, not in Hollywood or Washington. Now with the film ratings you will have the advance information needed to make proper choices. Henceforth, if children see something that offends your sensibilities, the responsibility is yours."

In less than two years, the MPAA's classification system so improved the climate of public opinion toward film content that the industry shed its role of substitute parent and focused its efforts as a supplier of entertainment. There are still problems: kids sneak into "R" movies; letter symbols don't differentiate between sex and violence; hypocritical games are played. But at least there is advisory information up front.

Led by president Jack Valenti, the MPAA was able to bring about a watershed shift of responsibility. They educated the nation to see the need and to use the service. They publicized the theme of family responsibility, made easier to assume by the ratings. Leading an all-out campaign toward major interest groups and concerned legislators, the MPAA won broad support. Waving favorable poll results of satisfied parents,[3] the film industry won the battle of public opinion. The institution of the MPAA code saved the movie industry from endless protest, and it improved conditions for moviegoers. It satisfied many critics and created conditions that allowed producers to provide the robust material sought by millions of people. Despite the fact that some MPAA ratings appear inconsistent and self-serving, the system realizes its aim: providing advance information, a dewline for parents.

The network television situation is both similar and different. Audience movement to alternative media outlets is similar. And despite the absence of anything exceeding many "PG" boundaries today, some in the television viewing audience have been alarmed by content they would rather not see. A major difference from film, however, is that networks must engage family core audiences while reaching out for cable audiences. At the same time broadcasters must retain the confidence of advertisers who feel vulnerable to public opinion.

Suppose such a system were offered to all four networks by a research organization as independent as Nielsen? How would it work? What would be its benefits?

A carefully crafted classification system suitable for everyday use in television program selection would improve the networks' ability to create programs that meet audience needs. By allowing advanced audience decisions, it would turn over the responsibility to individual viewers. It could reduce congressional and organizational protest and help to insulate networks and advertisers from the burden of defending every program that didn't square with moralistic critics or the "politically correct" crowd.

In large part, such a program review service would advance a viewer-driven concept of program development. Alerted to "coming attractions," the audience would determine the desired content. It would soften the objection that the "survival-of-the-fittest" approach ignores the sensitivities of innocent viewers who might tune to a show ignorant of its strong material. While this might happen only occasionally, it concerns people enough to be considered seriously. The availability of advance information is the best remedy. Forewarned is forearmed.

Viewers would know the level of intensity to expect; advertisers would know that their audiences would be less likely to be shocked; interest groups could relax, knowing their members had been safely diverted to other channels. The government could anticipate fewer complaints. Cautious viewers could be protected from offensive programming, and those seeking thrills could anticipate a freeing of some boundaries. Furthermore, it would be a comfort to all that the natural forces of large audience economics still would be in play. Programming content would push only to the point where audience support began to drop.

The benefits of this system would be greater than those of the film ratings, which accent the negatives. What about shows that glorify positive values? Some readers may be skeptical of the claim that primetime TV programs reflect universal values. Despite what NBC producer Susan Baerwald said, which was seconded by some of the writers interviewed, it might seem odd to hear from the academic community that network programs contain a healthy portion of traditional mainstream American values.

In a recent project we examined several weeks of network primetime programming for values content. Our instrument was built around eighteen teaching points used in a nationwide curriculum for values education in public and private schools. We discovered that the values synonymous with American culture are deeply embedded in network programming material. These values are played out in endless scenarios and in countless dialogues. They range in magnitude from subplot foundations to passing observations. They appear in many forms and are expressed by many types of characters at various levels of involvement.[4]

If we expect viewers to select programs on the basis of advance information, why not provide a more complete picture with which to make such decisions— offer a system that looks at both sides of the coin? A show with rigorous adult content may also have substantial values content. Perhaps to many viewers, an erotic program also high in human values would provide a pleasing balance. Such an approach shifts the decision from one entirely based on adult material to a more comprehensive account of the show. Adult material and values material are not at opposite poles on the same scale. Why assume more of one means less of the other? "Hill Street Blues," for instance, was known to display violence, sexual content and even strong (for television) language. It often happened that on episodes with some of the strongest material, however, there were well-developed values and positive themes. To obtain an accurate picture of such episodes, one needed a measure broader than one limited to adult incidents. We believe a system that offers two colors paints a better and more honest picture of program content.

Implementation of such a rating program is a manageable task. A computer-assisted coding system would allow the rapid content evaluation of television answer prints (or even rough cuts for programs pushing deadlines). Tested measures for adult and values elements would be used. Final scores for both categories would be calculated according to a precise formula. Scores would be converted into graphic symbols that describe the intensity of the two measures. This information would be provided for newspaper television logs and in publications such as *TV Guide*. We would expect routine calibrations of the system to conform the symbolic representations to the ever-changing tolerances of viewers. An advance rating system would not only assist viewers but also would accommodate the needs of special interest groups and advertisers. Advance information closes the loop, easing the progress of commercial television toward a viewer-driven system.[5]

WHO SHOULD MAKE NETWORK TELEVISION CONTENT DECISIONS?

In a free society the people should have access to daring and vigorous themes, to family fare and to special interest subjects of all varieties. The process would be ongoing and it would be simple. The game would be played between the programmers and their viewers, with advertisers, special interest groups and the government on the sidelines. It would be a supply-and-demand relationship unfettered by the selfish agendas of other forces that now affect commercial television content.

The viewer-driven theory of broadcasting currently operates in its purest form in pay-for-view cable stations. It is inhibited in any other environment because of economic conditions that require advertiser funding and political conditions that invite government intervention. We recognize this and tout the pay-for-view approach only as a point of comparison, a model and example of where we believe the industry will be moving in the next decade—particularly if a ratings system can be instituted for the protection of children and the unwary.

The proliferation of cable and the videocassette market has already given viewers more direct control over content than ever before. Microwave systems that emulate cable operations—without the cable—would lower costs, increase programming options and stimulate programmer competition, all of which would improve the viewer-programmer relationship. We expect the 1990s to expand the role of viewers and diminish the roles of other participants in program decisions. Despite all the talk about "people voting with their people meters," the truth is that key parts of the public—low-income and older citizens, for example—are left out of the market equation altogether.

MARKET-FORCES THEORY

On the surface it might appear that the deregulation "market-force" philosophies of the Reagan and then the Bush administrations have contributed to the environment of viewer control. In our judgment, the viewer-driven theory of programming and the market-forces theory are not natural allies. The market-force approach does not support the dominance of viewer control as much as it reduces government input. Conventionally, market enthusiasts are more against government input than they are in favor of the people's right to choose. In theory, removing government oversight increases viewer influence, but in practice, it grants more control to the interest groups, advertisers and the networks, which in turn reduces audience controls.

A big loser over the last twelve years has been the low-income viewer who does not have a cable choice. In the sixties, every big sports event came free in over-the-air broadcasts. Theatrical movies were also free, if somewhat sanitized by network censors. The enthusiasts for cable sang the praises of first-run films without commercial interruptions. A check of HBO, Showtime, Cinemax, Encore, Disney and others during a month's period of 1992 revealed that most movies were two years old, about one out of ten was one-year old and only the real bombs hit the pay screen immediately after the theatrical run. Oh yes, some of them were interrupted by commercials and all were heavy with ads before and afterward. The low-income viewer might not be all that grateful for those exponentially growing options at ever fancier prices. The pity is that many people below the poverty line, forced to choose between necessities and escape, choose entertainment, and who among the affluent is in a position to rebuke them? And more to the point, who in Congress speaks for them? Without the threat of government intervention, influence from special interests, particularly the merchants of greed, goes unchecked. When government withdraws from the equation, the formula does not shift in favor of the viewer.

The cases mentioned earlier involving Howard Stern and his fellow members in the scatological community illustrate the cut-off-your-nose-to-spite-your-face dilemma faced by the free-market enthusiasts.

The 1987 cases involved the FCC and three U.S. radio stations: KPFW-FM in Los Angeles, KCSB-FM in Santa Barbara and WYSP-FM in Philadelphia. For the first time since 1976, the FCC brought action against a broadcaster (in this case three broadcasters) for a content violation. Each of the stations was said to have aired indecent programming. WYSP-FM is the case most celebrated since it involves the notorious envelope pusher, Howard Stern, no stranger to controversy with his adolescent humor and blatant irreverence. Stern's show was also broadcast on station KXRK-FM in New York, which in combination with the Philadelphia station gave Stern an audience of at least 500,000.

Stern delighted enormous audiences in densely populated Philadelphia, New Jersey and the New York corridor who reveled in his bathroom humor, sexual innuendo, salaciousness, racial insults aimed at blacks and Hispanics and sexist attacks upon "broads," all interspersed with weather reports. Fellow jocks of his genre were no less offensive. The programming, however, offended the market-oriented Mr. Fowler, his fellow commission members and some in the Justice Department. Market-force philosophy notwithstanding, the FCC went after Stern (and the two other stations).[6] It brought action against the stations and threatened their licenses. In 1993 high fines lurk for stations and Stern.

The new militancy of the FCC, so quiet when the fast-money barons were buying up stations and networks, raises an important question: If the market is to decide what is airworthy, and if by the market the government means the listeners, why did the FCC challenge Stern and company? From the market viewpoint, Stern's show had the highest rating of any program in the three-state region. More people "voted" for his show than for any other, as Tom Shales said. What more evidence is necessary to identify the listener (market) force?

The only logical answer is that the FCC and Reagan-Bush deregulatory philosophers meant something else by market forces. In order to make a case against Stern, the FCC had to create a new set of guidelines. It hoped the ad hoc rules would offer some justification for an administration preaching deregulation, yet would impose the first round of broadcast sanctions in twelve years. The resulting guidelines were poorly defined, easily broken and ultimately embarrassing to the deregulators. The *New York Times*, for instance, said:

> For a decade the FCC has held out relatively clear guidelines to broadcasters . . . the rules have said, warn the viewer or listener of possibly objectionable program content, avoid seven dirty words and run the program only after 10 P.M., when children are less likely to tune in.
>
> For that relative clarity, the commission has now substituted vagueness. Forbidden now are the depiction or discussion of "sexual or excretory activities or organs" in terms "patently offensive as measured by contemporary community standards for the broadcast medium." And 10 o'clock is no longer a safe hour, but the commission won't say what the safe hour might be.[7]

To be fair to the commission and its staff, the *Pacifica* rules on obscenity and indecency, from which the FCC drew, were far from clear, no matter what the *New York Times* might claim. Diane Killory, general counsel for the FCC, and responsible for the 1987 guidelines on indecency, told *Broadcasting* magazine (April 20, 1987) that there had never been a "safe harbor" for obscenity on the air since obscene language is not constitutionally protected. Now the FCC was merely telling broadcasters that there was no longer a "safe harbor" for indecent language if there was a "reasonable risk" that children were in the audience. Even as late as 10 P.M., Killory said, millions of children are watching, especially on weekends. Therefore, following the 1976 Supreme Court decision in *Young* v. *American Mini-Theaters* that reasonable time, place and manner restrictions could be put on offensive material without violating the First Amendment, the FCC ruled that broadcasters should "channel" descriptions of sexual and excretory functions to more appropriate time periods. No longer would the Seven Dirty Words constitute the outer limits. "The interpretation," said Killory, "has been too narrow. We will apply the generic definition (as defined by the *Pacifica* case) and not limit it arbitrarily to seven specific words."[8]

Broadcasters and other industry participants were understandably perplexed by the government's resolve toward industry deregulation. Andrew Schwartsman, head of the Media Access Group, a consumer advocacy organization, found mixed signals in the administration's position. Talking about FCC chairman Mark Fowler, he said, "The irony is that he opposes the Fairness Doctrine, which promotes free speech, yet he is willing to suppress artistic expression."[9] Restrictions from such a market-force advocate as Fowler are indeed ironic.

The fact is, for government policy makers, "market force" does not mean "viewer (or listener) force." "Market force" means the absence of government. In practical terms, when the government removes itself from broadcasting activities (if it ever really can as the Stern case suggests), it would allow the other participants to share content determination, not equally and not necessarily with an augmented position for the audience.

THE BEST ALTERNATIVE TO VIEWER-DRIVEN CONTENT

Until the industry installs a ratings-review-and-advance-information system, and in the absence of affordable pay-for-view programming in which the viewer-programmer relationship is direct, the present contentious system involving government, viewers, networks, advertisers and special interests is workable. However awkward, it works and at times, it works very well. Can that system be fine tuned?

Surely it would help to seek ways of reducing the impact of fringe interest groups that represent few constituents, demand absolute compliance, and most notably, attempt to control not just some television content, but all of it in accordance with their dogmatic tenets. The best step in that direction was taken years ago by NBC-TV when it reached out for dialogue with the truly national, membership-based, responsible groups. Most public interest leaders loathe the crazies and resent the fact that the noisiest ones preempt the more moderate critiques by people who represent huge sectors of society.

Many of the writer-producers like Bruce Paltrow ("St. Elsewhere") who attended NBC seminars found the feedback from groups an asset to programming. In turn, interest group tolerance and recognition of the multiple network audiences contributed to greater harmony and a more cooperative environment. When the networks closed their doors to the interest groups, cut back the standards people who were liaisons with group leaders and then loudly announced their intention to depart from a philosophy of traditional responsibility to that of market forces only, their relationships with the groups soured. Feeling the cold draft, the lockouts are kicking hard to get back in. So far the bottom-line executives whose corporations run the networks have shown no inclination to re-cultivate friendships with their friendly critics, leaving them vulnerable to the not so tender but well-deserved mercies of the Irvines, the Rakoltas and the Wildmons.

More ominously for the networks, mainstream interest groups are beginning to adopt outsider tactics. The PTA joined with Tipper Gore and the Parents Music Resource Committee to impose a labeling system on a record industry that had to be dragged kicking and screaming every inch of the way. Now they brag about their public responsibility. If it worked on recording magnates, why not on network brass? And if the networks won't listen to the groups, then maybe they'll listen to advertisers who pay their bills. Long before anyone heard from Tupelo Reverend Wildmon, the major faith groups were storming into shareholder meetings and calling on advertisers. Should they return to those tactics, the networks will find their problems multiplied a thousandfold.

As laid out in chapter 6, the groups that were historically the most successful with the networks represented large numbers of constituents, and their values were reasonably in line with mainstream American beliefs. What they wanted, large numbers of viewers wanted. These groups might not have represented the desires of the "average reasonable viewer" but they represented the values that most viewers (who were also parents, churchgoers, civic servants and community stalwarts) found desirable.

The loudest interest groups today hold beliefs not often widely embraced by those outside their own circle. They do share some views with the majority, and on these common points occasionally strike a public chord. But the extension of their value system goes far beyond that held by average network viewers.

For instance, some decry the depiction of anti-Christian values, a groundless allegation and a matter of little regard to most viewers. Despite limited general support for this expressed concern, CLeaR-TV successfully manipulates some advertisers to act against the networks. When advertisers respond to threats of boycotts and bad press, the fringe groups wield power over the program content for everyone. This moves television content determination from the ideal viewer control to watchdog control.

What should be done? Speaking gratuitously to the industry, we would have the networks and the advertisers reevaluate the stock they put in the claims and threats of these groups. Sixth Avenue shies away from the problem, hoping it will go away. Afraid to confront their tormentors directly lest they give them even more publicity, they have settled for doing nothing. Occasionally an agency will reveal that a poll reported little support for the boycotters or that no boycott has ever worked. No one in top management, however, has tried to think through the threat to the viewers' freedom of choice, and consequently the industry's actions have been fragmentary and ambiguous. Professor James Kuhn, who has studied the economic impact of the boycotters, professes amazement at the impotence of executive suite and suggests that maybe the fleas are smarter than the elephants.

The effective interplay between responsible public interest groups and the networks, advertisers, affiliates and producers will hasten the day of total viewer control. The merit of the group input, however, should be measured not by the amount of press they can muster or the level of fear they can project but by the representativeness of their beliefs and the distribution of their constituency. Networks should seek more aggressively the counsel of mainstream interest groups that express a legitimate point of view about general values and content components. We say again: Networks once reached out to these groups because of a genuine interest in their views. They should reestablish contact. Networks need their help now more than ever. Indeed, if networks reestablish their liaisons with mainstream organizations, the radical fringe groups would be left whistling in the dark.

So far we have concentrated on interest group membership in this club of content shapers. What about viewers, the government and advertisers?

Viewers. Viewers are easy. Their input is measured moment by moment by the programs they select or avoid. If not a collective wisdom, then at least a collective preference emerges from the aggregate of their selections. There was a time not long ago when viewers had little choice but to switch among the three network stations. Their choices were limited and did not necessarily reveal their programming desires. ABC, CBS and NBC were indistinguishable except for ratings. Select one or the other, it made little difference, and it told little about content preferences. Today, with dozens of stations, a vote by program selection really means something. There are clear differences and many options. They cover the spectrum of subjects and formats and treatments from rough and ready themes and content to the squeaky clean. The Nielsen People Meters tell us much more about viewer preferences. The meters eliminate hidden agendas, constituency bases and ideologies found among other participants in the industry. (The only question is: how representative is a system which makes so many electronic demands on meter users?) Viewers don't confer, they don't consider strategies and they don't become philosophical. They watch what they like, and if they're satisfied they return for more.

In an industry dedicated to serving the needs of viewers, viewer preferences are the only real measures of what content ought to be. This is why we like the viewer-driven theory of content selection. If you want to know what people like, read the ratings. It sounds cut and dried, but it really comes down to identifying audience subgroups by demographics or other characteristics and programming for them.

Nonviewers. That's another book. But what about those whose needs are not met, who see scores of channels carrying the same stupid, irrelevent fare appealing to fickle consumers with the IQ of asphalt?

The Government. Deregulation or reregulation, what is the proper role of government? The FCC, ever massaged by the Congress and the executive branch, can make two contributions to the determination of content. First, it can maintain the spirit of the Fairness Doctrine. Now, only an act of Congress can reinstate this valuable tool. To be sure, the Fairness Doctrine has little to do with entertainment programming, except maybe in documentaries or docudramas, and it never brought about the marketplace of ideas it had hoped to foster. But it was a symbol. It did tell the industry that its licenses had to do with the variety and multiplicity of information and issues. As such it was treasured by many in Congress and by many public interest associations. Even though it has been attacked by political pirhanas for years, its recent demise at the hands of the FCC was too sudden a death.

Despite our lack of enthusiasm for the FCC's charge into the quicksand of indecency definitions, we see no reason why the government should not hold the stations and networks to minimal responsibilities in the areas of violence, sex and language, especially during early evening programs. (After 10 P.M., or at the outside 11 P.M., obscenity controls should be sufficient.) We like the metaphor Justice Stevens used when he said that broadcasters had the right to keep the pig out of the parlor. Adult content, then, may simply be "a right thing at a wrong place," or the wrong time.

The government also should maintain its watch over children's programming. The dust may have settled for now, but the smart money says we haven't seen an end to the exploitation on Saturday morning.

Concern for fairness and a variety of opinions, holding the broadcasters to their sworn duty of self-regulation and continuing oversight into children's programming—these will keep the government seated at the table for the next decade. When viewer control becomes stronger, the commission may wish to cash in its chips and go home. But not yet.

Advertisers. If networks adopt a ratings system, advertisers may once again fix on the bottom line and abandon recent preoccupations with program minutia. If an advertiser likes the demographics of a show and the price of airtime, it should buy in. The recent trend toward advertiser meddling in network programming decisions is unhealthy for the industry and far too reminiscent of the Red Channel days when people were blacklisted and self-appointed censors scrutinized scripts. At the moment, some big-ticket advertisers are vulnerable to boycotts and protests. They take the attitude, why bother to sponsor part of a show under attack when it is just as easy to buy into a harmless environment? Unfortunately such practices substitute advertiser (and interest group) preferences for network and viewer preferences.

The homogeneity of advertisers and the constrained value code of fringe interest groups will, if allowed to dominate the process, rob the medium of its creative spirit and water down viewer influence. In our scenario, the advertisers would allow the networks to develop the vehicles and then buy the audiences delivered by the programs. This suggests the need for a collective resolve among the major network advertisers to ignore fringe interest-group tantrums and breath-holding. Turning a deaf ear could easily wither some of the noisier groups for lack of attention.

In summary, both sponsors and networks must reawaken themselves to the value of reaching "everybody." At the moment, the obsessive concentration on the 18 to 38 audience is threatening to exclude half the nation. Because ad agencies are demanding young buyers only, the networks are filling 1993 with teenage shows. Ratings which reflect major shares are less desirable than smaller numbers of young adults. If this trend continues, broadcasting will become narrowcasting, and the networks will shrink down to cable size. By that time, there would doubtless be a "golden" channel for those over 40 or 50. Interestingly, the circulation of AARP's *Modern Maturity* is greater than most network hits, and a new "nostalgia channel" will try to co-opt this audience.

WHAT WILL THIS CONTENT LOOK LIKE?

In a viewer-driven plan for television, the industry freely develops content in response to the wishes of any audience subgroup of sufficient size to earn programmers a profit, while at the same time crafting mega-hits that appeal to that mainstream of almost all ages, groups and interests. Variety then becomes the hallmark of service to a diverse audience, large or small. Only the inveterate couch potato could find everything appealing, but all viewers would find something on the menu selections they could enjoy. American television programming would become a metaphor for the American culture—multilingual, multiracial, multiethnic. It would span the range of values and interests, tastes and philosophies that characterize a nation of nations.

Although cable stations and cable networks have expanded options for viewers, they pick up their audiences around the edges, appealing to a special interest here, a select concern there, bits and pieces across the fabric of preference. None of the cable networks has demonstrated the capacity to retain Big Three–size audiences, nor even those of Fox, the promising new kid on the block that is rapidly becoming the first new broadcasting competitor since the genesis of television. Indeed, now that Fox is programming seven nights a week, it's not too early to speak of the Big Four of broadcasting.

It makes little sense for the networks to try to out-cable cable with more sex and violence. Broadcasters must observe the values and expectations, the ethics and tolerance of middle America. Programming that strikes middle C and includes a couple of octaves on each side will please more ears than one that aims for the low notes of the Playboy Channel or the high notes of PBS. This does not mean mediocre, flattened fare. The middle embraces a wide variance on either side—toward those in favor of pushing the envelope and those favoring family entertainment. Must we remind networks to look to their ratings? At the moment, only CBS seems to realize that their market is the median and that shows like "Murphy Brown" grab the barely adult as well as the barely alive.

There is a school of thought in Hollywood that believes that extending the boundaries to an Anything Goes mentality will necessarily produce better, more original television. If this were true, the R-rated efforts of Geraldo Rivera would surely surpass in creativity the G-rated efforts of Marcy Carsey. A moment's reflection should remind us that Goldberg's "Brooklyn Bridge" demands more originality and insight than a recent network offering called "The Rape of Dr. Willis," in which the good doctor discovers that the man she is about to operate on is the one who raped her only the month before. Is that ever high concept?

No, the horizons of TV can be expanded by the future "Cosby"s as well as by the "Roseanne"s, the "Cheer"s and the naughtier "Married with Children," by the "Simpsons" as well as by "Seinfeld." Indeed, the most innovative new program of the 1992 season was pure formula chock-full of conventional values, but its writing was so sensitive to real teenagers that "Beverly Hills 90210" is a deserved hit.

Meanwhile, the Bochco bindings-pushers can take heart in the evolution of standards. Television has wisely positioned itself a step or two behind motion pictures and now presents themes, language and visuals that would have been shocking twenty or even ten years ago. For years, people have accustomed themselves to the rawer, more realistic content in theaters. Now with pay cable and video, the same material has made its way into homes. Some deplore the lowering of standards and the infusion of excessive violence, nudity and street talk. Others see it as the freshening of freedom. Whatever ones taste, the fact remains that the public still sees over-the-air broadcasting as so inherently intrusive, so freely available to children and so ubiquitous (even 55 percent is one hell of an audience) that it draws a large distinction between networks and cable/film/video.

The greatest change, described in chapter 5, is the matter of scarcity. The original impulse for regulating the electromagnetic spectrum arose from the interference of one frequency with another. There were only so many slots on the dial. This continued with television, particularly where access to UHF channels was limited. Today, many compete for existing channels but the public has an abundance of choices (if many of the same genre), remembering always that surging cable rates have priced out and will price the poor out of the market.

Nevertheless, the average viewer in 1993 gets more than 30 channels,[10] and the number keeps climbing. (Five cities have begun a 150-channel hook-up.) If the networks don't deliver, the viewer has a few dozen other choices. The irony is that one day the only "family" viewing option the public may have is network fare, and today nobody knows whether that is still a mass audience.

That is the networks' nightmare. A viewer-driven audience might decide to drive somewhere else. If that continues to happen at the rate of the last two years, the network share should stabilize at about 50 percent. (In 1992, cable lost audiences, probably to independent stations.) But if the four "webs" drop off into the forties or thirties, the nation loses a large chunk of national solidarity, the sense of a USA community. No other product in the history of the world has been so conspicuous, so integrated into the lives of so many people. When "everybody" gathers around the set during the Superbowl or the World Series—and as they used to for "Roots" and "I Love Lucy"— that makes for a curious sense of national togetherness. It's tantamount to spending one twenty-four-hour day each week doing the same thing at the same time. People talk about such experiences around the water cooler and over the breakfast table. Like New Yorkers who talk to strangers during snowstorms, they reach out and share what they all saw the evening before. Only network television (or war) has been able to bring that sense of identification to a nation that seems fragmented in almost every other way. If networks go under and mass audiences are chopped up into scores of channels each capturing a one share, America will then have lost something, a touchstone that broadcasting has provided since the early days of radio. All the more reason to think that a preoccupation with a "barely adult" audience is both suicidal and irresponsible.

This all-encompassing nature of broadcasting has created a cottage industry of social critics and university scholars. Academic courses, journals and conferences examine network programming with the measured cadence of publishers looking for business. With increasing passion and sometimes frenzy, the institutional leaders and the self-appointed watchdogs regard our national addiction from their own Rashomon perspectives. It is sometimes said that conservatives loathe sex on television and liberals loathe violence. Only the people like both.

Meanwhile the government maintains a wary presence; too wise to throttle free expression, too worried to leave it all alone and too equivocal to think deeply and prophetically about where it all leads.

Given the alternatives to commercial broadcasting, one must support the regu-

lated business system that brought networking this far. It is the strongest entertainer, the most capable of delivering the best shows to the greatest number of
viewers in the freest marketplace around. The tension between the bottom-line
reality of a business based on delivering audiences to advertisers at one pole, and
the public interest mentality of outsiders and critics at the other pole, has been a
healthy one. Just as the SEC makes the stock market safer for investors, so regulation has made television safer for viewers and therefore more sensitive to their
desires.

The government has tried to safeguard the rights of viewers (listeners during
the radio years) without invading the boardrooms of the networks or the work-
shops of writers and producers. Advertisers have occasionally applied speed
brakes to programmers who have expanded the boundaries too boldly or taste-
lessly. Interest groups representing mainstream constituencies have for years
served the constructive role as viewer emissaries and counsels to the networks.
We have been less kindly disposed toward the fringe groups, activists, boycotters
and watchdogs but have never bought the argument that such privately generated
pressure brought to bear upon station owners, networks and advertisers is somehow illegitimate or out-of-bounds in a democracy. At least it is a form of consumer pressure and what is more American than that? At the same time, many of
them seem to act as a restraint on the free trade of ideas and services.

Perhaps the "average reasonable viewer" can be compared to ticket buyers in
the old days of vaudeville. When they took seats it was with the intention of being
entertained. If unhappy with the fare, they did not sit there passively or demand
their money back or leave the theater. They either hissed, or if more deeply offended, threw cabbages and eggshells. When enough people joined the chorus of
boos, the management sent out the hook and replaced the rejected act with more
pleasing entertainers.

It seems to us that this kind of audience response is the nub of all popular programming. Ticketholders in television have already paid for their seats by buying
sets and enduring the commercials. Therefore, it is arrogant of management to
say to unhappy ticketholders, "Just turn it off if you don't like it." No, our average
viewer bought the set to keep it on and when something offensive or dull is aired,
that viewer has the right to throw a cabbage. If enough people protest, management will get the message and give that kind of entertainment the hook.

The problem is, how do you keep a single crazy with a rotten egg from running
an act off the air even if it appeals to tens of millions? That is the unfairness inherent in fringe-group protests. The only way we know to solve the problem is to
allow the viewers to drown out the unrepresentative cries of the whining narrow
interest groups. The best tool for that is a ratings system that takes the air out of
the balloon of demagoguery.

By the time the networks awaken, reach out to legitimate constituencies and
serve them with advance information, it may be too late. (Ralph Daniels has proposed an ingenious ratings system to the older networks, but the Three Blind
Mice have scurried to their holes.) If audiences dip far below 50 percent, the very
thing that attracted the mainstream critics and the pressure groups will be gone –

the audience of Everybody. Then networks will have the luxury of a completely level playing field with no fans in the stands.

The answer to viewers driven to other channels is the creative community, par-ticularly the writer-producers who have the greatest influence on primetime program content. They tell the stories about our affections and sympathies, about our loves and friendships, our hatreds and prejudices, fears and admirations. Their imaginations are inmates of a province of real things as broad and deep as that probed by the Hubble telescope in space. The writers serve the viewers whenever they stage a pageant of the world itself, the rise and fall of kingdoms, the lives of men and women great and small, the saints, the rogues, the clowns, the heroes and heroines, the Hamlets and Falstaffs, the Don Quixotes and Sancho Panzas and yes, an occasional game show with Vanna White on display if only to season the stew and appeal to the bustling, commercial, pleasure-seeking viewer.

All else is support, distribution, finance. At the core of our investigations of primetime content lies the viewer. Speaking from the armchair with a clicker, we offer some wishful advice to networks.

They must not lag too far behind or advance too far ahead of tolerances held by the large mainstream audiences. The must become increasingly more sensitive to the needs of the large viewer corps that is their stock and track. That base should include ex-viewers and nonviewers. If 80 million are tuned in at 8:00 P.M. on Mondays, what about the other 160 million Americans? While cable companies seek out and siphon off smaller audience subgroups, a place remains for a few giant programmers whose concern is for middle-of-the-road audiences. Viewer loyalties to networks have been the key to network success in the past. Network loyalties to viewers may be salvation in the network's future.

NOTES

1. Tom Shales, "Fowler's Way: Foul is Fair," *Washington Post*, April 20, 1987, p. B1.

2. David Levy quoted in Tom Shales, ibid.

3. Jack Valenti, "Art, Smut and Movie Ratings; We Don't Need a New Category between R and X," *Washington Post*, May 6, 1990, B7.

4. See Gary Selnow, "Values in Prime Time Television," *Journal of Communication*, 40(2) (1990), pp. 64–74.

5. We are grateful to the Television Program Services Company which has presented such a plan in pilot form to the networks. Some of the TPS material has been adapted from Selnow's content analysis research on values and Gilbert's values studies among special interest groups.

6. New York station KXRK, which carried Stern's show, was not included in the charge.

7. *New York Times*, Editorial, "Which Dirty Words? When?", April 22, 1987, p. A26.

8. Richard Zoglin, "Hill Street Hail and Farewell," *Time*, April 27, 1987, p. 89.

9. Reginald Stuart, "F.C.C. Acts to Restrict Indecent Programming," *New York Times*, April 17, 1987, p. 1.

10. A.C. Nielsen, Special staff research, March 5, 1992.

10

Public Expectations: Conclusion and Epilogue

Surely it's passing strange that public opinion gets so little attention when it comes to the boundaries of program content. Why is it that in this day of perennial polls so few address the public's own preferences about the actual content of its favorite pastime? What do most viewers want to see on the air and what, if anything, would they prefer not to see? Does the larger public feel it has the right to deny enjoyment to smaller publics in the name of the general welfare? Ethically, is there a distinction, indeed a conflict, between what the public desires and what it considers desirable?

One of the assumptions we have made, backed with objective content analysis and subjective experience in network standards, is this: the public wants *both* good entertainment *and* entertainment that is good. Paraphrasing a term from Supreme Court opinions—the average reasonable citizen—we posit that an *average reasonable viewer* would like to see primetime network fare strike a balance between exciting, interesting, diverting shows on the one hand, and shows that are "fitting" for the living room in terms of taste and values on the other. If you want more (or less) in the vein of unlimited porn and gratuitous violence, then buy pay cable.

Unfortunately, the polls that have tried to explore the average viewer's tastes and values have been hopelessly superficial. For years, *TV Guide* has been running national polls on program content, asking for responses on, among other things, the level of sex, violence and rough language. Their findings made good reading for preachers, teachers and pious politicians who have quoted the statistics so repeatedly that they have become mythic truth. Year after year, *TV Guide* reported that the majority of Americans say there is too much sex and violence on the air.[1] There appears to be a veritable Chatauqua of morality out there in viewers' land.

We have no doubt that these numbers are valid, although it would be nice to see a poll that warned readers about the distinction between "respondents" and "Americans." A quick review of the questions asked, however, reveals the problem in this kind of polling. Respondents were asked, in effect, how they felt about the level of sex on primetime television. Is there too much, about the right amount, not enough? Then they were asked the same kinds of questions about the levels of violence and profanity.[2]

Going along with the drift of the questions, the great majority agreed that, yes, there was entirely too much sex, violence and bad language on television. What did pollsters expect, a citizen's endorsement of evil? An ill-conceived methodology distorted the results.

For what little good it did in dislodging the myth of "too much," the networks complained that the very people who griped about the level of immorality on television were probably the same people who contributed to the success of every sexually suggestive or violent hit from "Miami Vice" to "Northern Exposure," to movies like the *Terminator* series.

For years, moralists had an answer. They said that people were locked into look-alike network shows and therefore had no other choices. Interest groups responded that given the option of cleaner, classier, less violent, less erotic content, viewers would become loyal followers.

Unfortunately for those like the National Council of Churches who made this argument, experience proved otherwise. The fifty-channel line-up gave viewers a lengthy menu of choices even if many were redundant. Remember all the arts and music channels and the great literature shows? Viewers measured these opportunities for uplift, whether ballet, opera or Shakespeare, and tuned in the familiar diet of soapy sex and action that had been entrees on the network menu. Those who really did dislike adult material merely switched to Andy Griffith reruns with nary a glimpse of highbrow programming. And those who really enjoyed watching unadorned sex and violence bought HBO, Cinemax and Showtime.

An NBC study conducted by Dr. Ronald Milavsky, now professor at the University of Connecticut, illustrated the network's point about generalized, ambiguous questions on sex and violence. He set up respondents with the same "too much" questions and got the same results, confirming with this methodology that people felt entirely too much of that material was coming into their homes!

Then Milavsky did something else. He listed the shows of the previous week and asked viewers to tag those that were objectionable and to list any examples of gratuitous sex or violence. Result: The large majority that had complained about too much sex or violence was unable to identify offensive shows, much less pinpoint incidents that illustrated their concern. In other words, viewers think there is too much sex and violent content generally but find very little in particular. Despite these revelations, the *TV Guide* myth lives on and doubtless inspires many to greater feats of moral censorship.

Faced with data like Professor Milavsky's, the networks and their suppliers have generally drawn a cynical conclusion: viewers deplore what they really enjoy. Agreed. At least sometimes. But puffing themselves up with righteous indignation, the creative community adds, "People are such hypocrites!" We disagree. This charge against the "average, reasonable viewer" betrays a misunderstanding of human nature.

It is not hypocritical to like things that war with one's values. The human condition has ever been so polarized. By contrast, people also love those shows ("Family Ties," "Full House," "Wonder Years") that confirm their values (i.e., good entertainment that is also morally good). Shakespeare marked this two-way pull of desire and principle when the praying Polonius said, "My words fly up; my thoughts remain below. Words without thoughts never to heaven go." True, Polonius, and out of that tension is drama born.

Look at viewer attitudes on fictional violence, for instance. Many of us get secret kicks out of a little vigilantism on police dramas even though we believe it to be illegal and immoral. We can tolerate it in a fictional setting for a very good reason. It appeals to desires we all know are undesirable. Our emotions and our ethics conflict but happily on the clouds of imagination. On the fictional level we enjoy Dirty Harry destroying the bad guys, even unconstitutionally, but in real life, we believe strongly in the right of a jury trial for the most heinous crimes.

Where children are involved the so-called hypocrisy is easily justified. Why should it be thought inconsistent to savor an erotic scene or laugh at adult jokes while at the same time wishing to protect our children from such fare?[3] In that context, parents are completely sincere when they say there is too much sex, violence and profanity on the air, especially before 10 P.M.

Viewers, who bought the set as an amusement appliance that dispenses news and information as well, want seemingly incompatible things – the protection of what is socially desirable and the programming of what they desire. If that last includes a few naughty shows or antisocial values, so be it. On a show like the old "Dallas," viewers are fascinated when undesirable values like hate and dishonesty are attractively portrayed. On a show like "Cosby," viewers revel in the affirmation of love and caring. J.J. Ewing and Dr. Huxtable – were there ever two better symbols of incompatible values?

We viewers stand in a no-man's land between two forces: those who in their superior wisdom would give us only what is best for us – informed by the teachers of morality and special interests – and those who would give us whatever we want – right on down to murderous "snuff" movies.

Nowhere are veiwers more ambivalent than on sex. Whereas most Americans agree overwhelmingly on values of honesty, freedom, loyalty, courage, justice and loving concern, they are hopelessly at odds over sexual ethics. Permissiveness and freedom war with responsibility and order. Networks share in the general ambivalence and moral confusion. Is it any wonder since so many of us fight a civil war of values within ourselves? We are caught in the tension between what we want and what we value. We value responsible human relationships built on trust and unselfish love; yet some of us may want instant sex – selfish gratification, variety, domination and hit-and-run encounters.

And when it comes to sexual themes — abortion, homosexuality, contraception, prostitution — America staggers from one booby-trap to another. Amid all the clamor and cacophony, television serves its role as storyteller. It hooks its audience with illicit love and fantasy passions. But it also does something redemptive, just as the old Hollywood films did. It lets the moral person within us eavesdrop on the immoral adventures of those who thumb their noses at our responsible behavior. It hooks us with voyeurism and leaves us with a moral lesson. Is that so bad?

Voyeurism is a way of life with people who watch soaps, those titillated by the very life-style they most condemn. Yet some psychologists suggest that the practice is not an unhealthy one, giving vent as it does to fantasies that might otherwise stay pent up within.

Scholars who investigate the phenomenon of soaps in America — like Robert C. Allen[4] at the University of North Carolina — point out that the soap is a morality play in which those who break the rules inevitably pay the price. Morality triumphs over all the relished naughtiness. Reflecting the opinions of writers interviewed by the authors, the world of soap opera is one in which the moral expectations of the audience play a major role in the shaping of content.

On balance, the problem for networks and public alike is making room on free television for shows that not only capture their time periods and age targets[5] but also cross the boundaries between mainstream values and material that may challenge these values? What about "undesirable" values that glorify violence, sex without love, intolerance, greed and selfishness, and that may honestly depict raw realism seen from the dark and seamy side of life?

At the moment of this writing, commercial television feels itself being pushed in a permissive direction by cable competition.[6] All the network talk about "a level playing field" is a euphemism for the freedom to follow theatrical film into these problematical areas. What will happen? If the primetime share of audience for networks sinks below 40 percent, there will be, in our judgment, no problem with a public backlash. But should the networks vigorously stretch the boundaries in the next five years while remaining the majority medium, the battle lines will be drawn between those who wish to preserve free TV as a predominantly family medium and those who would support the freedom of broadcasters to let the market alone decide.[7]

In the world of social criticism, it is a matter of faith that life imitates television. We have argued that television imitates life. Beginning with Gary David Goldberg's image of breathing in and breathing out, we have used the words of the TV-makers themselves to buttress the claim that they are profoundly influenced by public pressures outside their craft. And not only as reflectors of culture. Like any pop art, TV does reflect a pop society. It mirrors every fad from Valley Girl syntax to urban rap. And like the jet stream, that contagion travels from West to East, from Hollywood to everywhere USA.

From the other direction, however, a reverse breeze blows. The content of primetime entertainment follows coordinates set by the core values of American life, enforced directly by suits and censors, and indirectly by sponsors, interest groups and government regulators. Whenever primetime shows venture too far beyond these margins, they set in motion a critical backlash fanned by the press and worse, they probably alienate more people in the older mass audience (sending them into the eager jaws of Turner Broadcasting and USA Network) than they win back from the new cable audience. Public opinion, raised to a critical level, does affect TV content.

Closely connected to this stew of forces is the audience so well understood by TV-makers and often overlooked by critics. Culturally speaking, the tastes and values of the American public can be placed on three levels: highbrow, middlebrow and lowbrow. What most writers and too few of the network suits understand, however, is that the mass audience envelopes all of these tastes into one category; call it broadbrow.

The highbrow may prefer public TV and C-Span; the middlebrow may support the better sitcoms like "I'll Fly Away," "The Wonder Years," "Cheers" and "Murphy Brown"; lowbrows may tap into the wide world of wrestling.

But the rainbow that keeps writer-producers in Tinker's "nonbusiness" is the pot-of-gold gamble that they can somehow reduplicate a generic hit like "The Honeymooners" that clicks on all these levels of sophistication and then syndicates eternally. How can one show reach every audience? The answer is, the highbrows "dress down" to it mentally and get huge kicks out of something that is deliciously beneath them; middlebrows not only love the laughs but endorse the family values; and lowbrows, identifying with Ralph Kramden or Archie Bunker (much to the horror of the liberals who write sitcoms) feel the damn thing was written for them. That's broadbrow, and until cable divided audiences into fractions, that's what broadcasting meant.

Producing a broadbrow show takes simple genius and as Tinker noted, it ain't that easy to do. Try it sometime. It takes a talent that does not need to indulge in sleazy exploitation or brutal sensationalism to hook viewers en masse. How painful it must be to the networks when they realize that so many of their "off the wall" shows are being killed by those broadly appealing evergreens like "The Odd Couple," "Andy Griffith," "Mary Tyler Moore," "I Love Lucy," "Dick Van Dyke," "Sanford and Son," "Barney Miller," "All in the Family," and "Family Ties." And now that "Cosby" has left a Thursday hole in NBC, can "Cheers," "Murphy Brown," "Designing Women," "Full House," "Golden Girls," "Wonder Years" et al. be far behind in the syndication lottery? What then, big webs? What new shows do the networks have that can stand up to their own (former) shows?

NBC's "Law and Order" is solid and "Seinfeld" is funny. ABC's "Home Improvement" is refreshing and "Young Indiana Jones" could catch on, even if hourlong adventure programs don't syndicate well; CBS's "Northern Exposure" is weirdly innovative but what happens when "Murder She Wrote" begins to kill them in syndication? Fox is widening its niche between the series genre that made networks great and the specialized, young audiences that cable is attracting. "Beverly Hills 90210" is not only well-written but a solid choice for teens to thirties, and "In Living Color" could follow in the youth-oriented footsteps of "The Simpsons."

But where are the generic blockbusters for the broadbrow audience that the networks alone can serve? Is Newhart's "Bob" back for another fourteen years? How about the insider's pick of "Love and War"?

The promising shows listed above are suggestive. They seem to demonstrate that "off the wall" is not as effective as "tried and true" if the latter has good writing. Indeed, the newer hits just might prove that what the primetime industry needs is not shows that push the "ethics envelope," as *Variety* calls the exploitation shows, but those that push the talent envelope.

Food for network thought can also be found in the most aggressive of the basic cable networks, USA. Having built a solid base with off-network repeats and children's programming, USA is now commissioning thirty original made-for-TV movies each year, and according to the erudite Tim Brooks, research vice president for USA Network, they will soon be doing 60 percent new programming, including five new series. Granted that USA will skew toward the mystery-adventure motif that pulls in the kids on Saturday nights, the lesson for networks is clear: basic cable is not trying to out-pay pay-cable but trying to siphon off more of the mass audiences owned by the four webs. And they are doing it, by and large, with broadbrow shows with something in them for general audiences.

Often in network corridors you can hear people say that what they need is another "Hill Street Blues," because it was not only artistic and innovative by primetime standards but a ratings hit as well. Most of us would say Amen to that.

Arthur Price,[8] who ran MTM after Tinker left, demurs. He thinks networks need something else. He noted in an interview that "Hill Street" never got big numbers, and only began to win its time period after three years. Its value was purely innovative.

> Still, it was a wild scene every week. One time Renko (the white, redneck cop) walks into a bar. He's carrying his live pet mouse around with him in his upper shirt pocket. He loves that damn mouse. This time an old buddy comes over to him and says, "How are you, Renko,'" and hits him a hard wallop on the upper pocket. There is this horrible moment of silence. Renko looks sick. Everybody realizes that the fuckin' mouse is dead. Well, the censor on the show wonders if the animal lovers will be all over us the next day. We get a note of warning.
>
> So I call Ralph Daniels, who was then head of standards, and the world's classiest guy. In the game we play, maybe I've got one to trade him. I reach him at home at some ungodly hour from a public phone at the American Airlines Club. "Ralph," I say, "Bochco wants to do this scene with a character committing an unnatural act with an animal." I can hear Daniels snapping to attention. "Yeah, that's right, we're talking sodomy with an animal, and somehow that struck your guy on the coast as distasteful. But, see, it's off-camera . . . what? You won't discuss it further? Okay, Ralph, but there is this one small incident involving a mouse." I tell him about Renko's mouse, and by now, he'll agree to anything that doesn't involve unnatural acts. "Thanks," I say, "and I'll talk to you later about the animal sodomy" . . . and I hear this click in my ear. Well, by this time, half the club is eavesdropping on my conversation. I mean, what a business!

For a "broadbrow" audience – entertaining and wholesome – Price had only one model in mind. Reminiscing about the joys of doing "The Mary Tyler Moore Show," where boundaries were no problem, he said:

> Okay, like Grant [Tinker] says, its a crazy business. You worry about your ratings, you worry about renewals, you worry about deficiting, and uppermost in your mind is getting at least 66 shows in the can so you can sell the damn thing at the back end. But, I'll tell you, "Mary" was a joy to do. Sure the writers had to work seventy-two hours a week, but everytime any script was in trouble, all they had to do was have the team arguing about, say, the most irrational situation in the news business, whereupon Ted [the pompous anchor] walks in and says in that debonair manner of his, "Hi, Guys. . . ." And you get your laugh.

CONCLUSION

You get your laugh – that's what Goldberg called his compact with the public. Understand that and you understand why the public will influence TV as much as TV influences the public.

In this excursion into show biz, we have paddled upstream into the headwaters of TV-makers high in the canyons of Beverly Hills. We have discovered that programming is viewed by those who create it quite differently from those who study it. And the scholars who study it see it differently from those viewers who simply enjoy it.

We know what experts expect. Looking at their sets, educators see a classroom. Preachers see a pulpit. Advertisers see a showroom. Investors see a money machine. Auteurs see a theatre. Pressure groups see an image-maker. Newspapers, magazines and book publishers see something they wish would go away. And at the other end of the transmission line, viewers are searching desperately for what they bought the set for in the first place: entertainment.

The talents we talked with, people like Goldberg and Bochco, never forget that expectation. Unlike many critics, they know this: Tell a good story and all else falls into place.

EPILOGUE

Two heroes emerged from our Hollywood excursion: Ralph Daniels because he takes entertainment seriously and Grant Tinker because he doesn't. Both would probably get a chuckle out of Oscar Wilde who observed: "Give me the luxuries of life and I can do without the necessities." For Americans, however, the luxury and necessity of television are one and the same.

NOTES

1. The *TV Guide* polls have been reviewed most recently in "Television in the '90s," *TV Guide*, January 20, 1990.
2. Ibid.

3. In a 1978 report to NBC Research called "The Values of Viewers Seen in Focus Groups," this attitude was labeled "representational conservatism," wherein the parent takes umbrage at things seen with his or her children but wouldn't think twice about such material in company with adults only.

4. R.C. Allen, "On Reading Soaps: A Semiotic Primer," in *Regarding Television*, ed. A.E. Kaplan (Frederick, Md.: University Publications of America, 1983), pp. 97ff.

5. In 1990–1991 a 25 audience share will keep a show on the air, and on low viewing nights like Saturday, an 18 share is respectable enough to win renewal.

6. See chapter 8.

7. Undoubtedly, the issue would find its way into the Congress and Supreme Court. See chapter 4.

8. Price remembers this story as a two-parter; Daniels as printed below.

Selected Bibliography

Allen, R.C. "On Reading Soaps: A Semiotic Primer." In A.E. Kaplan, ed., *Regarding Television*. Frederick, Md.: University Publications of America, 1983.

Alschuler, G.C. and D.L. Grossvogel. *Changing Channels: America in TV Guide*. Champaign: University of Illinois Press, 1992.

"Annual Report on Broadcast Regulation." Washington, D.C.: National Association of Broadcasters, 1986.

"A Shock to 'Shock' TV." *Washington Post*, Editorial, May 8, 1989, p. A14.

Auletta, Ken. *Three Blind Mice: How the Networks Lost Their Way*. New York: Random House, 1991.

Barnouw, Erik. *A History of Broadcasting in the United States*. Vol. I, *A Tower of Babel*. New York: Oxford University Press, 1966.

Barwise, Patrick and Andrew Ehrenberg. *Television and Its Audience*. Newbury Park, Calif.: Sage, 1989.

Batra, N.D. *The Hour of Television: Critical Approaches*. Metuchen, N.J.: Scarecrow, 1987.

Berger, Arthur A. *Television in Society*. New Brunswick, N.J.: Transaction Publishers, 1986.

Berman, Ronald. *How Television Sees Its Audience: A Look at the Glass*. Newbury Park, Calif.: Sage, 1987.

Bower, Robert T. *The Changing Television Audience in America*. New York: Columbia University Press, 1985.

Buzzard, Karen. *Electronic Media Ratings*. Stoneham, Mass.: Focal Press, 1992.

———. *Chains of Gold: Marketing the Ratings and Rating the Markets*. Metuchen, N.J.: Scarecrow, 1990.

Cable and Television Fact Book. Services Volume. Washington, D.C.: Warren Publishing, 1991.

Cantor, Muriel G. *The Hollywood TV Producer: His Work And His Audience*. New Brunswick, N.J.: Transaction Publications, 1992.

Carter, Bill. "ABC Cancels Crime Show That Fails to Get Any Ads." *New York Times*, May 3, 1989, pp. D1, D21.

Communication Daily (12)171 (September 2, 1992), p. 6.

Davis, Richard H. and James A. Davis. *The Television Image of America's Elderly.* New York: Free Press, 1985.

Dougherty, Philip H. "TV Flipping's Effect on Ads." *New York Times*, October 7, 1987, p. D19.

Drummond, Phillip and R. Paterson, eds. *Television and Its Audience: International Research Perspectives.* Bloomington: Indiana University Press, 1988.

Duff, Evelyn J. "Homes without Remote TV Control (1985) vs. Homes with Remote TV Control (1986)." *TV Audiences,* Special Nielsen Report, 1986.

Fanning, Deidre. "The Return of the 'Sponsor.' " *Forbes*, April 17, 1989, p. 136.

Farhil, Paul. "Sikes Pushing for Deregulation at FCC by Year's End." *Washington Post*, February 7, 1992, p. F1.

Folkerts, Jean and Dwight L. Teeter. *Voices of a Nation: A History of the Media in the United States.* New York: Macmillan Publishing Company, 1989.

Frank M. Magid Associates, Inc. "New TV Viewing: Summary and Conclusions." (A study prepared for ACT III Communications.) June 1988.

Freitag, Michael. "Objections To TV Shows Win Support." *New York Times*, June 1, 1989, p. D19.

Garvey, E. Daniel. "Secretary Hoover and the Quest for Broadcast Regulation." *Journalism History* 3 (1976), pp. 66–70.

General Accounting Office. "Summary of Cable Television Rates and Services." April 1991. Washington D.C.

Gerbner, G., L. Gross, M. Morgan, and N. Signorielli. "Charting the Mainstream: Television's Contributions to Political Orientations." *Journal of Communication*, 2 (1982), pp. 100–127.

Ginsburg, D. *Regulation of Broadcasting.* St. Paul, Minn.: West Publishing Co., 1979.

Groller, I. "Should TV be Censored?" *Parents Magazine*, April 1990, p. 34.

Grover, Ronald. "Shootout on Hollywood and Vine." *Business Week*, January 8, 1990, p. 93

Hamamoto, Darrell Y. *Nervous Laughter: Television Situation Comedy and Liberal Democratic Ideology.* Westport, Conn.: Greenwood Press, 1991.

Himmelstein, Hal. *Television Myth and the American Mind.* Westport, Conn.: Greenwood Press, 1984.

Holden, Stephen. "Where the Laughs Are: Comedy is King on City Stages." *New York Times*, December 5, 1986, p. C1.

In the Matter of Editorializing by Broadcast Licensees. 13 FCC 1246, June 1, 1949.

Iyengar, Shanto and Donald R. Kinder. *News that Matters: Television and American Opinion.* Chicago: University of Chicago Press, 1989.

Jacobs, Jerry. *Changing Channels: Issues and Realities in Television.* Mountain View, Calif.: Mayfield Publishing, 1990.

Johnson, R. "New Targets for TV Sex Foes." *New York Post*, April 20, 1989, p. 6.

Jones, Louis B. "When People Collide." *New York Times Book Review*, March 1, 1992, Section 7, p. 7.

Kalish, E. "A Surprisingly Good Year for the Masses." *Channels,* January 1990, p. 32.

Kleinfield, N.R. "Stung by Cable Audience Claims, Networks Retaliate." *New York Times*, January 9, 1989, p. D6.

Kneale, D. "Zapping of TV Ads Appears Pervasive." *Wall Street Journal*, April 25, 1988, p. 29.

Kottak, Conrad P. *Prime Time Society: An Anthropological Analysis of Television and Culture*. Belmont, Calif.: Wadsworth Publishers, 1990.

Kozloff, Sarah Ruth. "Narrative Theory and Television." In Robert Allen, ed., *Channels of Discourse*. Chapel Hill: University of North Carolina Press, 1987.

Krasnow, G., L.D. Longley, and H.A. Terry. *Politics of Broadcast Regulation*, 3rd ed. New York: St. Martin's Press, 1982.

Krugman, D.M. and T. Childress. "Subscriber Use and Satisfaction with Cable and Pay Cable Services." In E.F. Larkin, ed., "Proceedings of the 1986 conference of the American Academy of Advertising." Norman: School of Journalism, University of Oklahoma, 1986, pp. R68–R71.

Kubey, Robert and M. Csikszentmihalyi, eds. *Television and the Quality of Life: How Viewing Shapes Everyday Experiences*. Hillsdale, N.J.: L. Erlbaum Associates, 1990.

Kunkel, D. "From a Raised Eyebrow to a Turned Back: The FCC and Children's Product-Related Programming." *Journal of Communications* 38(4) (1988), pp. 90–108.

Livingstone, Sonia M. *Making Sense of Television: The Psychology of Audience Interpretation*. Elmsford, N.Y.: Pergamon Press, 1990.

Lodziak, Conrad. *The Power of Television: A Critical Appraisal*. New York: St. Martin's Press, 1986.

Loevinger, Lee. "The Sociology of Bureaucracy." *Business Lawyer* 24 (November 1968), p. 9.

Lull, James, ed. *World Families Watch Television*. Newbury Park, Calif.: Sage, 1988.

Mahoney, W. "Networks' Share Drops 9%." *Electronic Media*, October 31, 1988, pp. 1, 41.

Marcus, Ruth. "Court Refuses to Reinstate Broadcast Ban." *Washington Post*, March 3, 1992, p. A4.

Marlowe, J., G. Selnow, and L. Blosser. "A content analysis of problem-resolution appeals in television commercials." *Journal of Consumer Affairs* 23(1) (1989), pp. 175–94.

Mellencamp, Patricia, ed. *Logics of Television: Essays in Cultural Criticism*. Bloomington: Indiana University Press, 1990.

Milavsky, Ronald J. et al. *Television and Aggression: Results of a Panel Study*. San Diego, Calif.: Academic Press, 1982.

"The Missionary's Position." *Manhattan. Inc.*, July 1989, pp. 84–91.

Montgomery, Kathryn. *Target: Prime-time*. NY: Oxford University Press, 1989.

Morley, David. *Family Television: Cultural Power and Domestic Leisure*. New York: Routledge, 1988.

Nielsen, A.C. Special staff research. March 5, 1992.

———. "Report on Television." 1990.

———. "Coping with the complexity of new video technologies." *Nielsen Newscast*. No. 1, 1980.

———. "Report on Television." 1980.

"Nielsen Media News." Nielsen Media Research. 1992.

———. Nielsen Media Research, April 1990.

Oskamp, Stuart, ed. *Television as a Social Issue*. Newbury Park, Calif.: Sage, 1988.

Palmer, E.L. *Television and America's Children: A Crisis of Neglect*. New York: Oxford University Press, 1988.

Papazian, E. "The Silent Majority: ABC, CBS and NBC." *Marketing & Media Decisions*, August 1988, p. 113.

Pearl, D., L. Bouthilet and J. Lazar, eds. *Television and Behavior: Ten Years of Scientific Progress and Implications for the Eighties*, 2 Vols. Rockville, Md.: National Institute of Mental Health, 1982.

Polan, Lois A. *Dailies: From Producers to Popcorn*. Beverly Hills, Calif.: Lone Eagle Publications, 1992.

Powers, Ron. *The Beast, the Eunuch and the Glass-Eyed Child: Television in the 90s*. San Diego, Calif.: Harcourt Brace Jovanovich, 1990.

"Protests get Saturday Night Live ads pulled." *New York Post*, March 19, 1989, p. X.

"Putting a Brake on TV 'Sleaze.' " *Time*, March 20, 1989, p. 51.

Quester, George H. *The International Politics of Television*. New York: Free Press, 1990.

" 'Reality' TV Shows Continue to Spread Despite Critics and Nervous Advertisers." *Wall Street Journal*, May 11, 1989, p. B1.

Robinson, Glen O. and Ernest Gellhorn. *The Administrative Process*. St. Paul, Minn.: West Publishing, Co., 1974.

"Roe vs. Wade Show's Ads." *New York Times*, May 11, 1989, p. B8.

"Screeners Help Advertisers Avoid Prime-Time Trouble." *New York Times*, January 20, 1989, p. C1.

Secunda, E. "Is TV's Golden Age at Its End?" *Marketing & Media Decisions*, February 1988, p. 128.

Seiter, Ellen et al., eds. *Remote Control: Television Audiences and Cultural Power*. New York: Routledge, 1989.

Selnow, G. "The Influence of Television on Language Production: Rules, Culture and Benjamin Whorf." *European Journal of Communication* 15(1–2) (1990), pp. 163–70.

———. "Values in Prime Time Television." *Journal of Communication* 40(2) (1990), pp. 64–74.

———. "A Content Analysis of Television Problems and Problem Resolutions." *Journal of Communication* 36(2) (1986), pp. 63–72.

———. "Television Viewing and the Learning of Expectations for Problem Resolutions." *Educational Studies* 12(2) (1986), pp. 137–45.

Shales, Tom. "Fowler's Way: Foul is Fair." *Washington Post*, April 20, 1987, p. B1.

Singleton, Loy A. *Telecommunications in the Information Age*, 2nd ed. Cambridge, Mass.: Ballinger Publishing Company, 1986.

Smith, F. Leslie. *Perspectives on Radio and Television*. New York: Harper & Row, 1985.

Span, Paula. "Quantity Time on Cable." *Washington Post*, February 12, 1992, p. C1.

Spigel, Lynn. *Make Room for TV: Television and the Family Ideal in Postwar America*. Chicago: University of Chicago Press, 1992.

"SRI Completes Review of Nielsen People Meter Service." *Media News*, December 1989, p. 1.

Stein, Ben. *The View from Sunset Boulevard*. New York: Basic Books, 1979.

Stengel, Richard. "Radio Daze; The FCC Tries to Clear the Air." *Time*, April 27, 1987, p. 32.

Stuart, Reginald. "F.C.C. Acts to Restrict Indecent Programming." *New York Times*, April 17, 1987, p. 1.

Stone, J. and T. Yohn. *Prime Time and Misdemeanors: Investigating the 1950s TV Quiz Scandal.* New Brunswick, N.J.: Rutgers University Press, 1992.

"Teens Tune Out TV." *American Demographics*, March 1988, p. 20.

"They Watch What We Watch." *New York Times Magazine*, May 7, 1989, pp. 42–65.

Tocqueville, Alexis de. *Democracy in America.* New York: Anchor Books, 1969.

"24 Advertisers Boycott 'Affair,' 'Edition,' 'Copy.' " *Variety*, March 21, 1990, pp. 1, 60.

Valenti, Jack. "Art, Smut and Movie Ratings; We Don't Need a New Category between R and X." *Washington Post*, May 6, 1990, B7.

Walley, Wayne. "Decency Debate." *Advertising Age*, March 6, 1989, pp. 1, 74.

Walters, H.F. and J. Huck. "Welcome to the Age of Viewer Lib." *Newsweek*, October 17, 1988, pp. 86–93.

Webster, James G. and Lawrence R. Lichty. *Ratings Analysis: Theory and Practice.* Hillsdale, N.J.: L. Erlbaum Associates, 1991.

"Which Dirty Words? When?" *New York Times*, Editorial, April 22, 1987, p. A26.

Wolfe, Tom. "Radical Chic." *New York*, June 1965 (entire issue).

Ziegler, Bart. "Two Electronics Giants Plan Satellite TV Broadcast System." *Washington Post*, February 5, 1992, p. D1.

Zoglin, Richard. "Hill Street Hail and Farewell." *Time*, April 27, 1987, p. 89.

Index

About the Authors

GARY W. SELNOW is a Professor at San Francisco State University. His writings have focused on communication policy research, mass audience research, and research components of strategic planning. Recent consultancies include the National Academy of Sciences, NBC, and Twentieth Century Fox.

RICHARD R. GILBERT is a senior partner in the Daniels Group. Until 1989, he had been Director of Policy Resources for NBC. In the last twenty years, Dr. Gilbert was an ethics consultant for all three networks, and did values research for ABC and NBC, and script analysis for CBS. He continues as a writer-consultant with producers Norman Lear, William D'Angelo, and others.